ADMIRAL
COCHRANE

The Audacious
ADMIRAL
COCHRANE
The True Life of a Naval Legend

BRIAN VALE

CONWAY MARITIME PRESS

For Margaret

© Brian Vale, 2004

First published in Great Britain in 2004 by
Conway Maritime Press
The Chrysalis Building
Bramley Road
London W10 6SP

An imprint of **Chrysalis** Books Group plc

www.conwaymaritime.com

ISBN 0 85177 986 7

A CIP catalogue record for this book is available from the British Library

Design and typesetting: Stephen Dent
Printed and bound in Great Britain by CPD

Contents

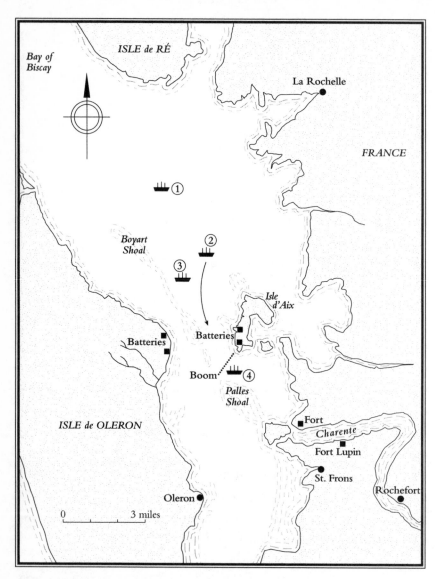

The Attack on the Basque Roads: 11–12 April 1809.

Key:
1. *English fleet at anchor, 11 April*
2. *Fireships, 11 April*
3. *English fleet at anchor, 12 April*
4. *French fleet, 11 April*

Wind: NNW to NW

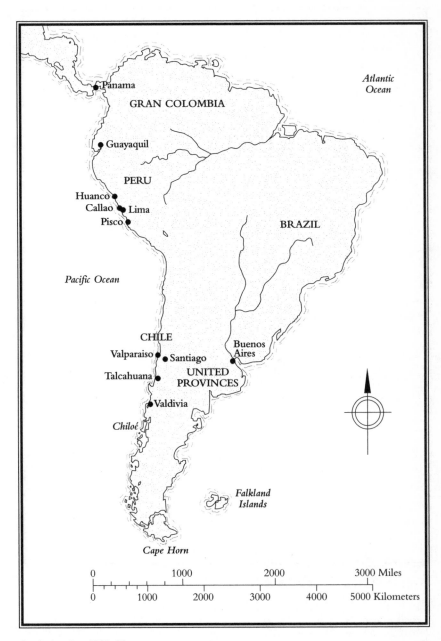

South America, 1818–22.

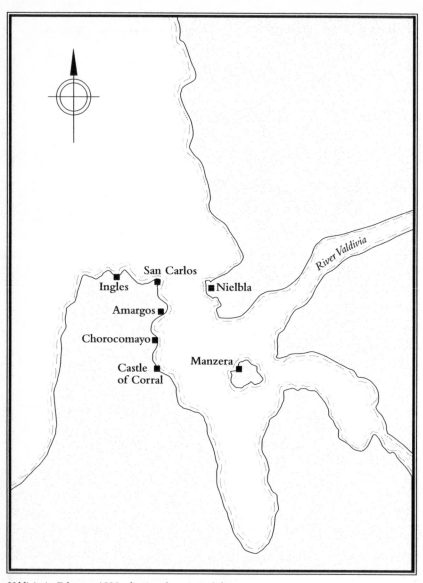

Valdivia in February 1820, showing the principal forts.

Brazil, 1823.

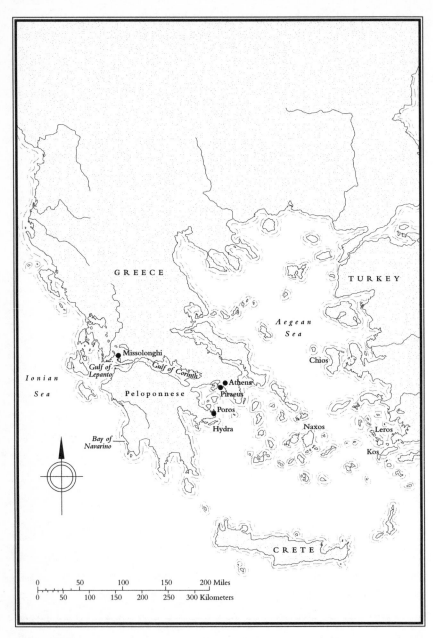

Greece, 1827.

Author's Note

LORD COCHRANE is a dominating figure in the maritime history of the early nineteenth century. His daring, personal bravery and powers of leadership made him one of the Royal Navy's most successful frigate captains during the Napoleonic Wars and a key participant in the naval campaigns which secured the liberation of South America and Greece. He was an aristocrat, but his dislike of the political corruption that underpinned the Georgian establishment turned him into a radical and a symbol of the reform movement. And his originality of mind and mechanical skills made him a pioneer of the new technological challenges which steam and iron posed for the navy of Queen Victoria.

But he was also a quarrelsome and complex figure who, in old age, published books that told the story of his life. His *Autobiography of a Seaman* and *Narrative of Services in the Liberation of Chile, Peru and Brazil* took events up to 1827, and within a decade of his death his son produced a two-volume *Life of Lord Cochrane* which completed the story. The purpose of these books was to ensure that it would be Cochrane's version of his dramatic and controversial life that was recorded for posterity. And it has been. Although they are filled with inaccuracies and are distortions of what actually took place, the story as told in these books has been repeated again and again by biographers who have been unwilling or unable to establish the facts.

This tendency to take Cochrane at his own evaluation has been reinforced by the fact that his most dramatic deeds have been used consistently as source material for naval fiction. Even during his lifetime, Cochrane was clearly recognisable as the heroic commander of Captain Marryat's midshipmen *Frank Mildmay* and *Peter Simple*, and, 50 years later G. T. Henty produced his gung-ho boy's adventure story, *With Cochrane the Dauntless*, based on his adventures in South America. In the twentieth century, the trend continued. It is impossible to read the logs of *Pallas* or *Imperieuse* without recognising the adventures of C. S. Forester's hero Horatio Hornblower when in command of *Hotspur* and *Sutherland* in the approaches to Brest and in the Mediterranean. And Patrick O'Brian went even further, integrating huge chunks of Cochrane autobiographies into his novels. In *Master and Commander*, Jack Aubrey's exploits in the tiny brig *Sophie* in the Mediterranean are a blatant re-write of Cochrane's adventures in *Speedy*; *The Reverse of the Medal* has Aubrey embroiled in a politically-inspired Stock Exchange swindle; while *Blue at the Mizzen* has him securing the independence of Chile by capturing Valdivia and seizing a frigate called *Esmeralda*!

This book breaks the mould. Rather than retelling Cochrane's version of events once more, it has gone back to original documents, newspapers of the time, objective contemporary accounts, and the work of the few scholars who have investigated incidents in the Admiral's life. It has been a lengthy task. Not only are three languages involved, but Lord Cochrane left behind him a mountain of personal and official papers in original, duplicate or microfilm form in numerous locations, principally the National Archives of Scotland, the Archivo Histórico Naval in Chile and in Peru, and the Arquivo do Serviço de Documentação da Marinha in Brazil. Footnotes and references in this book have been kept to a minimum but, for convenience, it is their location in the National Archives of Scotland that is given rather than the place where they may have been actually consulted. Likewise, if any document has been published, it is that source which is cited.

In relation to major incidents, the inaccuracies that appear in Cochrane's own works and in subsequent biographies have been noted in this book and compared which what actually took place. There are, however, scores of minor details where the true story is told without reference to the errors contained in the autobiographies. I leave it to the reader to make whatever comparisons with the 'Cochrane version' they wish.

I would thank the Directors and staffs of all the archival collections for the assistance they have given me over years of intermittent research, together with those of the National Maritime Museum, Greenwich, The National Archives in Kew, the University of Liverpool and Canning House in London. I am particularly indebted to Dr John Sugden for generously putting his unrivalled expertise on Cochrane at my disposal and providing invaluable comments and suggestions.

Brian Vale
Greenwich, 2004

CHAPTER ONE

Roots and Relations

OUR HERO was born on 1 December 1775, at the home of his mother, Anna Gilchrist, in Annsfield in Lanarkshire. He was christened plain Thomas Cochrane – but that was all that was plain about him. For Thomas was the eldest son and consequently heir to the Earldom of Dundonald, a title of Scottish nobility going back to 1648, whose family seat was located at Culross Abbey, some 12 miles across the water from Edinburgh. Built near the ruins of the Cistercian foundation which gave it its name, Culross Abbey was a dilapidated, flat-fronted mansion with towers set in the corners, occupying a ridge with a southerly view where the hills of Kinross descend to the Firth of Forth in a series of wooded bays. It was here that Thomas spent his early years. In the fullness of time, he was to succeed to the title as the 10th Earl of Dundonald, but for much of his astonishing and controversial life he was known as Lord Cochrane.

As the heir to an earldom and a landed estate, Lord Cochrane appeared to be the child of privilege. But reality was different. By the end of the eighteenth century, the Cochranes had dissipated most of their wealth and power over family disputes, endowments, the fashion for 'improvements', and sheer extravagance. One by one the family's scattered estates had been sold to pay off their debts, and one by one their sons were forced to turn to military and government careers in order to support themselves. By the time Thomas was born, the family fortune had sharply declined and what remained was being rapidly frittered away by his father, Archibald, the 9th Earl of Dundonald. The Earl was a gifted if eccentric scientist and was one of the leading figures of the Scottish Enlightenment. With extensive reserves of coal, salt and fire clay beneath his estates, and farms above, he applied his inventive and curious mind to the scientific challenges of both, producing, in 1795, a pioneering *Treatise showing the Intimate Connection between Agriculture and Chemistry*. He invented a process for distilling tar and varnish from coal; he discovered coal gas; he investigated the malting of grain for cattle; he made bread from potatoes; he devised an improved method for making sailcloth; and he worked on many processes which were fundamental to modern industry, such as the manufacture of salt, of sal ammoniac for dying, and white lead for paint. Unfortunately, although Dundonald was a resourceful scientist, he lacked any flair for practical business.[1] All his attempts to save Culross Abbey and repay the family debts by developing his coal mines and salt deposits failed, either through poor management or his inability to raise the capital needed to achieve industrial take-off. His inventions lost money rather than made it, and it was left to others to become rich by developing their commercial applications. Dundonald was also unlucky. Experiments had convinced him that coal tar was an ideal waterproofing material for wood and iron, and he became convinced that a generous application to a ship's bottom would solve the problem of the *teredo navalis* – the shipworm which ate its way through ships' timbers necessitating frequent repairs. As a result the Earl invested heavily in the production of coal tar and, by 1783, was ready to make his fortune. Alas, it was not to be. The private yards lived on repairs as much as building and did not want ships to be too durable; and the Navy Board had come to the conclusion that the answer to the *teredo* problem lay in sheathing its ships in copper. With neither private nor public sectors interested in his new invention, his expensive venture failed and Dundonald slid further towards bankruptcy. At Culross Abbey, belts were tightened and family life was governed by strict economies.

Thomas inherited his father's scientific curiosity, and was practical and good with his hands. Throughout his life he produced inventions; some of them – such as convoy lamps – were small; others – such as machines for chemical warfare and steam-driven warships – were large. In old age he followed even more closely in his father's footsteps by allowing a fortune to be consumed by technical innovations that never paid their way. To be an aristocrat with social position but no money to sustain it must have been an embarrassment; and Thomas's youth was spent among financial crises and parsimony. It is hardly surprising, therefore, that money-making became a major pre-occupation in his adult life. Indeed, he was notorious for it. What is more surprising, in view of the economic lifestyle at Culross Abbey, was the difficulty he seemed to have in controlling his expenditure. In his later naval career he earned plenty of money, but regularly lived way beyond his means.

In 1784, the Cochrane family was hit by the death of Thomas's mother, Anna. He was then nine years old, with three younger brothers, Basil, Archibald and William. Four years later, the Earl married a rich widow, Mrs Isabella Mayne, which enabled him to stave off financial disaster and launch another visionary – but unsuccessful – scheme to make money through the production of alkali salt. Culross Abbey became a happy place once more. But the sudden loss of their mother had left its mark on the children, and Dundonald himself was too engrossed in his experiments and his problems to give either encouragement or praise to his sons. It is small wonder that, in later life, Thomas seems to have developed a craving for the approval of his superiors and feared the worst when it did not arrive.

But now arose the problem of education. Lacking the funds to put them into public school with other boys of their class, the Earl entrusted the education of his sons to a series of tutors who were more memorable for their eccentricities than for their teaching. One responded to Thomas's first question by clipping his ear, while another, who was both French and a papist, further scandalised the good Presbyterians of the neighbourhood by blasting the magpies in the Dundonald orchard with a fowling piece on the Sabbath when they were in church. Neither lasted long. As a result Thomas's education was unstructured and disorganised, but he made up for it by ranging at will round the Culross Estate, indulging his own interests, developing practical skills rather than intellectual interests, and learning to sail on the Firth of Forth. These childhood experiences developed in him a sturdy self-reliance, an independent spirit, and a mistrust of authority.[2]

The Earl of Dundonald may have had a flexible and creative mind when it came to science, but in other areas he was opinionated and stubborn. He had had unhappy experiences himself in the navy as acting lieutenant on the sloop *Weasel* off the coast of West Africa, and had resigned in a huff when his commission had not been confirmed. As such, he was determined that Thomas and Basil should go into the army. To obtain the necessary training, in 1789 the boys were sent to Mr Chauvet's military academy in Kensington Square, and to provide for their future, commissions were bought for them in the 104th Regiment of Foot. When they left by stagecoach on the long journey to London, the Earl's agent famously remarked as he saw them off, 'it is true that they have not had very much education, but they are strong and fine to look at and very sensible and will go anywhere'.

The contrast between the freedom of Culross and the regulation cramming of Kensington Square was bad enough, but to make matters worse, Thomas had been provided with a uniform of the eccentric Earl's own design, which included trousers and a long waistcoat in mustard yellow – the colours of the Whig party of which Dundonald was a supporter. Worn with gaiters, hair greased down and a pigtail, the thin, gangling, red-headed Thomas, by his own description, looked ridiculous. After six months of tedium in the academy, interspersed with humiliation at the hands of the local street urchins, Thomas had had enough. He returned to his father and flatly refused to have anything to do with a loathsome army career. The Earl was beside himself with anger, but Thomas stuck to his guns and got his way. But what was he to do for a career? He had become convinced that the navy was the life for him. His maternal grandfather, James Gilchrist, had been a frigate captain, the technical aspects of ships appealed to him, and he had enjoyed his sailing excursions on the Firth of Forth. But how was he to enter the Royal Navy? His relations were to provide an easy answer.

The Cochrane family was an extensive one, with close links to other branches of the Scottish nobility.[3] The 9th Earl had seven brothers who survived infancy, and the family's penury meant that each had to earn a living. George and Charles went into the army, the latter being killed at the siege of Yorktown in the American War of Independence. John went into business, acted as Agent for the British army's bankers in Canada, worked in India, and ended his career as Commissioner for Customs in Scotland. James went into the Church, presiding as Vicar of Mansfield and then as Rector of Horsely in Northumberland. The most successful – that is, the richest – of the brothers was probably the Honourable Basil. Joining the East India Company as a Writer at the age of 16, he worked his way skilfully and profitably up the ranks, becoming successively Paymaster for Fort St George in Madras, Assistant Commissary for grain in Nagore, and Head of the Company's affairs in Negapatam. There, in 1784, he discovered two Indian employees embezzling funds and had them flogged so severely that it was said one died as a consequence. An inquiry was held, and Basil was forced to resign, but with good contacts and ample capital he stayed on in India. In 1791 he took over a contract held by his brother John as Contractor and Victualling Agent for the navy in the East Indies. It was a profitable venture, and over the next 15 years, goods and money totalling over £1,348,000 passed through his hands. He returned to Britain in 1807, purchased an estate in Auchterarder in Perthshire and a large town house in London, and began to enjoy the life of a rich bachelor 'nabob' while indulging in a 10-year battle with the Victualling Board over his accounts. As the most successful of the Cochranes, Basil slowly assumed the role of head of the family.

At the other end of the spectrum was the sixth of Thomas's uncles, the Honourable Andrew – known as Cochrane-Johnstone following his marriage to Lady Georgiana Johnstone, daughter of the Earl of Hopetoun. A cad and a scoundrel, he was the blackest of the family's sheep and was to be the eventual cause of Thomas Cochrane's disgrace. Originally following an army career in the Light Dragoons and the Royal Americans, in 1797 Cochrane-Johnstone was appointed Governor of Dominica and left for the West Indies determined to make his fortune. The following year he broadened his base by purchasing the colonelcy of the 8th West India Regiment and set about achieving his ambition. Active in the slave trade and allegedly keeping a local harem, Cochrane-Johnstone embarked on a five-year career of what the *Dictionary of National Biographical* calls 'tyranny, extortion and vice'. On his recall to England in 1803, he was court-martialled for embezzlement on the instigation of an officer who had been unsuccessfully set up to take the blame. To the dismay of all concerned, the prosecution failed and although Cochrane-Johnstone was in disgrace, he remained rich and unrepentant. He bought the pocket borough of Grampound in Cornwall and sat intermittently as its Member of Parliament until he was expelled from the Commons in 1814 following the Stock Exchange scandal. But his West Indian career was not over. When his brother Alexander was made naval

commander-in-chief there in 1807, Cochrane-Johnstone was back
exploiting to the full the lush opportunities for personal enrichment and
graft offered by an appointment to the customs house in Tortola, then as
the fleet's agent for the prize property taken on the capture of the three
Danish islands of St Thomas, St Johns and St Croix. The case was a
complex one, and to ensure a favourable decision he resorted to bribery
of the prize court officials, and then distributed the booty before the
court of appeal could intervene. Arrested, he promptly broke his parole,
returned to Britain under a cloud and embarked on further shady business
deals. This time they involved supplying sub-standard weapons to the
governments of Spain and her rebellious colonies at grossly inflated
prices, and using his parliamentary immunity to escape prosecution.

When Thomas began to look around for the means to launch his career
in the early 1790s none of these uncles was on hand to help, but there was
one who was. This was Captain the Honourable Alexander Cochrane
RN, then a frigate commander, who had served and gained his early
promotion in the West Indies during the American War of Independence
under the patronage of Lord Rodney. Like so many of his family,
Alexander was quarrelsome and opinionated, but he was a fine fighting
officer. In command of the two-decker *Ajax* in the Mediterranean in
1800, he orchestrated the successful landing of the British army in Egypt
under General Abercrombie. On becoming a rear admiral, he took part in
Sir John Duckworth's victory at San Domingo in 1806 during which his
ship, the 74-gun *Northumberland*, engaged and forced aground the finest
three-decker afloat, the 130-gun *Imperiale*. In 1809, he was commander-
in-chief in the Leeward Islands. Then, with the American War of 1812–14
going badly, he was sent out as commander-in-chief to bring new vigour
and boldness to the campaign. With his aggressive instincts sharpened by
the memory of the death of his brother, Charles, at Yorktown, Alexander
threw himself into the task – converting the blockade to an economic
stranglehold, masterminding a devastating attack up the Chesapeake
which led to the burning of Washington, and mounting an unsuccessful
assault on New Orleans after the war was technically over. Throughout his
career, Alexander was lucky, aggressive and successful. He was also tireless
at getting his sons and relations into the navy; pushing remorselessly for
their promotion once they were inside and, indeed, ignoring naval

regulations when they were inconvenient. Such manipulations of the system were common, but Alexander was an expert. One major beneficiary was his son, Thomas John, who enjoyed a meteoric career, becoming a lieutenant at the age of 16, a commander at 17, and a post-captain at 18!

Entry into the navy at the time was not under central control, but lay in the gift of individual captains. There were, it was true, a growing number of young men who were appointed by the Admiralty and called first class volunteers, but most entered the service in their early teens at the invitation, and under the sponsorship, of a captain. They were rated in the ship's books as captain's servants, boys, or even able seamen, but they were clearly 'young gentlemen', destined for the quarterdeck and for command. Inevitably, captains used these appointments to advance the sons of relatives or friends and to oblige the politically influential, and they formed part of the patronage system which was so important in Georgian times. Once they had learned the ropes, these young men were promoted to midshipmen, after which – as long as they had a minimum of six years' sea time and were 19 years old – they were eligible to become lieutenants. Knowing the advantages of a naval career, Alexander had, in fact, already taken the precaution of entering Thomas's name on the books of the various ships he commanded even though Thomas never set foot on any of them. This practice was called 'false muster' and was not uncommon as a way of acquiring sea time without the necessity of being on board ship. Thus, in 1780 when he was five years old, Thomas was technically a captain's servant on the bomb vessel *Vesuvius*. At the ages of seven and nine, he was filling the same post on *Caroline* and *Sophie*.[4] Although he did not know it, Lord Cochrane was already acquiring the seniority that would be so useful if he chose to join the navy.

With his uncle's assistance, Thomas persuaded the Earl of Dundonald to allow him to follow a naval career. It certainly seemed more suited to his temperament than life in the army with its mechanical drill movements and the raucous camaraderie of life in the officers' mess. The freedom and independence of Lord Cochrane's early life meant that he would never be a good team player. In fact, a naval career offered great advantages for families like the Dundonalds who were perpetually broke. In the army, commissions had to be purchased, and the pay was notoriously inadequate in view of the cost of mess bills, uniforms and keeping up appearances. This was not true of the navy, and the possibility of war with France brought the promise of fame and fortune to active officers who were lucky enough to capture prizes. Eventually the Earl was convinced, and once he had realised the advantages, he became so enthusiastic that he allowed his next two sons, Basil and Archibald, to follow Thomas into the navy. Basil later transferred into the infantry, but only the youngest sibling, William, was destined to become a soldier from the beginning. Basil ended up Lieutenant Colonel of the 36th of Foot, and William as a major in the 15th Hussars.

With Thomas's future decided, on 8 July 1790 Captain the Honourable Alexander Cochrane entered his nephew's name once more as a captain's servant on the muster roll of his sloop *Hind*, although as before he never appeared on board.[5] In May 1793, with war in the offing, Thomas's name was re-entered as Able Seaman while the sloop was at Leith, but this time it was more than a token entry, and when *Hind* sailed for the English Channel, Thomas received instructions to travel south to join the ship and begin his naval career in earnest. But first he had to prepare himself. He needed a sea chest, uniforms, nautical instruments and manuals. As usual, his father was short of money, but he managed to obtain a loan of £100 from the Earl of Hopetoun. This was more than enough to pay for what he needed, and with what was left over Thomas was provided with a gold watch. Thus equipped for his new life, in July 1793 Thomas set out on the high road to London, keen to join the *Hind* at Sheerness.

CHAPTER TWO

—◦◦◦—

Learning the Ropes

IN EARLY 1793, the reverberations of the French Revolution finally crossed the English Channel. The execution of Louis XVI and the installation of a Republican regime determined to export by force its principles of liberty, equality and fraternity had shattered the peace of Europe. Britain, always disturbed when the balance of continental power was threatened, had inevitably been drawn in. On 2 January 1793, the brig *Childers* was fired on in the approaches to Brest and hurried home carrying a French 48-pounder cannonball as proof that the war had started. The resulting conflict with the Republican and Napoleonic regimes was to last 22 years, and was the climax of the struggle for maritime supremacy between Britain and France which had occupied so much of the eighteenth century. Britain emerged politically and economically triumphant, with a world-wide dominance guaranteed by a powerful navy, a far flung network of supporting dockyards and naval bases, an extensive foreign trade, a growing manufacturing industry and a massive merchant marine ready to export its products. The war was to be marked by a series of dramatic naval triumphs such as those at St Vincent, the Nile, Copenhagen and Trafalgar, and by a multitude of victorious actions by small squadrons and individual ships. It was a conflict in which Lord Cochrane was to achieve justified and well-publicised fame.

But on 29 July 1793, when Thomas was rowed out to the *Hind*, this seemed far from inevitable. He was an unlikely figure as an entrant to the Royal Navy, being 17 years old at a time when young men normally joined the service at the age of 11 or 12, and knowing nothing of the sea or its practices. Indeed, his developing personality – already marked by a strong individualism and an inability to keep his opinions to himself – hardly seemed suited to the discipline and teamwork needed on a man-of-war. The one advantage he did possess was that he was captain's nephew. His uncle, the Honourable Captain Alexander Cochrane, had so far had a good war. *Hind* was a 26-gun sloop armed with 9-pounders, and was the smallest vessel with three masts and a single gun deck to be counted as a post-captain's command. Originally occupied on tedious patrols off the Scottish coast, on the declaration of war *Hind* had been redeployed to the Channel where she had promptly captured five French privateers. Due for a refit, on 26 July she arrived at Sheerness, a bleak and unpopular naval base set among the mudflats at the mouth of the Medway. The Captain immediately left for London, and the task of refitting the *Hind* was left to his first lieutenant, Jack Larmour. Within days, her guns and powder had been ferried ashore, her yards and masts swayed down and her rigging removed. Such was her situation when a nervous Thomas Cochrane arrived.

Lieutenant Larmour was a no-nonsense seaman and one of the few officers who had been promoted from the lower deck. When Thomas boarded the sloop he found him personally directing the refit, scruffy in seaman's clothes with a marlinspike round his neck and a lump of grease in his hand. Larmour was clearly unimpressed with the newcomer. After a cursory interview, Thomas was ordered below to find accommodation suitable to his nominal rank of Able Seaman[1] (not even Captain Cochrane had dared to rate such an inexperienced youth as a midshipman) but was soon disturbed by the sound of sawing. Larmour, astonished by the size of Thomas's sea chest and unaware of the financial sacrifices that had been made to fill it, had ordered a seaman to cut the thing in half so it could be fitted into the storage space in the orlop. Thomas returned on deck to find his chest in pieces and his precious possessions scattered over the planking. It was an inauspicious beginning.

Thomas was nevertheless fortunate to be on the *Hind*. In most vessels the midshipmen's berth was inhabited by a mixture of young boys who were learning their trade and experienced mature men who had failed to get promoted. Thomas would have fitted in with neither group. The *Hind* was different. None of her midshipmen was older than 22 years and Thomas was in fact the youngest. Likewise, Captain Cochrane was a leading member of the navy's Scottish 'mafia' and, of the 11 lieutenants and 'young gentlemen' aboard, all but one were Scots like himself.[2] And it was one of their number, Jonathan Murray, son of the Earl of Dunmore, who generously loaned Thomas some of his clothing to make up for what he had lost.

Thomas's second stroke of luck was that his first five months in the navy were spent in the dockyard. *Hind* was not only receiving a refit while afloat, she had to be put in dock to have her copper repaired. This gave ample opportunity for him to study all the details of how ships were constructed and maintained. With his inherited interest in technical matters and his skill with his hands, he threw himself into the task, learning from the expertise of the crew and the dockyard artisans and determined to master the skills involved. Indeed, his efforts and his obvious willingness to get his hands dirty won Larmour's grudging admiration and ensured that when his uncle and the crew of the *Hind* were transferred in October to the 36-gun frigate *Thetis* – also refitting in Sheerness – Thomas was rated as a full midshipman.[3]

Thetis was typical of the frigates that were to ensure Britain's mastery of the seas. She was one third bigger than *Hind*, with a crew of 280 men and a formidable battery of 18-pounder guns on her main deck. Her refit complete, she sailed on 23 December 1793 bound for Leith where she brought her complement up to strength, then headed east to Norway with orders to flush out any French privateers preying on Britain's vital trade with the Baltic. Thomas was enchanted with what he found in Norway. The dramatic contrast between the deep fjords and the towering snow-covered mountains was stirring, and he and the other midshipmen enjoyed their trips ashore, hunting, shooting and fishing or racing over the winter landscape in a silence only broken by sleigh bells. But what impressed him most was the egalitarian nature of Norwegian society. Unlike in Britain where the rural population were largely subservient tenants of aristocratic landowners, Norway's peasants and farmers were sturdy independent proprietors. When he and the officers of the *Thetis* were entertained ashore to tables groaning with food and a seemingly endless succession of dishes by the more affluent members of society, he was struck by the comparative absence of servants and became convinced that their hosts had both prepared and cooked the bulk of it themselves. This hospitality was returned by invitations to visit the frigate, but was marred on one occasion by the malice of *Thetis*'s resident parrot. The bird had learned to imitate the calls given on the boatswain's whistle to convey commands, and when one unfortunate lady was being lifted by block and pulley from a boat alongside, Polly suddenly piped 'let go'. The sailors obediently did so, and the guest was dropped hysterical into the sea. What happened to the delinquent parrot, Thomas does not record.[4]

Her assignment in Norway completed, in May 1794 *Thetis* headed west across the North Atlantic to join the Royal Navy squadron based on Halifax. *Thetis* remained on this station for four years, ceaselessly patrolling the North American seaboard, from the foggy Banks of Newfoundland to the blue tropical seas of Bermuda, on the lookout for enemy vessels. They made themselves far from popular with citizens of the newly independent United States by detaining American ships carrying supplies to France, or searching them for deserters from the British navy. It was, however, the period during which Thomas added a mastery of seamanship to his knowledge of ship construction and maintenance. Life on a wooden ship was hardly healthy, and officers were regularly invalided out. Thus within six months of arriving on station Thomas found himself promoted to the rank of Acting-Lieutenant and transferred to the 64-gun *Africa*. No doubt his obvious competence contributed to the promotion, but the fact that the local commander-in-chief was Rear Admiral George Murray, another Scot and a relation of the Earl of Athol, was clearly a factor. Thomas's experience was no doubt broadened by a year on the *Africa*, but the transfer meant that he lost the chance of action when, in May 1795 while he was absent, *Thetis*, in company with the frigate *Hussar*, engaged a convoy of five French armed ships at the entrance to Chesapeake Bay and captured the *Prevoyante* and *Raison*. In January 1796, Cochrane was posted back to the *Thetis*, successfully passing his examination for Lieutenant and being confirmed in the rank.

Lord Cochrane was comfortable on his uncle's frigate, and it is not surprising, because at that time there were no fewer than five members of his family on board. In addition to himself, there was the Captain and his wife Maria, their seven-year-old son Thomas John (later the recipient of such rapid promotion) and his own brother Basil, who was rated as Captain's Servant. A sixth joined the ship's company on 29 October when the Captain's wife gave birth to a son at sea off Cape Sable. His return to *Thetis* also gave Cochrane his first smell of action when, in August 1796, the ship formed part of a squadron under Admiral Murray which pursued a French flotilla off Cape Henry and captured the frigate *Elizabet*.

Cochrane was to stay off the American coast for two more years, but in June 1797 he was transferred to the 74-gun *Resolution*, flagship of the newly-arrived commander-in-chief, Vice Admiral George Vanderput. Life on a flagship was a new experience, but Cochrane seemed to enjoy it. There were plenty of shore trips for hunting and entertainment and he began to make up for the deficiencies in his formal education through a programme of voracious reading. Cochrane established a good relationship with his new admiral once he overcame his awkwardness. Overcompensating at dinner and forgetting that junior officers did not speak until spoken to, he made a poor start by offering to pass his chief a dish only to be told curtly that he was perfectly capable of serving himself. There were two other occasions when he sailed close to the wind. The first was to arrive at one of his Admiral's dinners disgracefully late. All was made well when he explained that he had gone ashore to shoot a wild boar for the feast only to be turned on by his infuriated prey and forced to take refuge for hours in the branches of a tree. The second was when, knowing Vanderput's partiality for tall girls, Lieutenant Cochrane embarrassingly proposed a toast to his current favourites, 'the Misses Tibbs'. It was received in silence. Fortunately the good-humoured Admiral took it in good part and Cochrane's career did not suffer.

Transferred back to the *Thetis*, Cochrane returned to England in the middle of 1798 and began to look for another appointment. The Scottish connection once more stood him in good stead. In the Mediterranean, due to the solid efforts of that gouty disciplinarian, Admiral the Earl of St Vincent and his brilliant subordinate, Rear Admiral Sir Horatio Nelson, the tables had been turned on the French at the Battle of the Nile and their Mediterranean Fleet effectively destroyed. Spain was still hostile and the great naval base of Toulon also remained a constant threat. By the end of 1798, the health of the 63-year-old St Vincent was problematic and the Admiralty chose a successor to lead the Mediterranean Fleet. It was Admiral George Elphinstone, Viscount Keith. Keith was reputed to have joined the navy with nothing but a £5 note in his pocket and, due to an abundance of prize money, left it the richest man in the service. His long and distinguished career included service in the American War of

Independence, the capture of Toulon and the suppression of the great naval mutinies; then went on to see him successively as commander-in-chief of Britain's most important naval stations – the Mediterranean, the North Sea and the Channel. He was never associated with a great battle, and never achieved public fame or popularity. But his gifts as a self-effacing and efficient administrator made him well suited to the task of managing the long, low-key struggles with the French that followed the dramas of the Nile, Copenhagen and Trafalgar.

Keith sailed for the Mediterranean at the end of 1798, taking with him a group of 31 'followers' comprising one captain, nine lieutenants, 19 midshipmen and master's mates, and two clerks.[5] This was quite normal. At that time it was customary for senior figures to have groups of adherents, or 'followers', around them who would receive favours and promotion in return for loyalty and support. A patron needed to attract followers who were able and efficient; and a follower had to find a patron who was professionally successful and – most importantly – survived. There were instances when all the officers on a flagship resigned upon the death of their admiral seeing their chances of preferment suddenly vanish. Since Keith was not only a distinguished admiral but the navy's most senior 'Scotch' officer, he inevitably acted as a patron to numerous promising young fellow-countrymen. As a result it is no surprise to find that Lord Cochrane was among the entourage who accompanied him.

Upon their arrival in the Mediterranean during January 1799, Keith and his followers were transferred to the *Barfleur*, displacing an equal number of officers and men as they did so. On the flagship, the insubordinate tendencies and the lack of judgement that were to mark Cochrane's character throughout his career showed themselves for the first time. Unadvisedly he developed an antipathy for the flagship's particular and fussy first lieutenant, Philip Beaver, being especially critical of his superior's habit of keeping the hides of bullocks slaughtered on the *Barfleur* for the use of the fleet in old beef casks so that they could be sold for the benefit of the senior officers. The result, as Cochrane graphically explained, was that 'as the fleshy parts of the hides decomposed, putrid liquor oozed out of the casks, and rendered the hold of the vessel so intolerable, that she acquired the name of "the stinking Scotch ship"'.[5]

Returning one day from a duck-shooting expedition ashore, Cochrane failed to report his arrival to Lieutenant Beaver on the quarterdeck and returned to his cabin, ostensibly to change before doing so. Beaver went below, found him in the wardroom and demanded an explanation, stating that such conduct made him 'look ridiculous'. Cochrane replied sarcastically that he could not help it if the First Lieutenant looked ridiculous, and when Beaver remonstrated further, replied ambiguously, 'we will, if you please, talk of this in another place'. Beaver was furious and, interpreting Cochrane's reply as a challenge, took the matter to Captain Elphinstone. Cochrane was asked to apologise, and when he refused, Beaver demanded, and was granted, a court martial. Cochrane was ultimately acquitted but the dour and punctilious Lord Keith was seriously annoyed by the whole affair, reflecting bitterly that at a time when the wind was fair to seek out the enemy, the captains and flag officers of the fleet were wasting their time establishing whether Lord Cochrane had been rude to the First Lieutenant!

For the next eighteen months, the routine of life on the flagship continued, while the fleet maintained its control of the Mediterranean, watching Toulon and Cadiz and trying to prevent a junction between the Spanish fleet and a French force which had evaded the blockade of Brest. In mid-1799, Keith moved with his followers to the massive 100-gun *Queen Charlotte* and there was a brief return to England. But within months they were back, enforcing the blockade, watching the French and Spanish, and visiting Palermo where Cochrane was impressed by a brief meeting with Nelson and by the Admiral's simple advice, 'Never mind manoeuvres, always go at them!', but he was scathing about the seamy Neapolitan port which was his base.

One by one, the followers who had come with Keith to the Mediterranean achieved their expected promotions, and at the end of March 1800 it was Cochrane's turn. It was the fortuitous result of the capture of the *Genereux*, one of the last survivors of the Battle of the Nile which, on 18 February, after a brief action with the frigate *Success* and the 74-gun *Alexander* – commanded in the absence of Captain Alexander Ball in Malta by Lieutenant William Harrington – hauled down her colours on the arrival of Nelson with the *Foudroyant*, *Northumberland* and *Lion*. The job of taking the ship to Port Mahon was entrusted to Cochrane.

With a weak prize crew and appalling weather, it was a task that tested his seamanship to the full. It is likely, however, that the move to the *Genereux* saved the lives of both Cochrane and his brother Archibald, who had recently joined him. On 17 March, the *Queen Charlotte* accidentally caught fire while laying off Capraia and within hours was completely burnt out. It was an appalling tragedy, with 673 of the 829 officers and men on board either perishing in the flames or in the water afterwards. If the Cochrane brothers – and Lord Keith for that matter – had not been away, their chances of survival would have been slim.

The incorporation of *Genereux* into the Royal Navy triggered a wave of promotions: a captain had to be found to command her, another captain appointed to fill his vacancy, a commander promoted to replace him, and a lieutenant promoted to fill his post. The lucky lieutenant was not William Harrington of the *Alexander*, whose efforts in capturing *Genereux* had been highly praised in Nelson's despatches: it was Lord Cochrane. On 28 March he received the crucial promotion to commander. Some have attributed this vital career move to merit, others to Keith's anxiety to get rid of him. Neither explanation is convincing. There had been few opportunities for Cochrane to distinguish himself on the flagship: indeed, in one memorable incident, he had failed to carry a privateer because a boat's crew from *Queen Charlotte* refused to board the vessel. Likewise, although Keith was becoming increasingly irritated by the behaviour of both Cochrane and his uncle – writing three years later that 'Captain [the Honourable Alexander] Cochrane is a crackheaded, unsafe man…and his nephew is falling into the same error – wrongheaded, violent and proud'[6] – the patronage system was driven by influence and not by personal likes and dislikes. Harrington was a man without 'interest' who was destined to die a lieutenant. Cochrane was a peer and a member of the Scottish mafia, and it was Keith's patronage that ensured this vital step in the promotion ladder. Certainly this was the view of many in the fleet, including Captain Henry Blackwood, who resented the way in which 'the Irish peer [Keith] has monopolised all the promotions which the well-timed exertions off Lord Nelson had thrown his way' and used them to reward his own followers, including Lord Cochrane.[7] Not that Keith received any thanks for his efforts on Cochrane's behalf. Captain Alexander Cochrane wrote sourly to say that he owed Keith nothing for the gesture as Lord Spencer (the First Lord) had already promised to secure his nephew's promotion;[8] and Cochrane himself grumbled that he should have been given the smart 18-gun ship-sloop *Bonne Citoyenne* rather than the humble brig *Speedy*.[9] In his memoirs, Cochrane was bitter about the pernicious effects of what he called 'parliamentary' influence in securing appointments and advancement. But of the effects of the type of interest from which he benefited, he says nothing. Nevertheless, whatever the reason for his promotion, it put Cochrane at last in a position to demonstrate his extraordinary skills and prowess as a naval commander.

CHAPTER THREE

Master and Commander

LORD COCHRANE'S first independent command was HMS *Speedy*, a cramped 14-gun brig of 158 tons with tiny 4-pounders and a crew of 90 officers and men. Complaining that *Speedy* was a 'burlesque of a ship of war' and that he could walk the deck with a full broadside of 28 pounds in his pockets,[1] Cochrane tried to improve her fighting abilities by installing two 12-pounders as chase guns. However, the brig's scantlings were too frail to take heavy artillery and the guns had to be returned. Persuading the dockyard to replace *Speedy*'s mainyard for a much bigger spar from *Genereux* was a more successful alteration that did much to improve her sailing qualities. There was nothing Cochrane could do to change the brig's diminutive size: Cochrane was over six feet in height and his cabin was so low that the only way he could stand upright to shave was to open the skylight and use the deck as a toilet table. But Cochrane's other complaints were exaggerated. *Speedy* had never been intended to stand in the line-of-battle or to take on regular warships: her job was to harry the coasting trade, attack gunboats and generally cause mayhem. And the success with which both her previous captain, the able and aggressive Jahleel Brenton, and Cochrane carried out these tasks showed her suitability for the role.

Cochrane was almost immediately in action. On 10 May 1800, while escorting 14 merchantmen to Leghorn, menacing sails lifted over the horizon and headed straight for the convoy. It proved to be the 6-gun privateer *Intrepide* which seized a straggling Danish brig. Cochrane immediately sped to her assistance, freed the brig and captured the *Intrepide*. She was his first prize. Four days later, in a flat calm and almost within sight of their destination, there was another attack, this time by five armed boats packed with men who swarmed aboard and seized the sternmost two ships in the convoy. Fortunately for Cochrane, a breeze then sprung up which enabled him to board and recapture the stricken vessels while the rest of his flock headed safely for port. It was a promising start, and Cochrane's success was rewarded by Lord Keith with orders to harry enemy commerce. It was an assignment that perfectly suited his fighting instincts and his ingenuity. For a year, *Speedy* patrolled the Italian and Spanish coasts, seizing cargo carriers by the score, attacking lonely harbours and overwhelming smaller armed vessels. The ship's log provides a clear insight into the constant effort Cochrane put into his operations and the number of prizes he took:

June 16 – Captured a tartan off Elba. Sent her to Leghorn in the charge of an officer and four men.

June 22 – Off Bastia. Chased a French privateer with a prize in tow. The Frenchman abandoned the prize, a Sardinian vessel laden with oil and wool, and we took possession…took the prize in tow and on the following day left her in Leghorn where we found Lord Nelson and several ships at anchor.

June 25 – Quitted Leghorn.

June 26 – Off Bastia, in chase of a ship which ran for that place and anchored under a fort three miles to the southward. Made at and brought her away. Proved to be a Spanish letter of marque *Assuncion* of 10 guns and 33 men… On taking possession, five gun-boats left Bastia in chase of us; took the prize in tow and kept up a running fight with the gunboats until midnight, when they left us.

June 29 – Cast off the prize in chase of a French privateer of Sardinia. On commencing our fire she set all sail and ran off. Returned and took the prize in tow.

July 4 – Anchored in Port Mahon.

July 9 – Off Cape Sebastian. Gave chase to two Spanish ships standing along the shore. They anchored under the protection of the forts. Saw another vessel lying just out of range of the forts: our boats cut her out, the forts firing on the boats but not inflicting damage.

July 19 – Off Caprea. Several French privateers in sight. Chased them.

July 20 – Captured the *Constitucion*, of one gun and nineteen men. Whilst we were securing the privateer; a prize she had taken made sail in the direction of Gorgona and escaped.

July 27 – Off Planosa, in chase of a privateer.

July 28 – Saw privateers lying in a small creek. On making preparations to cut them out, a military force appeared and commenced a heavy fire of musketry. Fired several broadsides at one of the privateers and sunk her.

August 3 – Anchored with our prizes in Leghorn Roads, where we found Lord Keith in the *Minotaur*.

Valuing the element of surprise, Cochrane invariably slipped inshore at night and attacked at dawn. And to avoid the attention of larger ships Cochrane devised a variety of stratagems. He escaped from one pursuing frigate by running until nightfall then launching a raft and a lantern to act as a decoy; and from another by posing as a familiar Danish coasting brig, the *Clomer*, fresh from plague-infested Algiers. Keith, who received one eighth of Cochrane's haul of prize money, was pleased with his success and his uncle, Alexander, began – typically – to pull strings to get him promoted yet again.[2] But his actions had also attracted the particular attention of the Spanish authorities, and early in April 1801 a naval Goliath was sent to the area to put a stop to the depredations of this insolent David. The ship selected was the 32-gun frigate *El Gamo* commanded by Don Francisco de Torres and carrying the distinctive southern Mediterranean xebec rig, a main armament of twenty-two 12-pounder guns and a crew of 319.

The encounter between the two ships was to establish indelibly Cochrane's reputation. It came on 6 May 1801, when dawn broke to find them sailing in sight of each other. *El Gamo* immediately raised the red and gold of Spain while *Speedy* responded with the stars and stripes. Torres was not fooled, loosed off a long-range broadside and moved in for the kill. Cochrane, however, did not run. Realising that his pop-guns were ineffective and that his only hope lay on boarding and surprise, he headed straight for the frigate. By the time *El Gamo*'s broadside crashed out again, *Speedy* was so close that the shot screamed harmlessly over her low-lying hull, allowing her to reach the frigate's side without damage. Sheering off again momentarily to frustrate a Spanish attempt at boarding, Cochrane brought *Speedy* grating alongside, locked their yardarms together, and fired a broadside at maximum elevation. Cochrane's men then swarmed up on to El Gamo's decks under the cover of smoke, Lieutenant William Parker leading a boarding party on one side, Cochrane's brother Midshipman the Honourable Archibald on the other, faces blackened and yelling like banshees to cause maximum alarm. The death of Torres in the first moments of the engagement, the bloody casualties as Speedy's broadside sprayed El Gamo's decks with splinters and shot, and the ferocity of the British attack caused panic and confusion. And when, at Cochrane's orders, the Spanish ensign was cut down, many of the Spanish seamen dropped their weapons thinking the ship had been captured. Finally, when Cochrane calmly called down to Surgeon James Guthrie (the only person remaining on board the Speedy) and told him to send over another 50 men, a Spanish officer stepped forward and surrendered the ship. It had been an astonishing victory, and at a small cost. Of the 54 men who had been aboard Speedy at the beginning of the action, only three had been killed, and eight wounded including Lieutenant Parker.

Cochrane returned to Port Mahon with his prize in triumph. Even in a naval war already replete with victories, the Speedy's action in attacking and capturing a vessel so superior in size, guns and men stood out as an outstanding achievement. Cochrane could now look forward to promotion to post-captain as a result of his efforts, possibly taking command of El Gamo itself if the ship was purchased for the Royal Navy. Unfortunately for him she was not, and he returned to Speedy, self-confidence increased, to await the inevitable news from the Admiralty of his promotion. There was prize money to look forward to. As a vessel built for the Mediterranean, El Gamo was bought by the Algerines. The price is not known but Cochrane and his men received £1394 in 'head money' for the capture plus £814 for her cables and cordage,[3] and the value of the hull and the ordnance stores could not have been less. Thus even at the lowest estimate, Cochrane's share of the money paid out would have been £1000. His bank balance was increased still further by the value of the huge number of smaller prizes that Speedy had taken on its year-long voyage of destruction.

For the next two months Cochrane continued to wreak havoc in the western Mediterranean, on one occasion seizing a prize in the neutral waters of the Dey of Algiers. In June 1801, Speedy, in company with the

18-gun brig *Kangaroo*, mounted an attack on a Spanish convoy sheltering in the Spanish port of Oropesa, destroying a shore battery, sinking or driving off seven gunboats, and carrying off three brigs laden with rice, wine and bread. Under the command of Captain Christopher Pulling of *Kangaroo*, who was senior to Cochrane, the raid was a success, but took place without subtlety in broad daylight so that the enemy were prepared and casualties high.

Speedy's next assignment was the routine one of escorting the packet boat that carried official mails from Minorca to Gibraltar. To add some excitement to the task, instead of taking the direct route Cochrane insisted on following the coast so that he could go off to look for prizes. But dawn broke on 3 July to reveal an alarming situation. Gibraltar was in sight to the west, but between Cochrane and his destination were the silhouettes of three French ships of the line under Admiral Linois, which had slipped out of Toulon and were making for Cadiz. Linois had already stumbled on the packet and knew that the vessel he could see to windward was not an insignificant trading brig but was the notorious *Speedy*. Desperately, Cochrane tried to escape by throwing his guns overboard and setting every scrap of sail, but the prevailing light winds favoured his pursuers. Every tack brought the French broadsides closer until, by nightfall, the brig had been overwhelmed and was in enemy hands. As fate would have it, Cochrane was not to remain a prisoner for long. Linois put into Algeciras where his squadron was attacked by a British force of seven ships of the line under Sir James Saumarez flying his flag in *Caesar*. But the French position was strong, and when the *Hannibal* went aground the attempt was abandoned. An exchange of prisoners was agreed the following day, and Cochrane found himself at liberty once more. By September he was back in London.

The Britain to which Cochrane returned was different to the one he had left two years before. First, the possibility of peace was in the air. Secondly, in February 1801 William Pitt had fallen and had been replaced as Prime Minister by Henry Addington. Another government was in power and the new First Lord of the Admiralty was none other than that grim old disciplinarian, Admiral the Earl of St Vincent. St Vincent was one of the greatest fighting seamen of his generation. Joining the navy in 1749, he had distinguished himself in engagements going back as far as the capture of Quebec by General Wolfe, and his first achievement in the Revolutionary and Napoleonic Wars was to capture a string of important and rich West Indian islands. But his greatest achievements came in the years after 1795 when, at the age of 60, he had been given command of the Mediterranean Fleet. In 1797 he had defeated a much superior Spanish force off Cape St Vincent, and in 1799 had secured the destruction of the French at the Battle of the Nile by sending the bulk of his fleet under Nelson to seek out the enemy in the eastern Mediterranean. St Vincent had all the prejudices of a fighting admiral, and came to his new office with an agenda that included purging dockyard inefficiency, stamping out corruption among the navy's timber suppliers, and sorting out the string-pulling which had been such a feature of the officer corps during the tenure of his predecessor, Lord Spencer.

Immediately swamped by letters from patrons asking favours for their protégés, the new First Lord was annoyed to find that most of the lieutenants and commanders who had been promoted following St Vincent, Camperdown and other victorious engagements were unemployed while appointments had gone to those with influential friends and relations.[4] He determined that there would be no more promotions except in cases of some outstanding service.[5] In Lord Cochrane's case, St Vincent accepted his victory over El Gamo in May 1801 as just that. In a letter to Keith explaining his decision, he wrote, 'the list of post-captains and commanders so far exceeds that of ships and sloops, that I cannot, consistent with what is due to the public and to the incredible number of meritorious persons on the half-pay list, promote except for very extraordinary service such as those of Captain Dundas and Lord Cochrane'.[6]

Despite this, Cochrane's promotion hit a technical snag. The interception of the mail packet by Linois in July 1801 meant that Captain Manley Dixon's letter of 9 June announcing the capture of El Gamo was delayed, and arrived in the Admiralty at exactly the same moment as news of the capture of the Speedy, a loss for which Cochrane would have to face a court martial. Since the Admiralty could not promote an officer who was facing such an inquiry, his promotion would have to wait. The court martial was held at Gibraltar on 10 July 1801, before Captains Samuel Hood, John Keats, Askew Hollis and Jahleel Brenton, sitting under the

presidency of Captain Charles Stirling of *Pompeé*. All were experienced
fighting officers and they had no hesitation in honourably acquitting
Cochrane and his officers for the loss of *Speedy* and in commending their
actions.[7] News of the verdict reached London on 8 August, and Cochrane
was immediately promoted to post-captain.

Cochrane was only 26 years old, with just eight years of actual service.
Now he was a captain and would, unless his career was compromised by
disciplinary action, automatically become an admiral. Most people would
have been delighted, but not Lord Cochrane. He and his family were
aggrieved, arguing that he should have been promoted on the day of *El
Gamo*'s capture and that the Admiralty had deliberately cheated him. The
fact that he had 'lost' three months' seniority, during which 10 individuals
– including his former adversary Philip Beaver, and Christopher Pulling
– had been promoted above him, dominated their thinking.[8] St Vincent
explained the technical problem in response to pressure from the Earl of
Dundonald, but he refused to bend the rules.

All things being equal, Cochrane should have been a supporter of St
Vincent who, like him, disliked 'influence' and was a scourge of
corruption. But things were not equal. Cochrane saw the world and its
inhabitants in terms of black and white – those who were not for him
must be against him, and St Vincent now fell into this category. He
became convinced that the First Lord was an enemy and, against all the
evidence to the contrary, that he was on the Admiralty's 'black books'.[9]
And when, in accordance with his declared policy, St Vincent refused to
promote Lieutenant William Parker, Cochrane felt that his fears had been
confirmed. St Vincent was a stern disciplinarian who was always prepared
to put the needs of the nation above the interests of individual captains
or, indeed, the condition of their ships. But for Cochrane to imagine that
St Vincent, carrying as he did the weight of the Admiralty on his
shoulders, had the time to persecute a junior commander such as himself
was an act of supreme arrogance.

In 1802 came the Peace of Amiens. There was little chance of
employment in a demobilised navy, so Cochrane retreated to Edinburgh,
enrolled in the university and began in earnest to fill the gaps in his
education and to hone his radical, anti-Establishment principles. Just two
years later, war was declared once more. Cochrane and his Scottish friends

lobbied St Vincent for a command and after some hesitation the First Lord gave him one: it was an unprepossessing Sixth Rate called *Arab* deployed in the Channel as part of the squadron that was blockading Boulogne, the key base for Napoleon's anticipated invasion of England. Cochrane was dissatisfied. He later denounced his service in the *Arab* as having been 'devised by official malevolence', describing it as 'naval exile in a tub…and a dreary punishment', attributing it to St Vincent's malice.[10] Cochrane exaggerated. *Arab* was not an ex-collier (yet another of Cochrane's criticisms) but a French prize. He also overlooked the fact that only a minority of junior captains had been given any kind of employment and that he was one of the chosen few. Nor do his memoirs mention the fact that he immediately got himself into trouble. A collision with the brig *Bloodhound* off Boulogne was not in itself serious, but Cochrane's intemperate refusal to accept the need for an inquiry into the incident caused displeasure at the Admiralty.[11] Then he caused a diplomatic incident by boarding the American merchantman *Chatham*, telling the captain that his place of destination, the Texel, was under blockade and redirecting him to the Downs. There was, of course, no such blockade, and James Monroe, the United States minister in London, delivered a stiff protest.[12] Small wonder that *Arab* was ordered to convoy the whaling fleet to Greenland waters and then to position herself so as to protect it from marauding privateers. Cochrane was scornful about performing this necessary duty, complaining – unjustifiably and inaccurately – that he was forced to cruise 'where no vessel fished and consequently where there were no fisheries to protect'.[13]

In May 1804, the government fell, Pitt became Prime Minister again and St Vincent was replaced in the Admiralty by Henry Dundas, Lord Melville. Fortunately for Cochrane, the Scottish connection once more came into play. Melville was Pitt's party manager in Scotland and sat like a spider at the centre of a huge web of political patronage and mutual obligation. It took only the slightest pressure from influential Scottish friends and from his uncle, Alexander, to get Cochrane assigned to one of the navy's new 32-gun frigates, the 670-ton *Pallas*. He also seems to have secured an unofficial assurance that a lucrative cruise would be arranged.

Cochrane set about completing his frigate's fit-out in Plymouth, then turned his attention to finding a crew. With the supply of seamen drying up as they were swept into a rapidly expanding navy this proved difficult. He tried to raise volunteers with a recruiting poster that hinted at Spanish treasure and plentiful opportunities for prize money. The poster, which can be seen in the National Maritime Museum to this day, jauntily concluded: 'None need apply but SEAMEN, or stout hands, able to rouse about the Field Pieces, and carry a hundredweight of PEWTER without stopping, at least three miles!' But the appeal had little success and he was forced to fall back on the press gang, causing problems with the civil authorities in Plymouth and provoking a fight with the mayor and constables. But by the end of January 1805 all was ready: *Pallas* weighed anchor and disappeared over the horizon heading for the Azores.

In the voyage that followed, Cochrane's ship won prize money to the grand sum of £300,000 and earned the nickname the 'Golden *Pallas*'. Those who had been enticed into his crew by the promise of wealth on the recruiting poster were not disappointed. They took a Spanish privateer; two merchantmen carrying rich cargoes of sugar, logwood, indigo and silver, and less valuable but interesting bales of Papal indulgences; and a fourth vessel, *La Fortuna*, which had on board half a million Spanish dollars.[14] On 5 April 1805 the *Pallas* returned to Plymouth with, in true Elizabethan fashion, huge gold candlesticks lashed to her mastheads.

Cochrane's two-eighths share of the prize money came to £75,000. He was a rich man. But in what would become a recurring theme throughout his life, he felt he had been cheated out of the full amount. The culprit on this occasion was Admiral William Young, commander-in-chief at Plymouth. Cochrane convinced himself that *Pallas* had actually been sailing under Admiralty Orders, and that Young had intercepted and copied them so that he could pretend the ship was under his command and claim one eighth of the prize money.[15] This became an issue on which Cochrane brooded for the rest of his life and which his biographers have repeated. Young was notorious for being one of the navy's most venal admirals, but in this instance he was innocent. *Pallas* was not sailing under Admiralty Orders, and letters from the First Lord to Plymouth and to Cochrane himself clearly show that the frigate had been put under Young's command.[16] Cochrane's life-long grievance against him was a figment of his imagination.

Six weeks later, *Pallas* sailed from Plymouth as escort ship for the convoys that sailed between Spithead, Halifax and Quebec. It was unexciting work, but Cochrane was never idle. He compensated for the tedium of the voyage by applying his mechanical skills, inventing a special lamp that would enable convoys to keep together more effectively, and experimenting with a giant kite which he felt would somehow assist a ship's forward propulsion. At the end of the year *Pallas* returned to the dank wintry chill of Sheerness dockyard for repairs and re-provisioning. It was there, on Christmas Eve, that all work stopped so that Captain and crew could pay their respects as the *Victory* passed carrying the body of Nelson after his death at Trafalgar two months earlier.

In February 1806, *Pallas* was ordered to join a division of St Vincent's Channel Fleet commanded by Vice Admiral Edward Thornborough deployed in the Bay of Biscay. The task was highly suited to Cochrane's skills, and to help in the expected cutting-out expeditions he had brought with him a fast 18-oared galley constructed at his own expense. For three months he caused uproar up and down the French coast. In April, near the Isle de Ré, he captured a lugger and three coasters filled with wine, and attacked a convoy of barges creeping round the Basque Roads to supply the great naval base of Rochefort. In April, under the command of Lieutenant John Haswell, his boats penetrated far up the Gironde and, in spite of tricky navigation and tides, boarded the 14-gun corvette *Tapageuse* in the mist and, running the gauntlet of the shore batteries, carried her off down river. Next morning, he beat off an attack by three gunboats, driving two ashore. In May Cochrane continued to create chaos in the approaches to Rochefort, destroying shore batteries, burning signal stations and – in company with the sloop *Kingfisher* – launching a gallant but ultimately unsuccessful assault on the big French frigate *Minerve*.

Cochrane's exploits were recorded in brief but dramatic detail in his log and in his despatches, which were forwarded to the Admiralty with increasingly glowing comments by Thornborough and, occasionally, St Vincent. But Cochrane remained uneasy. The insecure side of his personality seemed to need constant praise and reassurance. When the Admiralty – who had not the time to write glowing tributes to every successful captain – were silent, his conviction that he had enemies within was reinforced. Not even the implied compliment contained in the promotions of Lieutenants Haswell and Parker to commander in October satisfied him.

In June 1806 *Pallas* was back in Plymouth being decommissioned, and Cochrane had time on his hands. As his radical political views had developed and his bank balance had increased, so, like others of his class and background, he began to toy with the idea of entering Parliament. In May, when William Cobbett's anti-Establishment *Weekly Political Register* had appealed for a volunteer to come forward to fight the Devon constituency of Honiton in the radical interest, Cochrane had offered his services. Cobbett, realising that a dashing young naval officer was an attractive electoral proposition, secured his nomination. The hustings went well and Cobbett and Cochrane were eloquent in support of reform supported, ironically enough, by his supremely corrupt uncle, Cochrane-Johnstone, whose plausibility seems to have deceived both Cobbett and the Whig brewer Samuel Whitbread. Cochrane's opponent, Mr Cavendish Bradshaw – one of the government placemen he so despised, who had recently been appointed to the non-job of Teller of the Irish Exchequer – said little. He did not need to. Honiton was a 'potwalloper borough' of only 400 electors, and Bradshaw had secured his election in advance by paying the voters 2 guineas a head. Under the puritanical gaze of Cobbett, his political mentor, Cochrane had refused to follow suit and Bradshaw was duly elected. Cochrane, with an eye to the future, then threw a roast ox dinner for all the voters costing £1200 – instantly undermining his opponent's popularity and leaving Bradshaw's supporters with the feeling that they had somehow been cheated.

Four months later Cochrane was back. In October 1806, a general election was called and this time Cochrane was determined to win. He arrived in Honiton in great style accompanied by two uniformed lieutenants, a midshipman, and a cudgel-wielding boat's crew ready for action, and immediately sent the town crier to announce that he would pay 10 guineas a vote! Without Cobbett at his elbow, Cochrane had clearly decided that the ends would justify the means. In 1817, in the House of Commons, Cochrane admitted – and regretted – what he had done. But when he later came to record these events for posterity in his *Autobiography of a Seaman*, he realised that the bare-faced bribery to which he had – however justifiably – resorted sat uncomfortably with his much vaunted hostility to corruption. He therefore doctored the story by claiming that the voters of Honiton had voted for him not because he had promised to pay them 10 guineas a head, but because they *thought* he would do so due to his generosity after his previous defeat.[17] Recent research has shown this version of events to be untrue.[18] Nevertheless, Cochrane's ploy worked, and he was duly elected as Member of Parliament for Honiton.

CHAPTER FOUR

Captain of the *Imperieuse*

LORD COCHRANE may have been on the edge of a parliamentary career, but he was still a naval officer. Indeed, on 23 August 1806 he had been transferred with his crew from the *Pallas* to the *Imperieuse*, a captured Spanish frigate of the largest class carrying a total of 40 guns with twenty-six 18-pounders on the main deck. His appointment, and the deployment of the frigate in Atlantic waters rich with prizes and action, was a clear demonstration of the Admiralty's confidence. Unfortunately, Cochrane could not see it in this way. To him, it was merely a cynical move to muzzle him politically. The Lords of the Admiralty just could not win. If they failed to employ him, he complained of animosity and neglect; if they did, they were trying to get him out of the way! The three years during which Cochrane commanded the *Imperieuse* were the highest points in his life as a frigate captain; but they also brought him to the edge of self-destruction.

The cruise of the *Imperieuse* is also the best-known and best-recorded part of Cochrane's career, largely due to the later literary efforts of one of his midshipmen, Frederick Marryat. Captain Marryat's naval novels were to draw heavily on his experiences in the frigate and his heroic fictional captains are clearly based on Cochrane. There can be no doubt, for example, as to the identity of Captain Lord Edward in *Frank Mildmay*. He was, wrote Marryat,

> ...a sailor every inch of him, he knew the ship from stem to stern, understood the characters of seamen, and gained their confidence. He was besides a good mechanic – a carpenter, rope-maker, sail-maker, and cooper. He could hand, reef, steer, knot and splice; but he was no orator – he read little and spoke less. He was a man of no show. He was good-

tempered, honest, and unsophisticated, with a large proportion of common sense. He was good humoured and free with his officers; though if offended he was violent, but soon calmed down again.

In his memoirs, Marryat recalled and captured the thrills of life on the frigate.

> The cruises of the *Imperieuse* were periods of continual excitement from the hour she hove up her anchor till she dropped it again in port; the day that passed without a shot being fired in anger was with us a blank day; the boats were hardly secured on the booms than they were cast loose again; the yards and stay tackles were for ever hoisting up and lowering down. The expedition with which parties were formed for service, the rapidity of the frigate's movements day and night; the hasty sleep, snatched at all hours; the waking up to the report of the guns; the beautiful precision of our fire obtained by constant practice; the coolness and courage of our captain inoculating the whole ship's company...even now my pulse beats more quickly with the reminiscence.

Cochrane was fortunate in his officers in *Imperieuse*, all of whom played a leading part in the frigate's victories. As first and second lieutenants he had David Mapleton and Urry Johnson, and as midshipmen the Honourable William Napier, a Scots giant from a distinguished naval family, Frederick Marryat, Housten Stewart, who became an admiral, and Henry Cobbett, nephew of Cochrane's radical ally William, who, alas, became the bully of the gunroom.

Despite their later exploits, it was an inauspicious start. *Imperieuse* was commissioned on 8 September 1806 and spent four weeks in dry dock. In spite of the fact that Cochrane was busy with the Honiton election, the ship was fitted out in double quick time. Even so, Admiral Young in Plymouth had become increasingly impatient and forced Cochrane to take *Imperieuse* to sea on 16 November. In the persona of Admiral Sir Hurricane Humbug, Marryat has him watching the frigate disappear over the horizon with the exclamation, 'Damn his eyes! There he goes at last! I was afraid the fellow would have grounded on his own beef bones before we should have got rid of him!' But *Imperieuse* was not ready:

provisions cluttered the deck, rigging was slack and the compass uncorrected. Struggling to sort out the muddle at sea, the frigate was hit by a winter storm which drove her on to rocks near Ushant: it was only by sacrificing her false keel that she managed to escape. But by the beginning of December all was well and Cochrane had reached his cruising station off Rochefort and the Basque Roads. He fell upon the enemy with his usual vigour and, in two months of ceaseless activity, took over 50 merchantmen and destroyed eight gunboats and half a dozen coastal batteries. He returned to Plymouth in the middle of February 1807, leaving the usual trail of devastation behind him.

Politics now intervened. In April 1807, Parliament was dissolved and a new election was called. On this occasion, Cochrane looked around for a more respectable constituency than the rotten borough of Honiton. The two radical candidates for Westminster, the wealthy but idealistic baronet Sir Frances Burdett and a radical tailor called Paull, had quarrelled so violently that the outcome was a duel in which Burdett was wounded. Paull was dropped from the ticket and, on the recommendation of William Cobbett, he was replaced by Cochrane. Their opponents were the Whig playwright Richard Brindsley Sheridan, once a formidable wit but now a wine-sodden has-been, and a Tory nonentity called Elliot. Westminster was probably the most democratic constituency in the country: every ratepayer was entitled to vote and there were reputed to be 17,000 electors. The hustings were aggressive, raucous affairs, with voting done in public over 15 days while rival mobs good humouredly pelted each other with fruit and abuse. But the campaign went well for the radicals, and in the final count Burdett and Cochrane topped the poll. Both were duly elected.

Lord Cochrane was not overawed by the House of Commons. Indeed, on 7 July, showing the same impetuosity he used in battle, he tabled a motion demanding an inquiry into 'all offices, posts, places, sinecures, pensions, situations, fees, perquisites and emoluments…held by any member of this House'. This was followed by an attack on naval abuses and on reductions in the funding of naval hospitals, during which he criticised St Vincent's tenure as First Lord of the Admiralty accusing him of 'rash savings, unworthily made, endangering the lives of officers and seamen' and depicting him as sitting comfortably in London pocketing prize money won by the 'labour and blood' of others.[1] The Tories were delighted; but St Vincent's many admirers in the navy were not. And as Cochrane's vendetta intensified, St Vincent became increasing annoyed, giving vent to his memorable opinion that Cochrane, like others in his family, was 'mad, romantic, money getting and not truth telling!'

In September 1807, *Imperieuse* was sent to the Mediterranean where Vice Admiral Cuthbert Collingwood was in command. Regarded as irreplaceable as head of the Mediterranean Fleet since the death of Nelson at Trafalgar, Collingwood soldiered on, never able to put foot on land, nostalgic for his Northumberland home and growing daffodils in the great cabin of the *Ocean* as poor compensation. Exercising naval control of this vital and volatile area was a complex task and one which was given an extra dimension when the declaration of the French and British continental blockades made the interdiction of trade with the enemy a priority. It was a task to which Cochrane applied himself with enthusiasm.

Although on the whole successful, Cochrane's record was blemished by two lamentable episodes. The first happened one morning when daylight crept over a calm and hazy sea to reveal a small, suspicious-looking armed vessel. Cochrane hoisted British colours and sent two boats and a boarding party under Midshipman Napier to investigate. The vessel was found to be the British privateer *King George*, working out of Malta and manned by a scruffy multinational crew. Her captain, worried by the foreign appearance of *Imperieuse* and assuming that the British flag was a trick, hung out the union flag and tried to resist. The result was a bloody scuffle between the crews of two allied vessels with one killed and 15 wounded on each side. It was all a ghastly misunderstanding. Cochrane was dismayed by the mistake, but there was a minor irregularity in the ship's papers, so he sent her into the Vice Admiralty prize court in Malta. The judge there agreed with Cochrane and confiscated the *King George* but, finding equally that Cochrane's attack on a friendly vessel had been unjustified, he awarded her value to the crown.[2] Cochrane, incapable of accepting the criticism, reacted angrily, claiming that the *King George* was a well known 'pirate' manned by the scum of the Mediterranean, and that £500 had been offered for her capture[3] – a claim for which no evidence has ever been produced.

The second incident occurred when Cochrane was ordered to take

over from Captain Patrick Campbell as senior officer in the Adriatic. On
his way he intercepted three enemy merchantmen carrying illegal licences
to trade, which Campbell – who was well known for such advantageous
devices – had issued. But Cochrane's hopes of commanding a squadron
were never fulfilled. Even before he reached the Adriatic, Collingwood
had decided to reinforce the flotilla in the Adriatic with the 64-gun
Standard whose captain, Thomas Harvey, was senior to Cochrane. By the
rules of seniority, he automatically took command. It was just one of those
things. Cochrane, however, sprang to the conclusion that Campbell had
been so annoyed by the exposure of his 'licence' scheme that he
deliberately engineered the cancellation of his appointment.[4] It was an
early example of Cochrane's assumption that personal malevolence must
be behind every setback, however small. Thus Campbell, too, became an
'enemy' to be denounced anonymously in the *Autobiography of a Seaman*.
Nevertheless, Cochrane learned from the experience, and used licences as
a useful money-making scheme when he was in South America.

Transferred in the spring of 1808 to the western Mediterranean,
Cochrane fell on the coast of Spain and of the Balearic islands with his
customary energy. In the single month of April alone, he blew up the
battery at Citadella in Minorca, captured a French supply vessel taking
wine to the fleet, seized another cargo of enemy wine from a neutral,
bombarded a barracks full of troops, raided Alucia Bay and carried off
sheep, pigs and bullocks, destroyed a second battery at Jacemal, and caused
havoc among coasters on the mainland.

But in June 1808 the situation changed radically when Napoleon
abducted the King of Spain and put his brother Joseph on the throne.
There was widespread resistance. Spain changed allegiance and became a
British ally, while Napoleon was forced to occupy the country in order to
prop up his brother's rule. The main invasion route for the French was the
high road which wound south from the border along the rocky coasts of
Catalonia, round the Bay of Rosas to Gerona and Barcelona, then down
to Tarragona and the flat lands of the Levante as far as Alicante. The coastal
road became a major British target, and from the summer of 1808,
Cochrane harassed the French along its length. His actions over the next
six months revealed him to be a master of amphibious warfare. With the
French occupying fixed positions, he used his sea-borne mobility to

launch lightning raids up and down the coast by boats backed up by the rolling broadsides of the *Imperieuse*. Keeping in constant touch with Spanish patriots – from whom he heard of the destruction and sickening atrocities occasioned by the guerrilla war – he attacked isolated French units, destroyed coastal batteries, levelled signalling stations, blew up whole sections of road, and sent boats filled with seamen and marines into isolated ports to carry out what ships and goods could be removed and burn what could not. At the end of July, he cooperated with Catalan guerrillas in the seizure and destruction of the Fort of Mongat, which controlled communications between Barcelona and Gerona. Collingwood's reports to the Admiralty became more and more lyrical in tone. In October 1808, he wrote that 'nothing can exceed the zeal and activity with which his lordship pursues the enemy. The success which attends his enterprises indicates with what skill and ability they are conducted'; and in January 1809 that 'the heroic spirit and ability which have been evinced by Lord Cochrane…is an admirable example of his lordship's zeal'.

Cochrane's time with the *Imperieuse* confirmed that he was a true leader of men. He led by example and personality and never needed to resort to the lash to establish his authority. It was universally agreed that some level of flogging was necessary to the maintenance of discipline and morale at sea, but Cochrane's logbooks show him to have been among those captains who used it least.[5] He was also fearless and cool under fire, but was never rash, and ensured by careful planning that casualties were kept to a minimum. Captain Jahleel Brenton later wrote, 'I have never known anyone so careful of the lives of his ship's company as Lord Cochrane, or any who calculated the risks attending any expedition. Many of the most brilliant achievements were performed without the loss of a single life'. The men would follow Cochrane anywhere and there are many anecdotes to show it. One told of his asking the coxswain of a boat returning after an unsuccessful attack on a battery if it was impossible to take the objective. The reply was, 'No my Lord, not impossible: we can do it if you will go!' Cochrane immediately jumped into the boat and the battery was taken.[6]

In September 1808, Cochrane and Brenton in the frigate *Spartan* carried the offensive into the French province of Languedoc, blowing up

14 army barracks and severing French communications by destroying the
string of six signalling stations that were vital to the safe movement of
convoys along the coast. Mounting one such raid on the gun battery at
Port Vendres, Cochrane and Brenton first sent the defending cavalry force
galloping in the wrong direction by dressing the ships' boys in red coats
and feigning a landing further down the coast. They then launched the
main assault on the battery while the frigates moved in close to where the
road wound round the rocky headlands above the sea and decimated the
cavalry with grape shot when they hurried back to assist.

Cochrane's best-known operations during this period, however, were
during the defence of Rosas, a major strongpoint on the road south.
French attacks on the town had already been frustrated by the Spanish
defenders with the assistance of Captain John West of the two-decker
Excellent and the bomb vessels *Meteor* and *Lucifer*, and the enemy had been
forced to mount a regular siege. When Cochrane arrived on 22
November, the defences had already been pulverised by a steady
bombardment from batteries erected in the rocky heights around, but the
town, its citadel and the adjacent three-towered castle of Trinidad
continued to hold out. West had already accepted the inevitable and had
taken off his men. Cochrane had other ideas. A quick reconnaissance
convinced him that further resistance was possible and that *Imperieuse* was
better suited to in-shore work than the unwieldy 74-gun *Fame*, which
had just replaced *Excellent*. He also noticed that the cliff on which
Trinidad was built dropped straight down to the sea, making a last minute
evacuation using ladders feasible.

On 24 November, a boatload of over a hundred men led by Cochrane
himself landed to reinforce the defenders of Rosas. And while the heavy
guns of *Imperieuse* and the bomb vessels began to silence the more
exposed of the French batteries, Cochrane threw all his ingenuity into
converting what was left of the castle into a vast mantrap. Breeches in the
walls were piled with rubble and with hammocks and canvas awnings
filled with sand; barricades were erected using an early form of barbed
wire made from chains festooned with fishhooks; and on the slopes of the
glacis a device was built, which was made of planks covered in cook's
grease so that once the attackers had breeched the first line of defence,
they would lose their footing and slide into a 50-foot hole in the centre.

It was, as Marryat wrote, 'a very good bug trap!' But Cochrane could only delay the inexorable French assault. A week later it came. Covered by precise gunfire, which even Cochrane had to admire, a thick column of enemy infantry curled its way steadily down the valley and hurled itself into the breach. The defences held out, and the attack was repelled with heavy losses.

The siege of Rosas continued with a steady bombardment and desultory attacks by the defenders while the French paused to regroup. Then, on 4 December, they came again, this time in overwhelming strength. Marryat recalls wryly through Frank Mildmay how Cochrane, who had led his men forward to pepper the enemy lines with musketry, made a hasty but dignified retreat.

> The captain then ordered his men to run into the castle which they instantly obeyed, while he himself walked leisurely along through a shower of musket balls.... I felt bound in honour as well as duty, as an aide-de-camp, to walk by the side of my captain, fully expecting every moment that a rifle ball would have hit me where I should have been ashamed to show the scar. I though his funereal pace confounded nonsense: but my fire eating captain never had run away from a Frenchman, and did not intend to begin now. I was beside him, making these reflections, and as the shot began to fly very thick, I stepped up alongside of him and so by degrees, brought him between myself and the fire.... He laughed and said, 'I did not know you were here, for I meant you to have gone with the others; but since you are out of your station Mr Mildmay, I will make use of you which you so ingeniously intended to make of me. My life may be of some importance here; but yours very little; and another midshipman can be had from the ship only for the asking: so just drop astern if you please, and do duty as breastwork for me!'

In anticipation of the assault, Cochrane had already booby-trapped the castle with delayed action grenades and demolition charges. Next day, as the French prepared their final advance, he blew up the castle's strong points and effected a flawless evacuation, sending his men, both British and Spanish, scrambling down the cliff to the waiting boats of the

Imperieuse, *Fame* and *Magnificent* which had arrived to help. It was now time to return to England. But there was one more action when, in December, *Imperieuse* caught a convoy of victuallers in the harbour of Cadaques, sinking two escort ships, destroying a protective shore battery and carrying off eleven vessels filled with supplies for the French army.

The voyage of the *Pallas* had made Lord Cochrane a rich man: that of the *Imperieuse* made him famous. *The Naval Chronicle* printed a potted biography together with stories of his bravery and ingenuity;[7] and *The Times*, marvelling at what he had done with one ship, suggested that he be sent back at the head of a squadron to do more.[8] Cochrane was of the same mind, but his grasp of strategy never matched his tactical skill, and he was way off the mark when he later claimed that if he had been deployed against the French army's western lines of communication, the Peninsular War could have become a minor campaign rather than a major conflagration.[9]

Back in England, Cochrane's first objective was to enjoy a period of relaxation. The second was to press his strategic ideas about the war in Spain on the government. He was also keen to use his position in Parliament to expose another issue, namely the activities of the Vice Admiralty prize court in Malta. His interest had begun with the *King George* incident, but it had been stimulated by the widespread dissatisfaction that existed among his fellow naval officers with the court's activities and the huge fees it levied. But none of these plans were realised. No sooner had *Imperieuse* arrived at Plymouth in March 1809, than Cochrane found himself in a post chaise speeding up the road to London in answer to an urgent summons from Lord Mulgrave, the presiding First Lord of the Admiralty.

The Admiralty had a problem. Winter storms had driven the Channel Fleet off station, which had allowed a French division to escape from Brest and meet up with the Rochefort squadron. The combined force, comprising 10 ships of the line and five frigates under Vice Admiral Zacharie-Jacques-Théodore Allemand, was now sheltering in the Basque Roads awaiting an opportunity to head for the West Indies. Outside, a British force under Admiral Lord Gambier, totalling 11 ships of the line and a dozen frigates and smaller fry, was waiting. But the Admiralty was determined to do more than just wait. It wanted action. The Bay of Biscay was notoriously treacherous, and a spell of bad weather might enable the French to escape again. Likewise, although the tides and sandbanks of the Basque Roads made the normal method of assault extraordinary difficult, Captain Richard Keats had pointed out two years previously that it was vulnerable to 'an attack of bombs, fire-ships and rockets, covered and protected by the squadron…which should be kept…as close to Isle d'Aix as possible in order that it may be in constant readiness to act decisively'.[10] Gambier had accepted the idea, even though he thought it was 'a horrid mode of warfare, and the attempt hazardous if not desperate',[11] and a number of officers, led by the tough Trafalgar veteran Rear Admiral Eliab Harvey, immediately offered their services.

In London, the Admiralty was convinced that fireships were the answer. The arrival of Lord Cochrane at Plymouth therefore seemed providential. Here was an officer who was not only familiar with the Basque Roads, he excelled in unusual methods of fighting and knew all about pyrotechnics. Cochrane did not disappoint Mulgrave, and offered a much improved plan whereby fireships would be complemented by explosion vessels. Mulgrave was delighted and invited Cochrane to take charge of the forthcoming attack. For once in his life, Cochrane's impulsive nature was tempered by caution. He guessed that there would be senior officers in Gambier's fleet who were yearning for such a chance and would resent the arrival of a young captain from London to snatch all the glory. He refused the offer. But Mulgrave was insistent and Cochrane eventually had to accept. At the end of March 1809, he sailed in *Imperieuse* to join Gambier's fleet.

CHAPTER FIVE

The Basque Roads Affair

ADMIRAL JAMES GAMBIER was not a popular commander. He had certainly seen action, having commanded the *Defence* at the Glorious First of June and been responsible for the seizure of the Danish fleet in Copenhagen in 1807, but he was better known for the years he had spent as a cold and punctilious Admiralty bureaucrat. He was also a member of the evangelical movement, and exhibited a self-righteous religious zeal which annoyed veterans such as Eliab Harvey who believed that officers of the fleet would be better employed surveying the Aix channel than distributing tracts, mustering for prayer meetings and trying to suppress bad language. His nicknames 'Dismal Jimmy' and 'Preaching Jemmy' said it all.

Gambier welcomed Cochrane on 3 April 1809 with studied courtesy. But in the fleet, Cochrane's appointment had exactly the effect he had feared. Harvey in particular was furious, assuming that the decision had been Gambier's and stomping the flagship's deck in a fury, cursing the Admiral, accusing him publicly of being unfit for command, and claiming that he had been passed over because he was 'no canting Methodist, no hypocrite, no psalm singer!'[1] Harvey then hauled down his flag in disgust and returned to England to face the inevitable court martial.

Gambier carefully observed the Admiralty's instructions. His orders said that Cochrane was to mastermind the fireship operation 'under your lordship's direction', but neither officer took that literally. Gambier never tried to impose his authority over Cochrane. Likewise, Cochrane had no desire to have his hands tied by Gambier, and acted as if he were responsible directly to the Admiralty.[2] As a result there was little real communication between the two men and they entered the action with different ideas on both the tactical situation and how the attack was to unfold.

The Basque Roads is made up of a vast bay running roughly north-west to south-east, bounded by the Isle de Ré to the north and separated from the sea by the sandy flats of the Isle d'Oleron to the west. The mainland lies to the east with the Charante river, site of the great arsenal of Rochefort, flowing into the southern corner beyond the Isle d'Aix. There was ample sea room for ships at the entrance to the bay where the British fleet was positioned. But any vessel going further had to follow a shallow channel less than 2 miles wide between the Boyart shoal on the right and the Isle d'Aix and its attendant shallows on the left. Once past the island, the channel then swung left to avoid the Palles shoal before opening into the estuary of the Charante. It was here that the French fleet had its anchorage, protected by a great boom across the channel and by gun batteries.

Cochrane began his preparations as soon as he reached the Basque Roads, packing his explosion vessels with casks of powder, and supervising the fireships which each vessel in the squadron was required to provide. When the rest of the fireships, explosives and rockets arrived from England on 10 April accompanied by their inventer, Colonel William Congreve, he was ready to go. Gambier refused to authorise an attack for that night, which was just as well because Vice Admiral Allemand, guessing the purpose of the new arrivals, had taken immediate countermeasures. Deploying three frigates ahead to watch the boom, he reorganised his heavy ships into two lines facing north, the first made up of *Foudroyant*, *Varsovie*, *Ocean*, *Regulus* and *Cassard*, the second of *Tonnerre*, *Patriote*, *Jemmapes*, *Aquilon* and *Tourville*. The ships in each line were moored in zigzag formation, and the right flank of each was covered by a frigate, the first by an ex-British prize *Calcutta*, the second by the *Elbe*. Topmasts were struck and sails unbent to reduce the amount of flammable material, while 73 boats packed with men were deployed around the fleet ready to board and tow off any threatening fireships.

The British launched their attack on 11 April.[3] In the afternoon, there was a briefing on the massive 120-gun flagship *Caledonia*, after which the ships took up their allotted stations. Towing one of the explosion vessels, *Imperieuse* headed for the southern end of the Boyart shoal accompanied by the schooner *Whiting*, two cutters armed with rockets and the frigates *Aigle*, *Unicorn* and *Pallas*, whose job was to pick up the crews of the fireships. Nearby, in a position to throw shells into the Isle d'Aix was the bomb vessel *Etna* protected by the frigate *Indefatigable* and the brig *Foxhound*. To the east of the island, three more frigates and three brigs were deployed as reserves. The rest of the fleet remained at its anchorage 8 miles away to the north-west.

At 8.30 p.m., 20 fireships and two explosion vessels – with Cochrane leading in the first – were unleashed on the enemy line. Driven by a fast flood tide and by winds from the north-north-west so strong that the protective boats around the French fleet had to be withdrawn, the British rushed down on the enemy. At 9.30 p.m., Cochrane detonated the first of the explosion vessels in a mighty blast which tore the boom from its moorings, turned the sky red and filled the air with shells and grenades. Observers in the fleet could then see fireships in flames hurtling down on the enemy, the rockets tied to their yardarms spitting fire in all directions. Fifteen minutes later, Captain James Wooldridge in the explosion ship *Mediator* smashed what was left of the boom and they were through.

To the watchers in the fleet, the attack already looked like a victory, but Cochrane was disappointed. The explosion vessels had detonated prematurely and only four of the fireships had managed to reach the enemy. Some had got lost in the darkness, some had been hampered by the boom, others had burnt out too soon. Cochrane later complained that their crews had ignited their ships early in order to escape but it is more likely that the strength of the wind made both fuses and charges burn faster than had been expected. Even so, the effects were devastating. Faced with these devilish weapons, the French had cut their cables in panic and been driven aground by the gale force wind and tide. And when Cochrane scanned the horizon at dawn next morning, he could find only two of the enemy's line-of-battle ships, *Foudroyant* and *Cassard*, afloat: the remaining eight were perched, some at crazy angles, on the mud of the Palles flats.

At first light, Cochrane made the first of a series of signals to the flagship, reporting the plight of the French as more and more of their vessels became stranded. At 5.48 a.m. he signalled, 'Half the Fleet can destroy the enemy'; at 6.40 a.m., 'Eleven on shore'; and at 7.40, 'Only two afloat'. But with the passing of low water at 8 a.m., the French prepared to haul themselves off on the rising tide. Gambier was also ready, and at

10.45 a.m. the fleet began to move. But to Cochrane's dismay, an hour later it anchored again, 3 miles short of the Isle d'Aix just out of range of the batteries. With the wind still strong from the north-west and the tide running fast, Gambier was unwilling to risk his clumsy line-of-battle ships any further until around 2 p.m. when the tide turned and the ebb could carry them out again if they got into trouble.

While the British fleet remained motionless, the French began to re-float their ships. Cochrane, watching with a frustration that was shared by many others, became convinced that Gambier had no intention of bringing his ships of the line down to attack the enemy. He was partly correct: Gambier's plan was to do exactly what Keats had recommended – namely, to use the fleet as a reserve and to rely on the smaller sloops, the frigates and the odd two-decker to complete the destruction of the French. Unaware of what Gambier intended to do, Cochrane embarked on a series of daring manoeuvres designed to force the Admiral into a major attack. At 1 p.m., he allowed *Imperieuse* to drift down stern first on the enemy, then made sail and began to engage the *Calcutta*, *Aquilon* and the 80-gun *Varsovie*, all the while sending up increasingly urgent signals. At 1.30 p.m. he signalled, 'The enemy ships are getting under sail'; at 1.40 p.m., 'Enemy superior to chasing ship'; and five minutes later, 'In want of assistance'.

Just before 2 p.m., as the tide was about to turn, the bomb vessel *Etna* and three gun brigs were ordered forward to bombard the enemy, followed by the frigates *Indefatigable*, *Emerald*, *Aigle* and *Pallas*, and the two-deckers *Valiant*, *Bellona* and *Revenge* under Captain John Bligh. It was all part of Gambier's plan, although Cochrane was convinced that Gambier had only acted because his signals had shamed him into doing so. With the British now on the move, *Foudroyant* and *Cassard* cut their cables and ran for it, both grounding out of range on the mud at the mouth of the Charante. By 3 p.m., all the British ships were in position and the firing became general, the French ships stranded on the northern tip of the Palles shoal bearing the brunt. At 4.10 p.m. the *Calcutta* struck to the exhausted crew of the *Imperieuse*; at 5.30 p.m. the *Aquilon* and *Varsovie* surrendered; and half an hour later *Tonnerre* was set on fire by her crew. Bligh in the *Valiant* tried to attack Allemand's flagship *Ocean*, but could make no impact on the big three-decker. Rear Admiral Robert Stopford arrived with reinforcements in the shape of the two-deckers *Caesar* and *Theseus* and three fireships to join the attack. But by this time the tide was falling fast, and first *Imperieuse* then *Valiant* and *Caesar* slid to a halt on the mud. They could not be re-floated until 10 p.m.

At dawn next morning, the wind hauled round to the west and Stopford, convinced that the big ships could do nothing more, raised the signal to withdraw, leaving the four gun brigs, *Pallas*, *Imperieuse* and the bomb vessel *Etna* to harry the enemy which was now heaving guns over the side, unloading stores and pumping out water. Gambier then hung out a signal recalling *Imperieuse*. Cochrane ignored it, replying, 'The enemy can be destroyed'. The Admiral tried twice more – once by letter – only to receive the enigmatic responses, 'We can destroy the enemy' and 'Shall we unmoor' while the frigates and smaller ships went on firing. Finally, Gambier lost patience. Next morning, 14 April, he sent Captain George Wolfe of *Aigle* to relieve Cochrane carrying a courteous letter, which ordered him to take Flag Captain Sir Harry Neale to England with despatches. Cochrane boarded the flagship in a state of high dudgeon, urging Gambier to complete the work of annihilation by sending Stopford back in order to 'prevent a noise being made in England'. Gambier bridled. Cochrane was all innocence: he spoke, he said 'as a friend'. But the threat was real enough. Hours later Cochrane and *Imperieuse* were at sea bound for home.

Four years after Trafalgar, the nation was hungry for a victory and the news was enthusiastically received. This time, the navy had not only destroyed five enemy ships and put the rest out of action, but had shown the French that even the most well-protected anchorage was not beyond its reach. The Admiral's victory despatch, which was printed in full in *The Times*, began, 'The Almighty's favour to his Majesty and the nation, has been strongly marked in the success. He has been pleased to give the operations of his Majesty's fleet under my command…', and continued by lavishing praise on Cochrane's ingenuity and skill.

I cannot speak in sufficient terms of admiration and applause of the vigorous and gallant attack made by Lord Cochrane upon the French line-of-battleships which were on shore, as well as his judicious manner of approaching them, and placing his ship in the position most advantageous to annoy the enemy, and preserve his own ship; which could not be exceeded by any feat of valour hitherto achieved by the British Navy.[4]

But the nation needed a hero as well as a victory, and the dashing Cochrane was a far better candidate than the dour evangelical Gambier. The King made him a Knight of the Bath, and the public sung patriotic ballads in his honour. However, the euphoria over the battle did not last long. Spreading from either *Imperieuse* or letters from the fleet, there were whispers that the victory had been only partial, and that Gambier had shown a lack of enterprise. Two weeks later, *The Times* published an article headed, 'Lord Cochrane's Victory', which dwelt at length on his daring and his nobility in victory and hinted that his triumph had been achieved in spite of jealousy and the obstruction of 'helpless seniority'.[5] It was the same theme that was to underlie all of Cochrane's later autobiographies. And from the amount of detail in the article, and the repeated demand that he be sent back to Spain at the head of a squadron, it is impossible to believe that the writer was not someone close to Cochrane. The obvious candidate was a new acquaintance, a legal clerk called William Jackson. Jackson was a shadowy figure, who was soon to became Cochrane's secretary and would remain with him for 50 years, producing the drafts for his innumerable letters and petitions, and having a major influence on the content of his memoirs. He also composed and had printed at Cochrane's expense a mock-classical poem lampooning the commander-in-chief called 'The Gambryad'.

Cochrane's annoyance with Gambier's caution is understandable. But what he did next is not. Instead of remaining discreetly silent and enjoying the reflected glory of what was seen as a huge success, he decided to make an issue of it and informed Lord Mulgrave that, if the customary vote of thanks to Gambier was to be proposed in Parliament, he would regard it as his duty to oppose it. Mulgrave was appalled. Not only would such an act undermine the government's triumph; public criticism of a superior officer by a subordinate would strike at the roots of all discipline. Cochrane's reply that his two personae as member of parliament and naval officer were quite separate was clearly nonsense. Mulgrave tried to dissuade him, even offering a plum command in the

Mediterranean. Cochrane refused to compromise. Clear headed as he was on a quarterdeck in time of war, his judgement seemed to desert him in time of peace. Now, convinced of his own rectitude and unable to see any point of view but his own, he embarked on a course of action which was to harm his reputation more than Gambier's.

Confronted with Cochrane's determination, and aware of the whispered criticism, Gambier demanded a court martial to clear his name. It was convened on HMS *Gladiator* in Portsmouth harbour on 26 July 1809. The President of the Court was Sir Roger Curtis, sitting with six admirals and four post-captains who had been assembled to act as interrogators and judges. The logs of all the ships involved were gathered as evidence and Gambier was invited to write a second despatch to amplify the brief details given in the first. To reflect the tenor of Cochrane's criticisms and, no doubt, to avoid any similarity to the 12th Article of War which lay down the death penalty for 'any person in the fleet who shall not do his utmost to take or destroy' the enemy, the charge was carefully drafted. But it pulled no punches, and concluded, '…it appears to us that the said Admiral Lord Gambier, on the 12th of the said month of April, the enemy's ships being on shore, and the signal having been made that they could be destroyed, did for a considerable time neglect or delay taking effectual measures for destroying them…'. The trial was lengthy, and on the eighth day, after 240 printed pages of evidence, Gambier was acquitted.[6]

Cochrane's reaction was predictable. Since he *knew* Gambier to be guilty, the only explanation for the verdict was that the court martial had been rigged. He accused the judges of bias, of failing to call witnesses who were critical of Gambier, of browbeating those who appeared, and of falsifying evidence and charts. And he went further, railing that 'ruin and inevitable damnation hangs over…the witnesses – all of whom fall under the penalty attendant on perjury, except Broughton, Malcolm, Newcombe and Seymour'.[7] Study of the court martial records, however, supports none of these accusations. There were certainly undercurrents, since the idea that a commander-in-chief could be court-martialled because a junior officer disagreed with his actions was anathema; and some members of the court – notably his old adversary Admiral Sir William Young – were openly hostile. The court refused to allow

Cochrane, who had difficulty remembering he was a witness and not a prosecutor, to go off at tangents; but no stone was left unturned, and every angle of both the prosecution and defence cases was exposed at length. In fact it all rested on two questions: should Gambier have moved against the stranded French vessels before 2 p.m.? And were his reasons for not doing so justifiable?

The case against Gambier – made at length by Lord Cochrane whose evidence took up a whole day – was that the attack should have taken place between 11 a.m. and noon, when the French were still helpless; and that the Admiral's assessment of the situation had been wrong. Cochrane maintained that the Aix channel was wider, and the batteries less effective than Gambier had claimed. He had also found an anchorage to the south of the Isle d'Aix in which six ships of the line could have sheltered from enemy fire. He argued that if the attack had taken place earlier, the likelihood of ships getting into difficulties was remote and the victory would have been greater. He claimed that

> There was no delay whatever to the best of my belief after the signal for assistance was made on the part of Lord Gambier, in ordering the vessels to our assistance; but had the attack been made in the morning when the tide was falling, until past 8 o'clock, and when the enemy's ships were all with the exception of two, fast aground…with their masts and yards apparently locked, in which position they continued until 1 o'clock, it is my opinion that seven sail of the enemy, including the three decker, might have been destroyed with facility by two sail of the line, assisted by frigates and smaller vessels, And it is my opinion, that after the hour of half past 11…the frigates alone, assisted by the smaller vessels, might have destroyed the whole of the above mentioned ships, the rear of which afterwards were attacked.

Cochrane offered to produce French charts that would prove his assertions, but they were disallowed on the grounds that their accuracy could not be established and that Lord Gambier's actions could only be judged on the basis of what he actually knew at the time.

Gambier's defence was that the narrowness of the Aix channel, the strength of the batteries, their ability to use red-hot shot, and the lack of an anchorage where his heavy ships could shelter, made any attack problematic at the best of times. On the morning of 12 April, it had been made even more hazardous because of the north-west wind and the tide. He had instead relied on frigates and smaller craft backed by a few ships of the line. No other course was possible, he argued in the court martial report, because

…the movements of the enemy's ships were not, as I submitted to the Court, to be prevented by any means I could adopt with the slightest chance of success, and without HM ships being put in unwarranted peril…. The wind blew in, so that in the event of our ships being crippled while the flood tide was running, it would have been impossible for them to have worked out, or to have retreated to an anchorage out of reach of the enemy's shot and shells; the consequence of which could scarcely have been less than their utter destruction.

These serious impediments induced me to delay the attack until the latter part of the flood, in order to give any ships, which might be disabled in their approach, a chance of returning by means of the receding tide. Had the wind been favourable for sailing in and out – or even the latter only – there could be no doubt that the sooner the enemy's ships were attacked the better.

Lord Cochrane has expressed opinion, that two or three sail of the line sent in on the morning of the 12th might, by running up on the verge of the Boyart shoal, have passed to leeward of the two French ships remaining at anchor. This I declare to have been absolutely impractical; as well from the raking fire of the two ships afloat and upright on the shoal, and the fire of the batteries… Had I pursued the measures deemed practical and proper in the judgement of Lord Cochrane, I am persuaded the success attending this achievement would have proved more dearly bought than any yet recorded in our naval annals.

Twenty-five witnesses were called, including 17 of the captains who had been present. Each was asked two questions: did he believe that line-of-battle ships could have entered the Aix channel on the morning of 12 April and then got out again if in difficulties? Did he think that Gambier had been negligent in attacking the enemy? Only five of the captains answered in the affirmative – Cochrane (*Imperieuse*), Seymour (*Pallas*), Newcombe (*Beagle*), Malcolm (*Donegal*) and Broughton (*Illustrious*). Maitland of the *Emerald* was on a cruise but was known to be of the same mind. All agreed with Cochrane that the attack should have been made at 11 a.m. They admitted, however, that although the victory would have been more devastating, it would have resulted in a greater number of British casualties.

Twelve of the captains who had been in action against the French ships with Cochrane south of the Isle d'Aix gave negative answers and supported Gambier. These included Wolfe (*Aigle*), Rodd (*Indefatigable*), Bligh (*Valiant*), Kerr (*Revenge*), Godfrey (*Etna*), Hardyman (*Unicorn*) and Beresford (*Theseus*). Beresford added that when he had boarded *Imperieuse* in the afternoon, he had said to Lord Cochrane that 'ships-of-the-line have no place here', and had been astonished by the reply that in the all-out attack he (Cochrane) favoured, he would have expected three ships of the line to have been lost but that 'it did not signify'. In addition, four of the captains of the watching two-deckers supported Gambier – Ball (*Gibraltar*), Burleton (*Resolution*), Douglas (*Bellerophon*) and Newman (*Hero*). And Rear Admiral Stopford agreed, saying that the conditions which had prevented earlier attacks on the Basque Roads by heavy ships had not been changed by Cochrane's success with the fireships, and that if he had been in command he would not have risked them in the Aix channel either.

The Master of the *Caledonia*, Stokes, and Master of the Fleet Fairfax, both of whom had watched the whole action from brigs anchored in the Aix channel, also answered in the negative. Fairfax was asked about the various charts in use. He explained that there were a number of discrepancies between the British charts, *Le Neptune François* and his own soundings, and that he was of the opinion that the navigational information was not reliable enough to justify the taking of risks.

Modern opinion tends to agree with Cochrane that Gambier was too cautious and that he should have sent his ships in earlier. A more aggressive commander in the Nelson tradition, it is said, would certainly have done so. The court martial reports on the French officers involved – who were better informed on local conditions – supported Cochrane's contention that if Gambier had acted more decisively, a greater victory would have been achieved. But the majority of senior British professionals who were on the spot, and who were not privy to this knowledge, backed Gambier's refusal to take risks. The Admiral's acquittal was therefore inevitable.

Even then Cochrane could not leave the matter alone. First, he tried to have the whole question re-opened by proposing that the court martial record be placed before Parliament. When that failed, he vehemently opposed the vote of thanks to Gambier that was presented in January 1810. In spite of his efforts, it was passed with an overwhelming majority.

CHAPTER SIX

———

Radical and Romantic

THE BASQUE ROADS AFFAIR confirmed Lord Cochrane's popularity with the press and the Westminster electorate, but it did him little good in the navy. His reputation for bravery and ingenuity was reinforced, but he was seen in senior circles as being responsible for the public humiliation of the worthy if unattractive Lord Gambier. Even Gillray joined in with a cartoon showing Cochrane and a British Tar eager to get at the French while Gambier gives priority to bible reading. Naval colleagues were disturbed by Cochrane's pursuit of the Admiral and by the barrack-room 'lawyerish' way in which he justified it. And what admiral would now want Cochrane under his command? Nevertheless, the Admiralty were still willing – indeed eager – to employ him afloat and repeatedly tried to do so – although not on his terms. They turned down two of Cochrane's requests: one to lead an attack on the Scheldt with explosion vessels and mortars, the other, to go to Flushing as an observer of the Walcheren expedition. To Cochrane of course, these were further examples of Admiralty contempt and persecution.

There is no evidence to support this accusation, and the fact that the Basque Roads was Cochrane's last assignment with the Royal Navy during the Napoleonic Wars was largely his own fault. At a time when the career of the average frigate captain was three-and-a-half years, he had not only served for six, but the Admiralty were ready to put him in that elite group of frigate commanders who were employed for seven or eight.[1] But in the first half of 1810, Cochrane was distracted by politics.

It all began in the Autumn of 1809 when the remnants of the British army limped back from its disastrous invasion of the Low Countries. The expedition had begun with high hopes and the aim of seizing the islands where the East and West Scheldt flow into the North Sea to use as a springboard for an attack on the arsenals of Flushing and Antwerp. But from the outset things had gone wrong. Gales had delayed the landing; there were conflicts between the leisurely habits of General the Earl of Chatham and his impatient naval counterpart, Sir Richard Strachan; and the French were found to be entrenched in unexpected strength. The British army quickly became bogged down in the mud and fogs of Walcheren Island, its numbers decimated by the effects of bad food, dysentery and malaria. Within months it was forced into ignominious withdrawal. In February 1810, the government decided to hold an enquiry into the fiasco in secret. 'Citizen' Gale Jones, a printer and chairman of a radical debating society, plastered the walls of Westminster with protest posters and found himself locked in Newgate prison charged with contempt. When Cochrane's constituency partner, Sir Frances Burdett, denounced the treatment of Jones in William Cobbett's *Weekly Political Register*, he was charged with the same offence.

To avoid arrest, on 6 April, Burdett fled to his house at 78 Piccadilly and barricaded himself inside. He was joined by his political allies, including Francis Place and Lord Cochrane. A mob of radical sympathisers gathered outside, chanting anti-government slogans, throwing mud at passers-by and smashing the windows of nearby ministerial residences. The disturbances lasted for four days until troops were called in. Cannon were placed in Berkeley Square and the Tower, and there was a cavalry charge by the Life Guards down Piccadilly to disperse the mob. Organising the resistance inside number 78, Cochrane was in his element, even producing a barrel of gunpowder to mine the facade with the apparent intention of bringing it down on the heads of anyone who forced an entry. Fortunately, Burdett's commitment to Liberty did not extend to blowing up his own house and Cochrane was asked to leave. Burdett was probably relieved when the following morning a constable managed to get in through a basement window and arrested him at the very moment he was translating the Magna Carta with his son.

Cochrane became a radical star – a leading speaker at meetings in the Crown and Anchor tavern in the Strand, who frequently arrived at the House of Commons on the shoulders of a cheering crowd. But the political background had subtly changed. A new Tory government had come to power in 1809 led by a modest lawyer called Spencer Perceval. There was a new team at the Admiralty with Charles Yorke as First Lord and a cynical Irish MP, John Wilson Croker, as Secretary. Croker, notorious for his acid contributions to the *Quarterly Review*, was to prove himself a highly efficient operator who was to keep the job for 21 years. None of these changes in personnel, however, blunted Cochrane's reforming zeal and in May 1810 he had his finest parliamentary moment. Rising to speak on a motion by Croker concerning naval expenditure, he began by giving a detailed list of the financial compensation given to naval officers for injuries and loss of limbs, then launched a cogent attack on the amounts paid out in pensions and perks to government supporters, compliant peers and the Wellesley family. 'An admiral worn out in the service,' he pointed out, to roars of approval,

...is superannuated at £410 a year, a captain at £210: a clerk of the ticket office retires on £700 a year! The widow of Admiral Sir Andrew Mitchell has one third of the allowance given to the widow of a commissioner of the navy! To speak less in detail, 32 flag officers, 22 captains, 50 lieutenants, 180 masters, 36 surgeons, 23 pursers, 91 boatswains, 97 gunners, 202 carpenters and 41 cooks – in all 774 persons – cost the country less than the net proceeds of the sinecures of Lord Arden (£20,358), Camden (£20,536) and Buckingham (£20,693).... All that is paid to the wounded officers of the whole British navy, and to the wives and children of those dead or killed in action, do not amount by £210 to as much as Lord Arden's sinecure, viz £20,358.

Is this justice? Is this the treatment which officers of the navy deserve at the hands of those who call themselves His Majesty's Government? Does the country know of this injustice? Will it be defended? I cannot suppress my feelings...

I find upon examination that the Wellesleys receive from the public £34,729, a sum equal to 426 lieutenants' legs, calculated at the rate for Lieutenant Chalmer's legs. Calculating for the pension of Captain Johnson's arm, viz £45, Lord Arden's sinecure is equal to the value of 1022 captains' arms. [And] the Marquis of Buckingham's sinecure alone will maintain the...victualling departments at Chatham, Dover, Gibraltar,

Sheerness, Downs, Heligoland, Cork, Malta, Mediterranean, Cape of Good Hope and Rio de Janeiro and still leave £5460 in the Treasury![2]

During this time, Cochrane's frigate, *Imperieuse*, was at sea under a substitute captain, the Honourable Henry Duncan, son of the victor of Camperdown and another Scot. It was normal procedure for a captain who also had parliamentary duties to be temporarily replaced by another. In June, Parliament was prorogued and the Admiralty was anxious to send Cochrane and the frigate to the western Mediterranean. The First Lord wrote to Cochrane to ask if he was willing to return to his command. After a lengthy and confused correspondence, Cochrane had to admit that he was not. A tedious period of blockade duty off Toulon was not to his taste and Cochrane declined to serve – although it did not prevent him claiming that his substitution had been 'forced'.[3] In his place Duncan was confirmed as captain of the *Imperieuse*.

Cochrane was now free to enjoy a period of leave, going to live in Hampshire, near the Hamble river and the Boteley farm of his friend, William Cobbett. There he revealed the other side of his complex and contradictory personality. In public he may have been a radical rebel and a scourge of the Establishment but in private he was very different. The novelist Mary Russell Mitford, who was there at the time, was amazed to find that although Cochrane was at

> ...the height of his warlike fame [he was] as unlike the common notion of a warrior as could be. A gentle, quiet, mild young man was this burner of French fleets, as one should see in a summer day. He lay about under the trees reading Selden on the Dominion of the Seas and letting the children (and children always know with whom they may take liberties) play all sorts of tricks with him at their pleasure.[4]

Twelve years later in 1822, another lady writer, Maria Graham, was to describe him in similar terms.

> His naturally powerful mind had received all the solid advantage and much grace of cultivation; and his singularly gentle and courteous manner, which veiled while it adorned the determination of his

character, was admirable calculated to conciliate all parties. Though not handsome, Lord Cochrane has an expression of countenance which induced you, when you have once looked to look again and again. It is as variable as the feelings that pass within; but the general look is of great benevolence. His conversation, when he does break his ordinary silence, is rich and varied; on subjects connected with his profession, or his pursuits, clear and animated; if ever I met with genius, I should say it was pre-eminent in Lord Cochrane.[5]

And these were not the only unexpected aspects to his character. As the Regency gathered its raffish, devil-may-care momentum, the life of the average young aristocrat became a cycle of vast meals punctuated with port, hock and sherry, followed by gambling sprees at White's Club or Newmarket and affairs with easy-going social hostesses. Lord Cochrane shared none of these vices. He drank remarkably little, never gambled, and there was never the slightest hint of any sexual impropriety or relationship. He played little part in the Regency social scene, and his penurious upbringing and Scottish sense of propriety resulted in a lifestyle that was almost middle class in its seriousness.

Cochrane's restless personality could not remain idle for long. In 1811, as a comparatively rich man, he decided to take a Mediterranean cruise in his yacht *Julie*. But there was a hidden agenda. While visiting Malta he wanted to take a look at the Vice Admiralty prize court. Lawyers are never the most popular members of any society, and naval officers at the time were convinced that the lawyers who ran the prize courts were growing fat at their expense – colluding in order to prolong actions and increase their fees, encouraging pointless appeals, and making excessive charges. Modern research has discounted most of these accusations,[6] but Cochrane, like his uncle, certainly believed them.

The saga began when Cochrane reached Malta and visited the court on 20 February 1811 to find that the table of fees was not hanging in open court where, according to law, it should have been. After a search he found it pinned up in the Judge's Robing Room – although he later claimed that it was in the judge's privy. Cochrane tore it down and took it away. The Judge, an experienced but fussy and meticulous man called Sewell, immediately issued a warrant for his arrest for contempt. When the bailiffs found him in the navy commissioner's office, Cochrane refused to surrender himself on the grounds that the arrest was illegal, but later allowed them to carry him downstairs in his chair, bundle him into a carriage and – to the cheers of the assembled naval officers – drive him off to gaol. Once incarcerated in a roomy apartment at the top of the building, Cochrane went on hunger strike and refused to pay for his food. Sewell, sensing potential embarrassment, countered by ordering that his food and drink be supplied free. Cochrane responded by throwing a succession of lavish dinner parties for his naval friends, whose appetites were made even sharper by the knowledge that the court was paying to satiate them. By now the situation had descended into farce. Finally, a file was smuggled into the gaol; Cochrane sawed his way through the bars, slid down a rope and escaped.

Returning to England, Cochrane recounted his adventure to a delighted House of Commons as part of an attack on the Vice Admiralty courts. On average, court fees amounted to only 20 per cent of a prize's value, but many of the fees were fixed so that, the amounts left in respect of low value prizes could be abysmally small. There was more to Cochrane's complaint about Malta than that. Normally, Vice Admiralty courts had four officers – a judge, a registrar who was responsible for the paperwork, a marshal who handled the prize goods and duties, and a proctor who acted on behalf of the crown and the captors. In Malta, Cochrane found that a man called Jackson held both of the last two offices, with the result that he was solemnly paying himself fees as proctor for services he provided to himself as marshal and vice versa! The fact that Malta was too small to warrant the whole legal team and that permission had been given to combine the roles of proctor and marshal was overlooked – as was the fact that the fees charged there were actually lower than elsewhere.[7] Nevertheless, Cochrane had uncovered such a flagrant abuse that the Admiralty judge, Sir William Scott, was forced to set up a commission to review the scale of charges in Vice Admiralty courts throughout the world.

Fresh from this triumph Cochrane threw himself into other naval causes. He spoke eloquently about the plight and conditions of French prisoners of war incarcerated in such places as Dartmoor; and strongly criticised the system whereby seamen were only paid in their home port at the end of a ship's commission. This was not so bad when the vessel was employed in British waters, but when a ship was absent overseas for years at a time it caused obvious problems. At the other extreme, he spoke on behalf of captains whose interests had been adversely affected by a change in the regulations which had reduced their share of prize money from three eighths to two eighths of the value and increased that of the lower deck proportionately. The captains objected strongly, arguing that they took all the risks of incurring huge fines if a prize was ruled illegitimate, and that their pay was so modest that prize money was a necessary incentive to performance.

Lord Cochrane saw himself as a highly effective politician, so much so that he repeatedly accused the government of trying to silence him by sending him to sea,[8] and later claimed that its agents had framed him in the Stock Exchange fraud. There can be no doubt that Cochrane was a thorn in the side of the administration at this time. But it is unlikely that he was viewed as much more than an irritant and a safety valve. The Tory government was quick to pursue and imprison subversive voices from outside Parliament – William Cobbett, the Leigh Hunts and Citizen Jones all paid the price for libelling, that is criticising, the status quo – but Establishment insiders seemed to be regarded as eccentric rather than subversive. Cochrane, after all, represented two familiar features of the British political scene – the political sailor and the noble son who espouses radical causes. But his independent spirit and his refusal to toe any party line also provoked suspicion among his political allies. He could be relied on to be supportive in terms of constitutional reform, but rode his own hobbyhorses for the rest of the time. In Parliament his effectiveness was compromised by the fact that he protested too much and frequently strayed way beyond the point. Indeed, when he stood up to speak he was as likely to shoot himself in the foot as wing the government. His speech over pensions and placemen may have been a masterpiece, but the motion he raised on 8 July 1813 in the middle of the American War, during which he blamed the series of British defeats in single-ship duels on maladministration and low naval morale rather than the huge size of American vessels, was a shambles. Captain John Surman Carden and the officers of the *Macedonian*, recently defeated by the greatly superior *United States*, arrived back in London two days before the unfortunate debate and were shocked.[9] Indeed, Cochrane's argument seemed even more uninformed when his attack on naval ineptitude in the same debate was interrupted by news of the stunning victory of Captain Sir Philip Bowes Vere Broke's HMS *Shannon* against the USS *Chesapeake*.[10] It is little wonder that the ghost writers of Cochrane's *Autobiography of a Seaman* were advised to omit any reference to the numerous occasions on which he was mauled by Croker in the House of Commons.

Concurrently, Cochrane's fertile mind was busy with schemes to discommode the French. He had been struck on his visit to the Mediterranean by the noxious fumes of the sulphur mines of Sicily. Accordingly, in May 1811 he submitted a memorandum to the Prince Regent (who had replaced his increasingly disturbed father, George III, as head of state in February) outlining a plan which would mean the easy reduction of any French arsenal by using what amounted to chemical warfare. The plan proposed a simultaneous attack by explosion vessels, mortars and ships loaded with burning sulphur, the fumes from which would be blown on to the target area and would effectively gas the defenders. The Prince prudently deflected the proposal to a committee of experts, chaired by the Duke of York and including Admiral Lord Keith, the recently ennobled Captain Edward Pellew and Colonel Congreve. The general opinion was that Cochrane's scheme was certainly advanced, but it was risky, ungentlemanly and seemed against the current rules of war. And when the Duke of Wellington pointed out curtly that 'two could play at that game', the plan was shelved in a cocoon of secrecy.[11]

There was also time for romance. After returning from Malta, Cochrane had divided his time between Holly Hill, his home in Hampshire, and the house of his uncle, Basil Cochrane, at 12 Portman Square, conveniently situated for fashionable London and the House of Commons. Basil was still a bachelor (although with a mistress and illegitimate children), who had added a touch of the orient to his surroundings by building a Turkish bath in his house. This brought a whiff of scandal when he was taken to court accused by a greedy former mistress of using the apparatus to induce an abortion. Basil claimed the opposite, arguing persuasively that he had used it to induce robust good health in the future mother. In spite of this incident, he was a solid citizen whose wealth effectively made him head of the family. The holder of that title, the 9th Earl of Dundonald, was by this time declining in a cycle of drink and scandal. His second wife had died, and he had been forced to sell Culross Abbey to settle his debts. He now occupied a modest house off the Edgware Road, lobbying for a government pension and living on an allowance from his brother who made sure it was not wasted on booze and scientific brainwaves. Basil knew that the Earldom was the fount of the family's prestige, and he had plans to restore its former glory and prosperity. Lord Cochrane, the heir, was cast to play an important role in this. In the long run he was to be the principal beneficiary of his uncle's will; in the short term, he was being lined up for an advantageous marriage. In fact, Basil had already picked a bride – the daughter of a merchant who had grown rich on the West India trade and on lucrative Navy Board contracts.

By 1812, however, Cochrane had other ideas. He had already secretly chosen his future wife. She was a 16-year-old orphan schoolgirl called Katherine Corbett Barnes, who lived with her guardian, Mr John Simpson of Fairborn House in Kent, just along the road in Portland Place. Cochrane later claimed that he did not have an ounce of romance in him, but he seems to have been smitten by Kitty, a petite, lively girl with corkscrew ringlets and jet-black hair inherited, it was said, from her Spanish dancer mother. So smitten was he in fact, that in August 1812 he carried her off to Scotland and married her in the Queensbury Arms in Annan with two servants acting as witnesses. Kitty was thrilled by the match, but she was worried about the legality of the brief civil ceremony. She was not the only one. In years to come the legitimacy of their first son, Thomas Barnes Cochrane, born in April 1814, would be called into question. To make absolutely sure, she insisted on being married twice more, once in 1818 under the rites of the Anglican Church, and again in 1825 by the Church of Scotland.

When news of the marriage broke, it exploded like a bombshell. Basil, himself recently married, was appalled. The civil nature of the ceremony was not the reason – indeed it was common for young bucks to elope to Scotland with love-struck heiresses before their infuriated relatives could intervene to prevent them. The problem was that Kitty was *not* an heiress; she was nothing of the sort. Basil, seeing his plans for the financial revival of the Dundonalds lying in ruins, cut Cochrane out of his will, and concentrated his energies on his on-going legal feud with the Victualling

Board which, six years later, was eventually concluded with an award of
£1280 in his favour.[12] The news of Cochrane's marriage left his father, the
old Earl, even more unbalanced. He had already disowned his son's radical
politics: now he accused him of failing to support his father, of stealing his
inventions, and even knocking him downstairs. Cochrane regretted
nothing, writing later, 'I did not inherit a shilling of my uncle's wealth for
which however I had a rich equivalent in the acquisition of a wife whom
no amount of wealth could have purchased.'[13]

CHAPTER SEVEN

The Stock Exchange Scandal

For THE FOUR YEARS after he relinquished command of *Imperieuse* in 1810 Cochrane was on half pay, but busy nevertheless with politics, his marriage and his inventions. At the end of 1813, it looked as if the situation might change. In 1812, Great Britain and the United States had gone to war over the high-handed way in which the Royal Navy was enforcing the blockade of Napoleonic Europe and searching American ships for deserters. To the British surprise, the war went badly. A succession of naval engagements between frigates and sloops resulted in American victories, and caused a national trauma in Britain – until it was realised that the ships of the United States Navy were bigger and more heavily manned. Then, in spite of a blockade of the US coast, the seas seemed suddenly full of privateers snapping up British merchant ships. The Admiralty decided that the commander-in-chief on the North American station, Sir John Borlase Warren, had to be replaced by someone who would put new vigour and aggression into the war. The man they chose was Lord Cochrane's uncle, now Vice Admiral Sir Alexander Cochrane. Alexander immediately invited his nephew to become flag-captain, then sailed for US waters at the beginning of January 1814, leaving Cochrane to complete the refit of his flagship, *Tonnant*, at Chatham Dockyard with the help of First Lieutenant Robert Forster. Everything augured well for Lord Cochrane's reappearance as an active naval officer – but calamity was lurking in the wings.

Work on the *Tonnant* progressed well and the ship was soon ready. In the middle of February, she was moved to Long Reach to complete her armament and munitions, while Cochrane returned to London on leave to finish his work on the convoy lamp, and to find a house for Kitty who was in the last stage of her first pregnancy. At the same time Cochrane bought £139,000 worth of shares in a government stock called Omnium at a premium of 28¼, selling consols in order to meet part of the purchase price. Omnium, although government stocks, were more volatile than consols and were particularly popular with speculators since it was possible to acquire them through 'time bargains' – that is, by a promise to produce the purchase price at a future date. It was thus possible to sell them during the interim, pay the original price at the settlement date, and pocket the profit. This was actually illegal but was widely practised.

In the misty dawn of 21 February 1814, a man wearing the red coat of a colonel, a silver star, and the badges of a staff officer arrived at the Ship Inn, Dover carrying momentous news: Napoleon was dead, caught and killed by Cossacks. Colonel de Bourg, as he called himself, stopped long enough to write to Admiral Thomas Foley who was commanding in the Downs, then took a post chaise and headed for London loudly proclaiming the news on the way. At Lambeth he disembarked and disappeared. Fog had prevented the Admiralty telegraph stations from transmitting the news to the capital, but rumours of Napoleon's death began to spread, and seemed to be confirmed when, later in the day, a coach carrying cheering French officers in white Bourbon cockades paraded across Blackfriars Bridge, up Lombard Street and down Cheapside. The Stock Exchange needed no further confirmation: share prices rose quickly at the promise of peace and, within two hours, Omnium went up from 26½ to 32. The conspirators promptly sold their shares and made a handsome profit. For Napoleon was not dead: the whole thing was a charade.

When the truth was confirmed, a shocked Stock Exchange appointed a sub-committee to investigate. Its first act was to identify the individuals who had sold substantial numbers of shares during the boom on 21 February. There were six: Andrew Cochrane-Johnstone, the stockbroker and former Navy Pay Clerk Richard Butt, three well-known stock exchange gamblers called Holloway, Sandsom and M'Rae, and Lord Cochrane. The two largest speculators had been Cochrane-Johnstone and Butt who had disposed of Omnium shares to the value of £420,000 and £200,000 respectively – all bought as 'time bargains' – as well as £100,000 and £178,000 each in consols. The third largest seller had been Lord Cochrane, who had disposed of his entire holding of £139,000 in Omnium, at least a third of which had been bought as a 'time bargain'.[1]

The immediate assumption was that some, if not all, of this group were behind the fraud. Indeed, Holloway, Sandsom and M'Rae were quickly identified as the false French officers. On 4 March, the Stock Exchange committee offered a reward for information on the false colonel. Within days, an anonymous informant claimed the reward, telling the committee that the 'colonel' was a foreigner called de Berenger, and that on arrival in London, he had gone straight to Lord Cochrane's new house at 13 Green Street. All this was included in the sub-committee's first report on 7 March.

Cochrane was alarmed by the report and, anxious to establish his version of the story, swore an affidavit on 11 March describing his movements on 21 February. He did this of his own volition, and did not consult any legal advisers as he later claimed. Its purpose was to explain why de Berenger had gone to his house – a fact which suggested the two men were intimates since Cochrane had only occupied it for three days – then to prove that while he was there he had not been wearing the red uniform of his imposture. The affidavit explained how at 8.30 a.m. Cochrane had breakfasted with Cochrane-Johnstone and Butt at the former's house in Great Cumberland Street, after which they had dropped him off at the metal works in Cock Street so he could check on his convoy lamp. There a servant had delivered a message with an unreadable signature and reported that a military officer had arrived at Green Street who was anxious to see him. Thinking that the man brought news of his brother William, then serving with Wellington in the Peninsular, he had hurried home to find that the officer was de Berenger. The two men were already acquainted both socially and professionally. It had been reported that American ships were employing sharpshooters in their tops to pick off enemy officers during engagements, and Cochrane was thinking of doing the same in *Tonnant*. De Berenger, who claimed some expertise with small arms, had offered his services, carrying a letter of introduction from Lord Yarmouth, in whose green-uniformed volunteer regiment he held a commission. According to Cochrane, de Berenger was in his uniform and was highly agitated. He claimed that he was a debtor to the tune of £8000, and begged to be allowed to board *Tonnant* immediately to escape his creditors. When Cochrane demurred, de Berenger asked for a change of clothes. He had, he explained, broken the restrictions on movement imposed on debtors by the Court of the King's Bench, and feared he would be recognised if he returned in his regimentals. Cochrane had then obligingly supplied him with a round hat and a civilian overcoat on which, in his presence, de Berenger had taken off his uniform and wrapped it in a towel. It was, he claimed, all perfectly innocent.

The Stock Exchange took a different view. Although their report was guarded, it implied that Cochrane-Johnstone and Butt were the guilty men. There were also facts that implicated Cochrane. First, he had acquired Omnium stock in the weeks preceding the fraud; secondly, he had not only bought Omnium at exactly the same times as his uncle and Butt, but he had left identical instructions with his broker as to their disposal; thirdly, the false colonel had gone straight to his new residence to change his uniform as soon as he had arrived in London; and lastly, Cochrane's radical politics made him perfectly capable of cocking a snook at the financial establishment. The case against him was circumstantial and clearly did not amount to undisputed proof. On the other hand, to claim – as Cochrane did – that he was demonstrably innocent, and that no further questions needed to be asked, was ludicrous. Another link between the two men emerged on 8 April when de Berenger, arrested in Leith trying to escape, was found to have bank notes originating from Cochrane in his pockets.

The Admiralty was inevitably drawn in. On 14 March, the Secretary, John Wilson Croker, asked Cochrane for an explanation, and told him that an acting-captain would have to be appointed to *Tonnant* until the matter was cleared up. Cochrane exploded at what he saw as an unjustified act; but Croker replied soothingly, and explained that the arrangement was only temporary. By this time Cochrane's naturally suspicious mind had began to develop the idea that he had been framed by a hostile Establishment. His radical friend William Cobbett thought so too, and in his *Weekly Political Register*, unwisely leapt to the defence, not only of Cochrane, but of Cochrane-Johnstone and Butt as well.

The question of Lord Cochrane's innocence or guilt split Georgian England, and has divided commentators ever since. Unfortunately for Cochrane, the case for him was as circumstantial as the one against and rested upon the common sense argument that if he *had* been involved, the plot would have been better organised! He would certainly not have permitted de Berenger, however panicky, to implicate him by coming to his house. And if he had, he would have despatched the false colonel to HMS *Tonnant* immediately to get him out of the way. Likewise, while Cochrane had certainly sold his Omnium shares on 21 February, it was the result of a standing order to sell when their value went up by 1 per cent: a real conspirator would have waited until they reached the top of the market (which occurred late in the afternoon of the 21st) and made twice the profit of £2470 he had gained. The problem with this argument is that a careful conspirator would have done exactly as Cochrane did to avoid suspicion. Cochrane-Johnstone and the others had all given instructions to sell when the price went up by 1 per cent.

The case was heard by Lord Chief Justice Ellenborough on 8 June 1814, the first day's proceedings taking place beneath the tracery of wooden beams and arches of London's medieval Guildhall.[2] The defence team included some of the finest legal brains in the country – men who would later reach the highest ranks in the profession, such as James Scarlett, Henry Brougham and William Best, later to be a Law Lord and father of a naval officer. The prosecution was led by another luminary, Richard Gurney, who was acting for the Stock Exchange. One of the solicitors assisting him was Germain Lavie who had acted for Lord Gambier at his court martial. For Cochrane, this confirmed his suspicion of a conspiracy. The defence team put much effort into the case and in May and June there were six meetings between the lawyers, the solicitors Farrer & Co. and Cochrane who – in spite of subsequent denials – closely supervised the defence.[3] The lawyers finally decided unanimously that the defendants should be tried together rather than individually. The reason for this is unknown, but it worked to Cochrane's disadvantage as he became associated with the guilt of his uncle as the evidence against him steadily accumulated. Another feature of the trial was that in order to spare the defendants the indignity of standing in the dock, they were not required to appear in person. This was just as well because Cochrane-Johnstone and M'Rae had fled the country, to be joined by Butt as soon as sentence was passed.

Richard Gurney began the prosecution case by recounting the events of 21 February, describing in detail the share dealings of the defendants, the appearance of the bogus French officers, and de Berenger's

movements. He traced the journey of the red-coated de Berenger from
Dover to London, through Canterbury, Rochester, Dartford, Bexley and
Shooter's Hill, announcing the news and liberally distributing gold
Napoleons on the way. As witnesses he called innkeepers, post boys, the
man who had sold the red uniform, the man who had fished it out of the
Thames cut into pieces, a coachman called Crane who had driven de
Berenger to Green Street, and bystanders who had seen him get into the
coach. He then turned to the role of Lord Cochrane. The case against
Cochrane was finely balanced, and clearly hinged on the colour of the
uniform de Berenger had been wearing when they met in his house. If it
had been the green of the sharpshooters, then Cochrane's explanation and
his protestations of innocence were plausible. If it had been red, then he
was obviously implicated and was lying. Gurney concentrated on this
point and brought forward witnesses, including the coachman Crane and
others at Lambeth, who swore that under de Berenger's overcoat, the
uniform was red.

Gurney concluded his case at 10 p.m. It had taken all day and lawyers
and jury were tired. But at that stage in the proceedings William Best
revealed that he intended to call defence witnesses. All were present in
court and included the second Lord Melville, who like his father was now
First Lord of the Admiralty, Colonel Torrens, Secretary to the Duke of
York, Under Secretary Goulburn of the Colonial Department and Lord
Yarmouth. They were there to confirm the relationship – or lack of it –
between Cochrane and de Berenger. Realising that the witnesses might
not be available the following day, Justice Ellenborough ordered the
defence to carry straight on. Henry Brougham later claimed that this was
a deliberate act to weaken the presentation of Cochrane's case, but at the
time Best did not object. Gurney's presentation of the prosecution case
had been compelling and Best may have preferred to get a rebuttal in
quickly rather than let the jury sleep on it. Best, who spoke on behalf of
Cochrane, Cochrane-Johnstone and Butt, was followed by Sergeant Park
for de Berenger, and Sergeant Pell for M'Rae and the other defendants.
The court was finally adjourned at 3 a.m.

The trial reconvened seven hours later, at 10 a.m., in the Court of the
King's Bench in Westminster. Best first called the distinguished witnesses
he had not had time to cross-examine the night before. Then he presented

the common-sense case for Cochrane's innocence with skill, but skirted round the question of de Berenger's uniform. Instead of trying to prove that he had worn green, he suggested that Cochrane might have been genuinely mistaken since he was used to seeing de Berenger in that colour. And to Cochrane's annoyance, he did not call his servants, Thomas Dewman, Mary Turpin, Isaac Davies and Sarah Colton, to testify. In fact Best had good reason for not doing so. It emerged that their affidavits were not in their own words but had been dictated to a lawyer's clerk by Cochrane himself on 20 March – the servants had merely signed them. All had said that the *collar* of de Berenger's uniform, visible above the overcoat, had been green, but when they had been interviewed by the solicitors who were preparing the defence brief on 11 May, Dewman and Turpin admitted that they thought the rest of the uniform had been red.[4] Cochrane complained in later years that the defence brief had been sloppily written when it had said that Turpin thought de Berenger wore red: it was not. Best realised that the two servants had probably made this admission because they assumed that all military officers wore red, but he also appreciated that under cross examination they would not support the contention that de Berenger had worn green, so decided not to call them.

Best's tactic did not work. Chief Justice Ellenborough's summing up brought the jury's attention back to the colour of de Berenger's uniform, asserting that it had been red and, by implication, that Cochrane had lied. *The Times* of 10 June reported his words as follows:

His Lordship [Ellenborough] then recapitulated the whole evidence, commenting thereupon as he proceeded. The Bricklayers Arms was too near the King's Bench for the defendant to stop at. Having hunted down the game, the prosecutors at last shewed what became of the skin: and it was a very material fact that the defendant de Berenger stripped himself at Lord Cochrane's. He pulled off his scarlet uniform there, and if the circumstances of its not being green did not excite Lord Cochrane's suspicion, what did he think of the star and the medal?…Did he ask de Berenger where he had been in this masquerade dress? It was for the jury to say whether Lord Cochrane did not know where he had been. This was not the dress of a sharpshooter but of a mountebank. He came before Lord Cochrane fully emblazoned in the costume of his crime.

Whether the Chief Justice's assumption of guilt was due to genuine conviction or to the instinctive distaste felt by a High Tory for a radical such as Cochrane has long been debated. But whatever Ellenborough's motivation, it was a jury of respectable city men who, after two hours' deliberation, found the defendants guilty. They had just not been convinced by Lord Cochrane's explanation of de Berenger's visit and the change of uniform.

Cochrane was stunned. But the rules of the court dictated that there should be a gap between verdict and sentence so that appeals could be lodged. Cochrane made his appeal on 14 June, having gathered more affidavits, some from new witnesses at Lambeth stating that de Berenger's uniform was green, others aimed at discrediting the original witnesses, such as Crane, who had said it was red. Cochrane put in one final plea of innocence, repeating the common-sense argument for his defence. He said,

It has been my misfortune to be apparently implicated in the guilt of others with whom I never had any connection, except in transactions, so far as I was apprised of them, entirely blameless. I had met Mr de Berenger in public company, but was on no terms of intimacy with him. With Mr Cochrane-Johnstone, I had the intercourse natural between such near relatives. Mr Butt had voluntarily offered, without any reward to carry on stock exchange transactions… The pretended de Bourg, if I had chosen him for my instrument, instead of making me his convenience, should have terminated his expedition and found a change of dress. He should not have come immediately in open day to my house. I should not rashly have invited detection and its concomitant ruin… Is it not next to impossible that a man conscious of his guilt, should have been so careless of his most imminent danger?… I look forward to justice being rendered my character sooner or later: it will come more speedily…if I shall receive it at your Lordship's hands. I am not used to injury: of late I have known persecution; the indignity of compassion I am unable to bear.

The plea for a retrial on the grounds of new evidence was rejected by the four judges of the King's Bench who were hearing the appeal – Le Blanc,

Bailey, Dampier and Ellenborough himself, and a week later, Mr Justice
Le Blanc pronounced sentence. Cochrane and the others were fined
£1000 and condemned to a year's imprisonment. They were also ordered
to spend an hour in the pillory in front of the Royal Exchange, but so
great was the outcry against this archaic form of punishment that it was
quickly dropped.

On 2 July, the House of Commons sat to discuss the expulsion of Lord
Cochrane and his uncle from Parliament. Cochrane's performance in the
debate did him little good. Convinced in his own mind that his innocence
was obvious, and thereby unable to appreciate the strength of the case
against him, he assumed – as in the Gambier court martial – that the trial
had been rigged. In his Common's speech, Cochrane cast aside his
carefully prepared statement and hit out violently against all concerned:
his solicitor had been idle, his advocates inept, the witnesses had perjured,
the jury had been corrupted, and the judge was not only vindictive but
the instrument of a government plot against him. Only Richard Gurney,
whose presentation of the prosecution case had been damning, remained
free from invective. The language of Cochrane's speech was as shocking as
its contents. The Parliamentary Record had to be filled with asterisks in
place of the swear words, and the Speaker warned the shorthand writers
that if the accusations were repeated outside the chamber they would be
held for libel. Cochrane's radical friends rallied round and, together with
others who were sympathetic to the travails of a hero, managed to raise
44 votes in his favour. But 140 voted against; and Lord Cochrane was
expelled from Parliament.

The final indignity soon followed. On 25 June 1814 Cochrane's name
had been struck from the Navy List. Now on 11 August, his arms as a
Knight of the Bath were unscrewed from Westminster Abbey, his banner
was kicked down the steps, and he was formally expelled from the Order.
Lord Cochrane's disgrace was complete.

CHAPTER EIGHT

Rebel at Large

THE STOCK EXCHANGE SCANDAL was a professional and social disaster for Lord Cochrane, but as a radical politician it took him to new heights. Although the evidence for the claim was flimsy enough, he saw himself as a political martyr – a judgement his radical friends were eager to support. William Cobbett carried bitter denunciations of Cochrane's treatment in the *Weekly Political Register,* and in the streets the mob was delighted to follow his lead. Cochrane's expulsion from the House of Commons meant that a new MP had to be elected in his stead. But there was no contest. A mass meeting attracted 5000 cheering supporters who nominated Cochrane again. The rival candidates withdrew – either out of loyalty to Cochrane or fear for their windows – and he was re-elected unopposed as Member of Parliament for Westminster by acclamation at the hustings on 16 July 1814.

First, Cochrane had to pay his debt to society. He and de Berenger – the only defendants who had stayed in England after the verdict – were imprisoned to serve their one-year sentences. The King's Bench was a prison for gentlemen, and for a modest fee, Cochrane was able to hire rooms on the upper floor where he could entertain friends and receive his wife and baby son Thomas, who had been born just as the Stock Exchange scandal was about to break. He could also have paid for the privilege of moving freely in the area half-a-mile radius from the prison, but did not do so lest his imprisonment look too comfortable. For a man of Cochrane's temperament, boredom was the greatest problem. He spent much of the winter of 1814–15 inventing an oil lamp for street lighting, and producing, with the aid of his secretary William Jackson, a lengthy denunciation of the Chief Justice called 'A Letter to Lord Ellenborough'. His mind was too active. Before very long, and quite erroneously, he managed to convince himself that his imprisonment was illegal because he was a Member of Parliament, and on 6 March 1815 he decided to escape. At midnight, he fearlessly traversed the gap between the prison buildings and the spiked outer wall using a rope, then lowered himself to the street. Unfortunately, either the rope broke or Cochrane fell, and he landed on his back, causing a temporary injury. Despite this, he managed to disappear into the maze of alleyways around the prison.

Next day, a hue and cry was raised. Wild rumours circulated as to where Cochrane had gone. In fact, he was in his house in Hampshire, but no one seems to have thought of looking there. Two weeks later, he sauntered into the House of Commons wearing his familiar pantaloons and grey frogged overcoat and demanded to speak. Astonished officials rushed to summon help, and a Bow Street Runner accompanied by a posse of tipstaffs arrived to arrest him. There was a struggle as he was taken into custody, and a search of his pockets revealed a box of snuff. With Cochrane's encouragement, word was soon circulating that this was another of his famous secret weapons!

Life was not so easy in the King's Bench Prison this time. Locked in a secure room without windows and below ground level, Cochrane's spirits began to decline, while the damp and lack of light had an adverse effect on his health. His term of imprisonment came to an end on 3 July 1815 and he was free to leave as soon he had paid the £1000 fine. At first he refused. But the arguments of his friends prevailed, and he handed over the money, though ensuring that the banknote was endorsed with a bitter protest at his treatment. 'My health', he wrote, 'having suffered long and close confinement, and my oppressors being resolved to deprive me of property or life, I submit to robbery to protect myself from murder, in the hope that I shall live long enough to bring the delinquents to justice'.

Lord Cochrane was ready to resume the political struggle. But first there was some unfinished business to attend to. In the opening session of the Parliament of 1816, Cochrane continued his vendetta against Ellenborough by unsuccessfully trying to have him impeached. Then, he had to stand trial for escaping from the King's Bench Prison. He was clearly guilty, but the jury recommended mercy, and nothing more than a £100 fine was imposed. Cochrane once more refused to pay and he went back to gaol until his constituents raised the money through a penny subscription. His temporary imprisonment, however, turned out to be a stroke of good fortune, since it prevented him becoming involved with his political ally, 'Orator' Hunt, in the violence and disorders that accompanied the Spa Fields riot of December 1816.

Cochrane's emergence from gaol coincided with the end of the Napoleonic Wars. But peace did not bring prosperity. The economy went into depression, unemployment soared as thousands were demobilised from the army and navy, the cost of living rose as laws were passed to protect the price of corn, and wages slumped. There was hardship and want throughout the land: protesting labourers rioted in the cities, Luddites smashed machinery in the industrial towns, and peasants burned hayricks in the countryside. Seizing the opportunity, the London radicals began deliberately to politicise the pauperised workers, organising political clubs and orchestrating mass protests. The mood of the radical movement moved left, demanding not just electoral reform, equal voting districts and the end to rotten boroughs, but universal suffrage. Parliament was flooded with petitions, with Westminster constituency's radical members Cochrane and Burdett acting as the principal channel through which they reached an unreformed House of Commons. Cochrane's stature and influence in the radical movement grew, and it was he who advised Cobbett and his fellow reformers to bring out a cheap weekly paper which the ordinary working man could afford – the famous 'Tuppenny trash'.

In the eyes of the government, Cochrane had become more of a dangerous demagogue than an aristocratic eccentric, but among the public he was never more popular. Carried to Westminster on the shoulders of cheering supporters, he enthusiastically presented petitions signed by thousand of people, on one occasion unrolling one vast document until it covered the floor of the House of Commons. He loved it, writing to Jackson, 'I am getting on famously; petitions and letters of thanks come from all quarters.'[1] Political ballads were written in his honour; one ran,

All hail to the hero – of ENGLAND the boast
The honour – the glory – the pride of our coast
Let the bells peal his name, and the cannon's loud roar
Sound the plaudits of COCHRANE, the friend of her shore

From boyhood devoted to ENGLAND and FAME
Each sea knows his prowess, each climate his name
While he hurls round the thunder, and rides in the storm
He is more than all this – He's the FRIEND of REFORM!

On a personal level, Cochrane may have been awkward and reserved with his superiors and people he did not know, but with friends and social inferiors he was affable and easy, inviting the representatives of the working men into his home and expressing genuine concern for their plight. Samuel Bamford, a humble Lancashire weaver who visited Cochrane to hand in one of the many working-class petitions, was struck by the difference between the sailor's easy-going manners and the aloof dignity of Sir Francis Burdett. Cochrane was, he recorded,

> ...a tall young man, cordial and unaffected in his manner. He stooped a little and had something of a sailor's gait in walking; his face was rather oval; fair naturally, but now tanned and sun freckled. His hair was sandy and his whiskers rather small and of a deep colour, and the expression of his countenance was calm and self-possessed.

Bamford was equally charmed with Kitty, 'a slight elegant young lady, dressed in white', he wrote, 'very interesting [who] served us with wine'.[2]

But the disputative side of Cochrane's character was also in evidence. In 1816, a group of philanthropists led by William Wilberforce formed the Association for the Relief of the Manufacturing and Labouring Poor aimed at raising funds to alleviate some of the misery caused by the economic slump. In July, it held a meeting in the City of London Tavern to raise money. It was a typical charity occasion, with the Duke of York in the chair supported by a group of celebrities, who included the Dukes of Kent and Cambridge, the Archbishop of Canterbury, the Bishop of London, the Chancellor of the Exchequer and other worthies. Lord Cochrane was there, too, but with a political agenda. There was a series of supportive speeches deploring the effect of the recession on the labouring poor, then a motion embodying the aims of the association was proposed as a preliminary to collecting money and pledges. At this juncture, Lord Cochrane rose and proposed an amendment declaring that the distress of the workers had nothing to do with any economic slump, but was entirely due to the corruption of the government. To alternate cheers and hisses, he launched into his familiar tirade against sinecures and placemen. The Duke of York tried to steer the meeting back to the philanthropic and away from the politically controversial, but Cochrane would not be deterred. Eventually, the meeting collapsed into disorder, the Royal Dukes withdrew in confusion, and the Chairman was forced to abandon it.[3] A well-meaning charitable event had been sabotaged. Cochrane was pleased, and his wealthy radical friends were convinced that he had struck a blow for liberty. None of them, alas, seemed to register the fact that he had prevented anything being done to alleviate the distress of the poor and needy.

Fresh from that 'triumph', two ghosts from Cochrane's past reappeared to distract him. First there was the Basque Roads. When naval vessels destroyed an enemy warship, head money reflecting the size of its crew was distributed among the captors in the same way as prize money. By tradition, these sums were paid not only to the ship that had been in action, but to any that had been in sight – the argument being that their very presence had affected the outcome. In 1817, a claim submitted on behalf of Lord Gambier's fleet in respect of head money for the five French ships which had been destroyed in the Basque Roads finally came to judgement. Cochrane opposed the claim, arguing that only *Imperieuse* and the ships that had been in action should receive the payment. The case was heard by the senior Admiralty judge, the capable and experienced Sir William Scott, who analysed the case in detail, repeated the traditional doctrine, and predictably rejected Cochrane's argument.[4] Raising such an objection had been a pointless gesture, but Cochrane could not resist the opportunity to rake over an old grievance. Then there was aftermath of the Honiton election. In 1806, Cochrane had refused to pay the £1200 cost of his banquet for the electors, and the unfortunate tradesmen and caterers who had provided it were forced to take him to law. Eleven years later, a court finally found in favour of the plaintiffs and granted an order on Holly Hill in Hampshire. When Cochrane refused to comply, there was a comic siege of the house by 25 constables, Cochrane pretending that he had mined the property with explosives before eventually surrendering and paying up.

By 1817, it was clear to Cochrane that, in spite of the passion with
which he pursued his liberal causes, he was achieving little results. Indeed
the situation was getting worse as the government responded to the
growing unrest and violence with widespread arrests and repression.
Habeas corpus was suspended, rioters were tried for sedition, a tax was
put on publications to gag the cheap political tracts that Cochrane had
advocated, and the printers of radical pamphlets were imprisoned.
Cobbett fled to America, and other leaders left for overseas. In the House
of Commons, Burdett's regular motion in favour of reform attracted less
and less support. Cochrane was becoming disillusioned with the political
scene and could not shake off his obsession with injustice. Paying a short
visit to Paris with Kitty during August 1817, he wrote, 'We will have great
rejoicing tomorrow. All Paris will be dancing, fiddling and singing. I wish
I could join in; but the cursed recollection of the injustice that has been
done to me is never out of my mind; so that all my pleasures are blasted,
from whatever source they might be expected to arise'.[5] Cochrane
needed a change. He was frustrated and short of money. He began to look
around for a profitable way of using his military talents. The opportunity,
when it arrived, came from an unexpected quarter.

Half way round the globe in South America, the Wars of Independence
were reaching their climax. The Napoleonic Wars had shattered the
Spanish colonial regimes, and from Caracas to Buenos Aires, local
politicians and military strong men had taken advantage of the situation
to mount armed struggles for independence. In the north, Simon Bolivar
was the dominating figure, establishing the Republic of New Granada in
1814. In the south, the radical junta in Buenos Aires took the lead,
organising an armed rebellion, which eventually ejected the last Spanish
viceroy from the River Plate. In 1813, it established a republic in what is
now Argentina, and began to send liberating armies against the royalists in
Peru northwards through the Paraguay river system. All were beaten off.
In 1817, another expedition was mounted, this time masterminded by the
leading figure of southern independence, General José de San Martin.
Born in 1778 in the north of what is now Argentina, San Martin had
joined the Spanish army as a youth, and had eventually risen to become
Lieutenant Colonel of the Walloon Guards and a staff officer with the
Spanish forces fighting with the Duke of Wellington in the Peninsular

War. He had returned to South America in 1812, where he had quickly allied himself with cause of independence. Five years later, he had been put in command of the fourth expedition against the Spanish royalists. But this time, instead of heading north, San Martin led his men west, crossed the high peaks of the Andes into Chile and, on 9 February 1817, surprised and defeated a royalist army at Chacabuco. Spanish power crumbled and Chile became an independent republic.

San Martin was a dedicated patriot, but he had no political ambitions and refused to become Supreme Director of the new state. Instead, he stood aside in favour of his friend, General Bernardo O'Higgins. O'Higgins was a local boy, the illegitimate son of an Irishman who had risen to become Captain General of Chile and later Viceroy of Peru. Educated in Richmond near London, on his return to Chile he had led a revolt against the royalists in 1814 but had been betrayed by rivals and defeated. O'Higgins had fled across the Andes to join San Martin, and had returned with his victorious army. Short and stout, with liberal principles that he acquired in England, O'Higgins was a popular figure, though time was to show that he lacked the ruthlessness so necessary for survival in Latin American politics.[6]

In Chile, San Martin began to prepare for the final push into Peru. But he faced a different situation. Up to then, the liberation struggle had been decided by land campaigns: now, the need to move his army up the coast introduced a new element – he would have to seize sea power from the Spanish. Operating from its base in Callao, the Spanish navy continued to command the Pacific even though the number of ships at its disposal was small. At the end of 1817, Commodore William Bowles of the British South America Squadron reported, 'the whole naval force of His Catholic Majesty in these seas consists of the *Venganza* and *Esmeralda* of 36 guns each, and three corvettes of 16 or 18 guns'.[7] In fact there were also a dozen small gunboats and armed ships in the area, but these were of little military use except for port defence. The Napoleonic Wars had crippled Spain's once proud navy, and there was a woeful shortage of ships to counter the rebellion in South America. The government in Madrid made desperate efforts to find more, and in May 1818, despatched a third frigate called *Maria Isabel* with a convoy of nine transports carrying reinforcements.

While Spain controlled the waves a successful invasion of Peru was impossible. The Chileans therefore set about creating a navy of their own. The task was entrusted to the newly appointed Minister of Marine, José Ignacio Zenteno, a cold but dedicated man with the training and temperament of a lawyer, who had suffered all the ups and downs of the campaigns of liberation as an army officer and was high in the esteem of O'Higgins. His performance as the architect of the new navy and later as Governor of Valparaiso more than justified the Supreme Director's good opinion of him.

Zenteno's first task was to buy and arm ships locally; his second was to create a *Reglamento Provisional de la Marina* from the old Spanish military codes, which would establish a rank structure for sea officers, pay and ration scales, and uniform regulations. He also found a commander-in-chief in a 28-year-old Chilean-born artillery officer called Manuel Blanco Encalada, who had been a midshipman in the Spanish navy before transferring to the army and joining the liberation struggle. As the only senior Chilean with any naval experience, Zenteno appointed him to the post of Commodore in June 1818.

Framing regulations was straightforward enough. The real problem O'Higgins and Zenteno faced was the severe shortage of manpower. In spite of their long coastlines, Chile and Peru were countries of miners, farmers and ranchers with a continental perspective. Few people were seafarers, and there was no maritime tradition. Where were they to find the officers and men they needed to fight and man their ships? O'Higgins and Zenteno had the answer: to send agents to the world's largest pools of maritime labour – Britain and the United States. Antonio Alvarez was sent to London and Manuel Hermanegildo Aguirre to New York, each carrying $100,000 (the equivalent of £20,000) with orders to buy warships and recruit officers and men.

In England, Alvarez had no difficulty in fulfilling his assignment. Following the post-war demobilisation, 90 per cent of the 5250 officers on the Navy List were unemployed and living on half pay, and many more midshipmen and master's mates were existing without even that compensation, so there were plenty of people interested in the opportunities offered by a foreign war. Naval officers were flocking to offer their services, some bringing demobilised warships, which they had

bought, armed and manned. Alvarez signed them up and sent them on to
Chile. The first vessel, an 850-ton East Indiaman called *Windham* arrived
in Valparaiso in March 1818, to be followed by another East Indiaman, the
Cumberland, under Captain William Wilkinson, and the former brig-of-
war, HMS *Hecate,* owned by Commander Martin Guise RN and
commanded by Lieutenant John Tooker Spry. Between them, these three
ships carried 400 officers and men. Although short of cash, the Chileans
purchased them all and took their officers and crews into the new navy.
The ships were renamed respectively *Lautaro, San Martin* and *Galvarino*.

In the United States, Aguirre was also successful. In November 1817,
the brig *Columbus* sailed from New York, fully manned and under the
command of Captain Charles W. Worster. She reached Valparaiso eight
months later to be purchased and renamed *Araucano*. In July, Aguirre
authorised the construction in New York of two fast 700-ton corvettes
each mounting 28 guns. In keeping with the classical taste of the time,
they were called *Horatio* and *Curiato*. The two ships were completed
quickly and, after last minute tussles with American neutrality laws, sailed
for the River Plate in September 1818. In the event, the cash-strapped
Chileans could only afford to buy the *Curiato*, which finally reached
Valparaiso in June 1819 under Captain Paul Delano to be incorporated
into the Chilean navy with the name *Independencia*. Her sister-ship,
Horatio, was eventually sold to the Brazilians.

Meanwhile, in England Alvarez had met Lord Cochrane. He had no
orders to sign up a commander-in-chief but Cochrane's military and
political credentials were compelling. Acting on his own initiative, Alvarez
offered him the post, and to his delight Cochrane accepted. On 12
January 1818, Alvarez conveyed the exciting news to Chile.

I have extreme satisfaction in informing you that Lord Cochrane, one of
the most famous and perhaps the most valiant seaman in Great Britain,
has determined to travel to Chile in order to direct our navy and co-
operate decisively in the consolidation of liberty and independence. He
is a person highly commendable, not only for the liberal principles with
which he has upheld the cause of the English people in Parliament, but
because he possesses a character superior to any ambition...and has been
watching with enthusiasm the progress of South America. As a

consequence, I have not hesitated one moment in using the plenary powers with which you honoured me, to offer him the rank of admiral and commander-in-chief of the naval forces of Chile; and to authorise him to select and nominate officers and men who will be capable of fulfilling their destinies in a manner satisfactory to the Supreme Director.[8]

Cochrane, too, was pleased. The offer was exactly what he was looking for and the cause of liberty in the Pacific fired his imagination – so much so that he did not even ask how much money he was to be paid. Indeed, so enthusiastic did he become that his second son, born on 8 March 1818, was christened William Horatio Bernardo in honour of O'Higgins.

And there was more good news. Alvarez announced that Cochrane intended to bring an armed steamship with him called *Rising Star*. The vessel was already being built by Brent's Yard at Rotherhithe on the Thames to a revolutionary design. She was of 410 tons with twin funnels, an internal retractable paddle wheel and 60-horsepower engines, although she could, as insurance, carry sail on two masts. So great was Cochrane's confidence in the vessel, that he had put £3000 of his own money into the venture.[9] Alvarez had clearly been convinced by Cochrane that with such an example of modern naval technology at their disposal, the Chileans would make short work of their enemies.

The adaptation of the *Rising Star* seemed likely to take some time and Chile needed Cochrane urgently. Alvarez persuaded him to leave the supervision of the project to his soldier brother William and to leave without delay. Cochrane concluded his preparations and wound up his affairs. In June, he made his last speech in the House of Commons. It comprised an expression of thanks to the electors of Westminster, a final swipe at sinecure and pensions, and a plea to the government for reform before it was too late. He then headed for Boulogne to embark on the merchantman *Rose*. With him went his wife Kitty, Thomas aged 4 years, William (nicknamed Horace) aged 6 months, and a group of servants and secretaries. On 15 August 1818, the party set sail for South America.

CHAPTER NINE

Vice Admiral of Chile

AT THE END OF NOVEMBER 1818, after a voyage of only three months from Europe, the *Rose* fought her way round Cape Horn into the Pacific, sighted the white jagged peaks of the Chilean Cordilleras and headed up the coast for Valparaiso. On the 29th, the brig rounded the rocky headland at its southern extremity and sailed into the bay on which the city was built. Valparaiso was a straggling town wedged on to a narrow semicircular strip of land between the sea and the slopes of the hills, which rose precipitously all around. In this space were huddled shops, churches, the customs house, meat and fish markets, and rows of one-storey whitewashed houses with red-tiled roofs which spread inland up a number of narrow ravines that cut into the hills. Driven by a brisk sea breeze, *Rose* passed on the right the fort that guarded the entrance to the bay, the stretch of flat land which the British used as a cricket ground, the Chilean navy's rudimentary arsenal with its half empty stores and small building slips, and dropped anchor in the glittering water before the port.

The news that Lord Cochrane had arrived spread rapidly. Bernardo O'Higgins hurried down the coach road from Santiago to greet him and inaugurate days of junketing and celebration. There was a special dinner at which the newly arrived British were entranced by the beauty and style of the local ladies who had 'dark abundant hair falling to the shoulders adorned with jasmine and other flowers', although according to Major William Miller, all were put in the shade by 'the two presiding belles…Lady Cochrane and Mrs Commodore Blanco, both young, fascinating and gifted'.[1] Cochrane reciprocated by throwing a lavish party on St Andrew's night, appearing in full highland dress. There was infectious good cheer, food, champagne and fine wines punctuated by innumerable toasts.

Eventually the partying drew to a close and the Chileans got down to business. On 11 December 1818, Lord Cochrane became a Chilean citizen and was appointed Vice Admiral and commander-in-chief, while Commodore Manuel Blanco Encalada was promoted to the rank of Rear Admiral.[2] Both officers were satisfied with these appointments which reflected exactly their respective ages and experience. There was never any chance of their positions being reversed nor is it accurate to say – as suggested by later biographers – that Encalada 'stepped down' in Cochrane's favour. Cochrane also learned at this time that his pay and allowances in the Chilean service would be $6000 a year – that is, the equivalent of £1200.

Cochrane was anxious to familiarise himself with the ships and men he was to lead. Thanks to the Minister of Marine's efforts, he found that his new command comprised three frigates, a corvette, four brigs, a schooner and numerous small craft – an even match for the Spaniards in the Pacific. In pride of place was the *O'Higgins*, formerly the Spanish frigate *Maria Isabel*, which had successfully brought its convoy all the way to the Pacific only to be captured in the Chilean navy's first exploit under Blanco Encalada. The recruiting campaign had also gone well, and had attracted 1200 sailors, 400 marines and 40 sea officers. The marines were entirely Chileno, but two thirds of the seamen and almost all the officers were North American or British, many of the latter with Royal Navy experience.

There were two other urgent tasks for Cochrane. He had to find a house and see his family comfortably settled. Then he had to appoint a staff. As commander-in-chief, Cochrane's duties were immense. He was responsible not only for the tactics and deployment of the Chilean squadron but for its victualling, maintenance and pay – tasks which were to prove formidable in view of the Chilean Treasury's impoverishment and the fact the navy's main field of operations was off the coast of Peru, 1500 miles from its home base. From England, Cochrane had brought his secretary, William Jackson, and a former Royal Navy purser called Henry Dean to deal with prize matters. In Chile, he recruited a local merchant called William Hoseason to handle his finances, and William Bennet Stevenson, a long-standing local resident, to act as his Spanish-language secretary. Cochrane certainly needed a staff – one who was experienced,

efficient and trusted. Alas, he seems to have picked the wrong men.
Hoseason knew little of his duties and only got the job because he was
Dean's father-in-law. The two were later to cause Cochrane endless
difficulties. Likewise, Stevenson had little experience of naval matters and
was a gossip. Jackson's influence is less easy to evaluate, but Lady Cochrane
later described him as 'the greatest enemy my husband ever had, the ruin
of his purse and character'.[3] In Chile, these men formed a shadowy and
distrusted inner circle around Cochrane who were suspected by many in
the squadron of self-interest, of spying on private conversations, and of
feeding his suspicions.

The tone was immediately set when Captain John Tooker Spry of
Galvarino and Captain Charles W. Worster of *Araucano* were overheard
discussing whether Cochrane should not use his formal title when in the
service of a republic. It was later reported that they were 'caballing' against
him and advocating that the Chilean navy should be led by two equally
ranking commodores and not by one commander-in-chief. According to
Stevenson, the idea was that Spry and Worster would then be able to
'control' Blanco Encalada who was inexperienced and spoke no English.[4]
There was not the slightest chance of the 'two commodores' idea ever
becoming a reality, and such comments – if they were true at all – were
nothing more than loose tap room talk.

There was another appointment to be made – that of the Chilean
navy's senior captain and, technically, third in command. This created a
predicament. Before Cochrane's arrival, the senior foreign naval officer
was Captain Martin Guise. Guise had arrived in Chile after the taking of
the *Maria Isabel*, but his service record in the Royal Navy gave him an
undisputed claim to the senior position. He was 39 years old, had joined
the navy in 1794 on *Marlborough*, and had served in the Channel and off
the coast of Spain in *Jason* and *London*. In 1801, he had been promoted
Lieutenant to spend 10 years in the *Ville de Paris* and *Conqueror* off Lisbon
and in the Mediterranean, and had finished the war in command of the
cutter *Liberty* in the West Indies. He had been promoted Commander on
29 March 1815.[5] Unfortunately for him, Cochrane wanted one of his
'followers', Robert Forster, to be senior captain. Forster was also a veteran.
As a lieutenant on the *Mars*, he had been present at the attack on
Copenhagen in 1807 and the capture of Anholt in the Baltic in 1809. He

had been appointed First Lieutenant of HMS *Tonnant* in 1814, the ship which – but for the Stock Exchange scandal – Cochrane would have taken to North America, and had subsequently joined the *Asia*, and had distinguished himself in land operations against the United States under Cochrane's uncle. Forster's seniority as a Royal Navy commander dated from only 13 June 1815[6], making him junior to Guise by three months – a small but important difference since Chile had by this time decided to use British rules to regulate its naval service. Nevertheless, Cochrane had recruited Forster personally in London and insisted that he got the position. He thus became flag captain of *O'Higgins*, while Guise went to the frigate *Lautaro*.

Although the Chileans were delighted to have recruited Cochrane as commander-in-chief, they did not regard him as a saviour who had come to take charge of the war. His reputation was in fact uneven. His sympathy with radical causes was well known, but so was his tendency to pursue his own agenda rather than stick to orders. His brilliance as a naval leader was also recognised, but in no higher rank than captain and in command of nothing larger than a frigate. How he would perform when in charge of a squadron was undetermined. Likewise, the liberation struggle in South America would clearly be decided by land campaigns, and what happened at sea was a subordinate part of a wider strategy. As a result, Cochrane was not given a free rein to take on the Spanish navy as he saw fit. His orders, when they arrived on 9 January 1819, were long and detailed. They began, 'the principal objective of this expedition is to blockade the port of Callao, to cut off the maritime forces of the Viceroy of Lima…and by so-doing enable them to be defeated in detail', and continued in 17 clauses to lay down exactly how this was to be done, with what forces, and for how long. They emphasised that the expedition was a preliminary foray aimed at weakening the Royalists through blockade (Article 1), to encourage patriot resistance (Article 6), to gather intelligence on military deployments (Article 7), to exchange existing prisoners of war (Article 9), and to seize all ships and property belonging to Spain (Article 12). To ensure that nothing should put at risk the invasion planned for the following year, Cochrane was ordered to keep clear of shore batteries (Article 5), and to avoid action with superior forces (Article 13).[7]

Cochrane's arrival in the Pacific was not met with universal joy. Commodore Bowles, the commander-in-chief of the British South American Squadron, was well aware of his enthusiasm for both action and financial gain, and feared an unscrupulous onslaught on neutral commerce in the interests of prize money. In December 1818 he wrote, 'It is not difficult to foresee that the class of foreigners entrusted with the principal naval commands are likely to use their power and influence for the gratification of their private interests.... Their Lordships will judge what sort of conduct may be expected from Lord Cochrane'.[8] Later, he added gloomily,

> I have little doubt, from the language used by Lord Cochrane that whenever a fair opportunity offers he will pay no more regard to neutral rights than to the orders of the government under which he serves.... He has come to this country, as he himself expressed to Mr Worthington [the United States agent], to live. He has brought a prize agent with him and professes the determination to keep everything in his own hands and distribute the proceeds of all captures himself.[9]

The United States Government shared Bowles's concern and, in response, sent the frigate *Ontario*, commanded by Captain James Biddle, to protect American interests in the Pacific.

On 14 January 1819, the Chilean squadron was ready for sea and Cochrane was eager for action. Indeed, no sooner had the boats carrying Lady Cochrane and other visitors left the *O'Higgins* for the shore than she began to weigh anchor. But when the boats returned, there was an unexpected passenger on board. In the confusion at the dockside, Cochrane's five-year-old son had been swept up in the excitement, deposited in the launch and brought back to the flagship. It was too late to send him back, so Thomas stayed on board as the squadron worked its way out of the bay, turned into the cold blue rollers of the Pacific and headed north.

They made good time reaching Peruvian waters and, by the middle of February, the ships were busy enforcing the blockade of Callao, a low-lying town built at sea level against a backdrop of hills that rose in successive ranges as far the distant peaks of the Andes. Its buildings and

Archibald, 9th Earl of Dundonald by Reaburn. He was a gifted scientist but a hopeless businessman. (The Earl of Dundonald)

Sir Alexander Cochrane by Beechey, the uncle who first took Cochrane to sea. (© National Maritime Museum, London)

Admiral Lord Keith, the navy's most senior 'Scotch' officer and Cochrane's early patron.
(© National Maritime Museum, London)

Admiral the Earl of St Vincent after Hoppner. He was a tough disciplinarian who Cochrane regarded as an enemy.

The capture of El Gamo *by the diminutive* Speedy *in 1801, by Pocock.* (© National Maritime Museum, London)

GOD fave the KING.

Doublons.

SPANISH
Dollar Bag
Consigned to Boney.

My LADS,
The rest of the **GALLEONS** with the TREASURE from LA PLATA, are waiting half loaded at CARTAGENA, for the arrival of those from PERU at PANAMA, as soon as that takes place, they are to sail for PORTOVELO, to take in the rest of their Cargo, with Provisions and Water for the Voyage to EUROPE. They stay at PORTOVELO a few days only. Such a Chance perhaps will never occur again,

THE FLYING
PALLAS,
Of 36 GUNS,
At PLYMOUTH,

is a new and uncommonly fine Frigate. Built on purpose. And ready for an EXPEDITION, as soon as some more good Hands are on board;

Captain Lord Cochrane,
(who was not drowned in the ARAB as reported)
Commands her. The sooner you are on board the better.

None need apply, but SEAMEN, or Stout Hands, able to rouse about the Field Pieces, and carry an hundred weight of PEWTER, without stopping, at least three Miles.

COCHRANE.

To British Seamen.

BONEY's CORONATION
Is postponed for want of COBBS.

J. BARFIELD, Printer, Wardour-Street.

Rendezvous, at the White Flag,

Cochrane's recruiting poster for Pallas. Anyone tempted to enlist by the hint of riches was not disappointed. (© National Maritime Museum, London)

Stroehling's portrait of Cochrane as a young captain in 1807.

Admiral Lord Gambier, whose caution against the French at the Basque Roads in 1809 provoked Cochrane's ire. (© National Maritime Museum, London)

The Imperieuse *attacking stranded French ships at the Basque Roads, after Dodd.* (© National Maritime Museum, London)

Cochrane as a naval hero in 1810 by Meyer, with fireships burning in the background.

Cochrane – 'the Friend of Reform' – as a politician, by Buck. (National Portrait Gallery, London)

Election-Candidates; — or — the Republican-Goose at the Top of the Pole —
the Devil helping behind! —Vide M.ʳ Paull's Letter į Article. Horne Tooke.
— also. an exact representation of Sawney M.ᶜ Cochran flourishing the Cudgel of Naval Reform
lent to him by Cobbett:— mounting Triumphantly over a small Beer Barrel — together with an Old
Drury-Lane Harlequin trying in vain to make a spring to y.ᵉ Top of the Pole, his Broad-Bottom always
bringing him down again! — į lastly, poor little Paull į Taylor dmw̃ over! wounded by h Goose, & not a Leg to stand on —

Gillray's cartoon of the Westminster Election in 1807. Sir Francis Burdett and Cochrane — with
a paper labelled 'Charges against St Vincent' in the pocket of his French revolutionary trousers —
are at the top of the greasy pole. Scrambling after them are the two other candidates — Elliot as a
beer barrel and Sheridan as an overweight Harlequin followed by the disgraced Paull with tailor's
scissors. (National Portrait Gallery, London)

Lord Chief Justice Ellenborough, who presided over the Stock Exchange Trial, by Lawrence. (© National Maritime Museum, London)

THE SEVERE
SENTENCE
ON
LORD COCHRANE & OTHERS,
TO
STAND IN THE PILLORY,
IN THE FRONT OF THE
Royal-Exchange,
FOR
A CONSPIRACY,
TO RAISE, BY FALSE REPORTS, THE PRICE OF THE PUBLIC FUNDS;
As pronounced by Sir Simon Le Blanc,
IN THE COURT OF KING'S-BENCH,
ON TUESDAY, the 21st of JUNE, 1814.

" That you, Sir Thomas Cochrane, commonly called Lord Cochrane,* and that you, Richard Gathorne Butt, do pay a fine of one thousand pounds to the King; and that you, John Peter Holloway, having also benefited from this infamous conspiracy, do pay a fine of five hundred pounds to the King.

" That you, the six several Defendants, Sir Thomas, commonly called Lord, Cochrane, Richard Gathorne Butt, John Peter Holloway, Charles Random De Berenger, Henry Lyte, and Ralph Sandom, be severally imprisoned in the custody of the Marshal of the Marshalsea of this Court for the term of twelve calendar months, and that,

* Member of Parliament for the City of Westminster, and late Captain of his Majesty's Ship Imperieuse.

during that period, you, Charles Random De Berenger, you, Sir Thomas, commonly called Lord, Cochrane, and you, Richard Gathorne Butt, be set in and upon the pillory in the front of the Royal-Exchange, for the space of one hour, between the hours of twelve at noon and two in the afternoon.

" And that, you, Sir Thomas, commonly called Lord, Cochrane, Richard Gathorne Butt, and John Peter Holloway, be further imprisoned until your several fines be paid."

The other two persons found guilty of the said Conspiracy, namely, Andrew Cochrane Johnstone and Alexander M'Rea did not appear in Court, consequently judgment was not pronounced upon them.

Published by John Fairburn, 2, Broadway, Ludgate-Hill.

A broadsheet announcing the verdict of the Stock Exchange Trial in 1814.

'Things as they are. Things as they might have been'. Cartoon contrasting Cochrane the naval hero with Cochrane the discredited civilian. (© National Maritime Museum, London)

Bernardo O'Higgins,
Supreme Director of Chile.
(Canning House)

The departure of the Chilean squadron for Callao in 1819, by Somerscales. (Club Naval de Valparaiso)

The capture of the Esmeralda. Captain Guise and his men are shown boarding from the port side. Three months later they were under arrest. (Club Naval de Valparaiso)

General José de San Martin, the liberator of Chile and Peru, with whom Cochrane clashed. (Canning House)

The Emperor Pedro I of Brazil.

Pedro's dramatic declaration of 'Independence or Death!' in September 1822. (Museu Paulista)

*Francisco Villela Barbosa,
Brazilian Minister of
Marine and a target of
Cochrane's hostility.*

*Cochrane in middle
age by Hayter.*
(The Earl of
Dundonald)

Vice Admiral Sir Edward Codrington, British commander-in-chief during the Greek War. Engraving from the original picture by Sir Thomas Lawrence.

The destruction of the Egyptian–Turkish fleet at Navarino, 1827. (© National Maritime Museum, London)

Kitty with Lizzie in the Italian mountains in 1830, by Hayter. (The Earl of Dundonald)

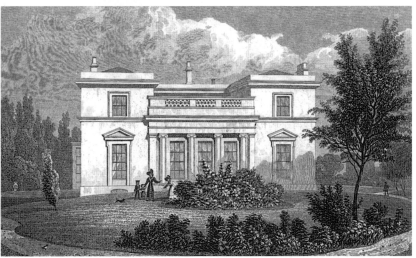

Hanover Lodge in Regent's Park, London, was the Cochrane family's home during the 1830s.

HMS Wellesley, *Cochrane's flagship in the West Indies, 1848–51, by Crawford.* (© National Maritime Museum, London)

Cochrane in old age wearing the uniform of a British Admiral. (The Earl of Dundonald)

defences were scattered round the curve of a semicircular bay, the seaward arm of which was dominated by the castles of the Real Felipe and the entrance protected by a heavy-chained boom. Cochrane devised a plan that would rely on the element of surprise by slipping into the harbour under American colours while the defenders were distracted by a local festival, and then to carry off one of the Spanish frigates anchored inside. On the morning of the attack the approaches were shrouded in a dense and impenetrable fog. It lasted a week. During a clearer spell of hazy sunshine on 29 February, there came the sound of guns from the shore. It was only the firing of salutes to mark a visit by the Viceroy but the Chileans, thinking one of their ships was in trouble, headed for Callao only to be enveloped in fog once more. When it lifted, they found themselves huddled together near the entrance with a Spanish gunboat caught in their midst. The gunboat was easily taken, but the Chileans were within range of Callao's formidable defences – 160 fixed guns on land plus a similar number on the broadsides of the Spanish armed ships which had been anchored in a protective semicircle. Sighting the intruders, the Spanish batteries erupted in thunder and smoke, and with shot whistling about their ears the Chileans turned and laboriously worked their way out of the bay to safety. It had been a bad moment for Cochrane – made worst by the fact that, in his miniature midshipman's uniform, little Thomas had escaped from the after cabin in which he had been locked and had made his way to the quarterdeck where he was found amid the carnage left by the Spanish cannonade.

With his initial foray against Callao frustrated, Cochrane sent Captain Forster to seize the adjacent island of San Lorenzo. Although nothing more than a treeless outcrop of rock, it would provide a useful base. Then, remembering his orders, Cochrane sent a letter in to Pezuela, the Spanish Viceroy, proposing an exchange of prisoners and complaining about the ill treatment suffered by those liberated on San Lorenzo. Pezuela, accustomed to the flowery courtesies of official Spanish correspondence, was offended by Cochrane's tone and answered by expressing surprise at seeing a British nobleman in the company of a bunch of rebels. Cochrane relished paper arguments, and for the next fortnight the two men indulged in a long-winded correspondence over the justice of the Chilean cause, the neutrality of Great Britain, and the right of a nobleman

to fight for justice wherever he chose.[10] It finished with Cochrane pleased
to have got the better of the argument. But by this time he had forgotten
the real objective: there was no exchange of prisoners.

Leaving Blanco Encalada in charge of the blockade, Cochrane then
spent four weeks raiding the Spanish settlements scattered along the long
desert coast. With the same skill he had demonstrated while commanding
the *Imperieuse* off Catalonia, he fell on the unsuspecting villages and
towns, distributing patriotic proclamations and seizing ships, property and
money. At Patavilca he took $67,000. At Paita he captured and plundered
the town, although – to the astonishment of the Chilean marines – he
was careful to return property that had been looted from a church. At
Guanbacho he seized a French brig called *Gazelle* carrying $60,000, and
at Supe his men ambushed a convoy of mules carrying $120,000 in gold
and silver which Cochrane claimed belonged to the Philippines
Company. Unfortunately, two thirds of it was the property of an
American called Elphalet Smith, whose schooner *Macedonian* Cochrane
had also captured. The American authorities protested at length over
Cochrane's action.

On 19 June 1819 Cochrane was back in the raw cold of the Valparaiso
winter, joining Blanco Encalada and the rest of the squadron, which had
been forced to raise the blockade of Callao by shortage of supplies. He
received a jubilant welcome. Whatever their initial caution, the Chilean
Government fully approved of Cochrane's aggressive approach. From the
outset, news of his successes had been published in the *Gazeta Ministerial
de Chile* – indeed whole editions were filled with his despatches.[11] The
National Institute of Santiago issued a eulogy of his operations off Callao
and the public responded with enthusiasm. O'Higgins came down from
Santiago to congratulate Cochrane personally, and to raise a loan so the
squadron could be supplied and paid. Cochrane's offer to use his prize
money for the purpose was politely declined. Preparations for the next
stage of the campaign were also agreed. This time, there was to be an
attack on Callao in true Cochrane style using pyrotechnics and the latest
technology in the shape of Congreve rockets and explosion vessels. A Mr
Goldsack, an assistant of Congreve, arrived from England to prepare the
rockets and bombs, and the various devices were carefully tested before
the squadron departed.

Cochrane's outlook was entirely positive at this time. In letters to his brother William, he reported that things were going well, and that he had high hopes of prize money. He even urged William to follow him to Chile, telling him that Forster had recently got married, and that there were excellent brides to be found for any of his friends who cared to come. But his optimism was already being undermined by money worries. As usual, his expenses were running ahead of his income. The costs of finding a house, of repairing it, of employing servants, and of providing the level of entertainment expected of an admiral on his flagship were well in excess of his pay. Cochrane explained the problem to O'Higgins and described the Royal Navy's system of command pay or 'table money' for official entertainment, which effectively doubled the income of British flag officers. The Supreme Director was sympathetic and agreed to raise Cochrane's emoluments to $10,000, or £2000 per annum It was made clear, however, that the extra $4000 was a personal gratuity payable only to Cochrane in recognition of his special circumstances and experience.[12]

But Cochrane was also concerned about prize money. In Britain the whole value of captured ships and property was shared among the captors, the commander-in-chief receiving one eighth; the captain of the ship concerned, two eights; the sea officers, warrant officers and petty officers one eighth respectively; and the rest of the ship's company the remaining two eights. In Chile only half of the value was distributed in this way, the rest being retained by the State. For Cochrane this meant that his share of prizes not only went down to one sixteenth of the value, but was reduced further, since he had to pay one third of the flag's share to Rear Admiral Blanco Encalada. Cochrane had already pressed the point to O'Higgins that prize money was 'the liberal reward for enterprise and exertion which has brought the Royal Navy to the pitch of Glory', and had urged Chile to adopt British practice.[13] Once more, O'Higgins was willing to compromise, and agreed that, in addition to his normal one-eighth share of prize values, Cochrane should receive one eighth of the government's half as well.

When the squadron set off for the next campaign, the only major change in personnel was that Captain Robert Forster went to the corvette *Independencia*, which had only recently arrived from the United

States via the River Plate. This left the *O'Higgins* without a captain, but Cochrane decided to take on the job himself as well as being commander-in-chief. The Chilean squadron reached the Peruvian coast on 28 September 1819, and began to prepare the rocket and mortar rafts needed for the great attack on Callao. Each was commanded by a marine officer, the mortars by Major William Miller and the rockets by Colonel Charles and Captain Henry Hind. On 2 October, Cochrane launched his first tentative sally. As night fell, the rafts were towed into position by the brigs *Galvarino*, *Araucano* and *Pueyrredon* and began to fire into the anchorage. They were answered by a hail of cannon fire, the shore batteries using red-hot shot. After a vigorous exchange, the Chileans withdrew. They had suffered only slight damage, principally when Captain Hind's rocket raft had blown up and a stray shot had killed Lieutenant Benjamin Bealy of the *Galvarino*, but the performance of the mortars had been poor and the rockets had performed erratically.

The days that followed saw more skirmishes, while Cochrane prepared for the main attack scheduled for 6 October. The rocket and mortar rafts were towed once more into position by three brigs and began to bombard the anchorage, while a fireship commanded by Lieutenant Ford Morgell was sent in to break the boom and flush out the ships in the harbour. This time light winds prevented Morgell reaching his objective, and the rockets missed their targets, going wildly off course or plunging into the sea. The attack was a failure. Cochrane remained surprisingly optimistic and urged the Chileans to persevere with the new technology, explaining that the artisans from England had failed to weld the rocket cylinders adequately and that the wood of which the tails were made was of inferior quality.[14] It was only later – when he was anxious to denigrate the Chilean authorities – that he blamed them for the failure by claiming that the Spanish prisoners used as labourers had filled the rockets with sand and manure to stop them going off.[15] It was an accusation the Chileans strenuously denied.[16]

Deciding that any further attack on Callao was doomed, Cochrane ordered Captain Guise to take the fort at Pisco and to seize the shipping sheltering under its guns. Guise successfully carried out the attack, but Major Miller of the marines was wounded and their commander, Colonel Charles, was killed. Then there was further cause for frustration. Before

Cochrane left Valparaiso, he had been ordered to look out for the Spanish reinforcements that had left Cadiz in May. This time they were substantial, comprising the 74-gun ships *Alejandro I* and *San Telmo* and the frigate *Prueba*. The arrival of such a powerful force would clearly mean a sharp swing of maritime power in favour of Spain. Fortunately for Chile, the *Alejandro I* was forced back before it left the Atlantic, and the *San Telmo* was hit by a storm so severe that she was lost with all hands. Only the *Prueba* managed to round the Horn and get as far as Peru. She was actually sighted by the Chilean blockading squadron off Callao, but she turned away and continued north before she could be recognised. Cochrane heard rumours that she had been seen in Guayaquil and immediately sailed in pursuit but could find no sign of the Spanish frigate. For Cochrane and his men, the campaign of 1819 ended with a whimper and not a bang.

—⇒●⇐—

CHAPTER TEN

Triumph and Tribulation

STILL PATROLLING the sea lanes off Callao, Lord Cochrane was despondent and assumed that his superiors would be dissatisfied with his efforts. The Chileans were disappointed but, as Bernardo O'Higgins explained, no one blamed Cochrane. As far as he was concerned Cochrane had done all that had been asked of him. He had driven the Spanish navy from the Pacific, confined the remnants to its base, and imposed a crippling blockade on the Peruvian capital. His despatches were once more featured in the *Gazeta Ministerial de Chile*; O'Higgins wrote repeated personal notes of support, and in a long letter dated 26 November 1819, the Minister of Marine, José Ignacio Zenteno, praised Cochrane's audacity and tactics, confirmed that he had the Supreme Director's total confidence, and demonstrated it by concluding,

> ...while reiterating that the squadron should (i) not return unless faced with an emergency it cannot overcome, and (ii) that it should operate in such a way as to avoid compromises but take advantage of any chance to destroy all, or part, of the enemy's forces – the Government does not wish to restrict you with any rules. It leaves you free to operate in its interests according to circumstances.[1]

Nevertheless, Cochrane continued to brood. When he picked up a rumour that the elusive Spanish frigate *Prueba* was heading south to Valdivia, it suddenly struck him that the best way to restore his reputation was to seize that fortress by *coup de main*. Valdivia was Spain's last remaining stronghold on the Pacific seaboard south of Callao. It was the first landfall for ships coming round Cape Horn from Europe and was a vital base and a major depository of supplies, arms and munitions. The scheme was typical of Cochrane's daring; it was also totally against his orders, which were to remain off Callao. Leaving a handful of ships on blockade duty, Cochrane sailed away in the *O'Higgins* alone to Valdivia – 2000 miles away from where he should have been. He told the Chilean Government nothing of his movements or plans. The flow of weekly dispatches simply ceased.

Cochrane reached Valdivia at dusk on 17 January 1820. His first task was to discreetly assess the chances of a successful attack. With the *O'Higgins* standing off the entrance of the bay flying the red and gold of Spain to avoid alarming the defenders, early the next morning Cochrane did a personal reconnaissance of the harbour in his gig.[2] After he returned, a boat carrying four Spanish soldiers and a pilot came innocently alongside the flagship deceived by her Spanish colours. They added to the intelligence Cochrane had already gathered. The suveillance completed, the *O'Higgins* made sail and disappeared as stealthily as she had come. Cochrane now had two objectives: first to capture the Spanish brig *Potrillo*, which he had learned was on its way from Callao carrying $20,000 in cash for the garrison of Valdivia; second to head for the nearest Chilean base at Talcahuana in search of reinforcements.

Cochrane was lucky. The *Potrillo* sailed straight into his hands as he headed east for the mainland, and he reached Talcahuana with her cargo of bullion safely in his possession. Arriving on 22 January, he immediately took command of the two Chilean warships he found there, the brig *Intrepido* and the schooner *Montezuma*. The local governor, General Ramon Freire, willingly supplied 250 infantrymen to augment his landing force, and a week later, Cochrane's flotilla headed back to Valdivia. Almost immediately, there was a crisis. On the first night out, the *O'Higgins* suddenly juddered aground off the remote island of Quiriquina. Her false keel was torn off, her pumps failed, and she began to take in water. Cochrane rallied his men, led them below, and carried out repairs to the pumps and hull with his own hands. The *O'Higgins* was re-floated and, with pumps going continuously, set her course once more for Valdivia.

For a sailing ship to run aground at night in poorly charted waters was not uncommon. But Cochrane's entourage thought that the incident would reflect badly on their patron and that they needed to manufacture

a defence. The excuse which subsequently appeared was that Cochrane
was exhausted with carrying out the duties of both commander-in-chief
and captain and went to bed giving orders to the officer of the watch,
Lieutenant Nicholas Lawson, to call him if the wind rose. Lawson,
however, also retired, leaving the deck to a midshipman who failed to
carry out his orders. Thus, Cochrane's partisans argued, he was blameless
for the accident. Alas, this excuse does not hold water. It was Cochrane
who decided that *O'Higgins* did not need a captain while he was on
board; and it was he who allowed the complement of lieutenants to fall
from four to one. The grounding of the *O'Higgins* showed Cochrane's
powers of leadership, his strength of character, his technical skills and his
seamanship at their best. It is a pity that his constant need for self-
justification did not allow him leave it at that.

Surrounded by apple trees and with an ample harbour, the town of
Valdivia was located on the low, heavily wooded banks of a long river
entered through a flask-shaped estuary with a narrow entrance 1200 yards
wide. Cochrane's translator, William Bennet Stevenson, described it as 'the
Gibraltar of South America', defended by 2000 men and over 100 guns.
This was an exaggeration. Unlike Gibraltar, the troops and guns defending
Valdivia were not located in a single fortress, but were scattered between
four different forts, four smaller gun emplacements, and the Castle of
Corral which dominated the interior of the bay.

The defences of Valdivia appeared formidable, but Cochrane's
reconnaissance had revealed their weaknesses. Not only was the garrison
scattered but the guns were positioned so as to resist an attack by sea. To a
man of Cochrane's tactical brilliance, the answer was clear. It was to land
unexpectedly by night and roll up the forts and batteries one by one before
a central defence could be organised. And this is exactly what he did. Late
on the afternoon of 2 February 1820, Cochrane's flotilla was within
striking distance of Valdivia. Leaving the damaged *O'Higgins* out of sight of
the shore, Cochrane embarked the landing parties on *Intrepido* and
Montezuma and, in a heavy sea, headed for a cove at the foot of Fort Ingles.
To gain time the Chilean ships flew the Spanish flag and even
communicated with the shore posing as friendly vessels fresh from Cape
Horn. The bluff was eventually called, but by the time the fort opened fire
it was too late. With Major Miller in the lead, the boats battled through a

rising wind and a crashing surf to reach the beach and drive off a picket of enemy skirmishers. Then, with the light fast fading, the rest of the troops and marines landed and began to file up the steep track to the heights. By the time they reached the top it was night. With the defenders firing blindly into the darkness, the Chileans bridged the ditch around the fort, stormed it in a two-pronged attack, and drove the defenders out at bayonet point. Fleeing in panic the Spaniards collided with a column of reinforcements and threw them into disarray. When the fort of San Carlos opened its gates to admit the refugees, a horde of pursuing Chileans followed them in and promptly captured that as well. The attack surged on, with Fort Amargos falling with equal ease. The castle of Corral could have been expected to mount a sturdy defence, but so great was the Spanish confusion and demoralisation that when the Chileans approached the defenders rushed for the boats and escaped. By daybreak, to Cochrane's astonishment, the whole of the western side of the bay was in his hands.

Next day, as the Chileans prepared to attack the fortifications on the eastern side the *O'Higgins* appeared from the sea. Ignorant of her condition, and assuming that she bristled with guns and was full of men, the Spaniards deserted their defences and fled up-river to Valdivia while *O'Higgins* was hastily beached before she could sink. The Chileans followed, and on 6 February Cochrane entered the town to receive the surrender of the Spanish forces. The fall of Valdivia was a major victory and confirmation of Cochrane's extraordinary military prowess. Not only did it remove the last potential threat to Chilean independence, but it put vast quantities of gunpowder, cannon, small arms, and other military equipment in the government's hands.

News that Cochrane had abandoned the blockade of Callao to pursue some scheme of his own was received with concern in Valparaiso and Santiago. So when news arrived of his triumph at Valdivia, the authorities were relieved and delighted. On his return to Valparaiso, the City Council and the National Institute of Santiago published messages of praise, and the government signified its pleasure by issuing a public letter from Zenteno on 27 February which ran,

If victories over an enemy can be estimated according to the resistance offered and the national advantages gained, then the conquest of Valdivia is, in both senses, inestimable – encountering as you did the natural and artificial strengths of that impregnable fortress – the memory of that glorious day will occupy the first pages of Chilean history and the name of Your Excellency will be transmitted from generation to generation by the gratitude of our descendants.

His Excellency the Supreme Director, highly gratified by that noble conquest, orders me to inform you that he experiences the most heartfelt gratitude at that signal achievement. The meritorious officers…and soldiers who, in imitation of Your Excellency, encountered such vast dangers, will be brought to the notice of the Government in order to receive a distinctive medal in gratitude for their gallantry and in proof that Chile rewards the heroes who advocate her cause.[3]

The minister repeated these sentiments in a private interview: but he was inevitably obliged to mention that the Vice Admiral *had* acted against orders, and that it had been a risky enterprise. In so doing, Zenteno inadvertently blighted his relationship with Cochrane. The Vice Admiral's tendency to think that anyone who offered the slightest criticism had to be motivated by malice meant that Zenteno was cast in the role of an enemy. Out of delicacy, the minister's comments had been made in private. It was Cochrane and his entourage who hastened to make them public. In the Cochrane version of the interview, the Minister of Marine is abusive, railing that he had acted like 'a madman…and that I should lose my head for attacking without orders and for exposing the patriot forces to such a hazard'. From this point forward, Cochrane regarded Zenteno as 'my bitter opponent, obstructing all my plans for the interests of Chile',[4] a man who all the while was secretly plotting against him.

It would be naive to expect a revolutionary official to be an angel of virtue, but Cochrane's distorted picture of Zenteno in no way conforms with his record as organiser of the Chilean navy or as governor of Valparaiso. An unemotional but dedicated man, Zenteno was clearly no charmer. Yet there is no evidence to substantiate Cochrane's accusations of jealousy, malice and obstruction – rather the reverse. During their four years of association, Zenteno sent Cochrane hundreds of orders; supplemented by scores of personal letters.[5] Even allowing for Latin American courtesy, their tone is amiable and so at variance with

Cochrane's description that even he feels obliged to explain away the discrepancy.[6]

Cochrane's suspicions of Zenteno soon extended to the Chilean Government as a whole. This is not on the whole surprising. Cochrane had a lifelong mistrust of anyone in authority and in Chile it was to be no different. Only O'Higgins was immune. In the *Narrative of Services*, Cochrane depicts him as an honest and well-intentioned patriot, while his ministers are described as corrupt, hostile, and so jealous of a foreigner achieving military glory that they deliberately undermined his efforts. Written in bitter hindsight, Cochrane's *Narrative of Services* claims that this animosity existed from the beginning, using the sensible precaution of his original orders to avoid action with the batteries of Callao to prove his argument. Furthermore, at the moment Cochrane was capturing Valdivia, Zenteno is accused of maliciously preparing court martial charges for insubordination – an accusation Zenteno's biographers vehemently deny. Cochrane's version of the events that followed the taking of Valdivia was later repeated by John Miers in his *Travels in Chile and La Plata*:

> Lord Cochrane on his return instead of being hailed by the government for the services he had rendered was annoyed by every possible vexation, the Minister of Marine declaring that instead of reward he deserved to have lost his life in the enterprise as it was the act of a madman!!! This Minister carried out a series of intrigues, the object of which was to degrade the Admiral and lessen the glory which his brilliant services so well deserved... He did not even receive public acknowledgement or thanks for this brilliant exploit. It was only when Lord Cochrane's indignation was raised at the ingratitude of the Government of Chile and it was feared he was about to retire in August, that the requested form of thanks was conceded, that medals were distributed to the victorious troops, and a nominal reward of the grant of an estate was given Lord Cochrane for his brilliant services.[7]

This distorted account bears no resemblance to reality. O'Higgins and the Chilean Government in fact regarded Cochrane's presence as indispensable to victory, were pleased with his activities, and said so frequently and publicly. Their private views were no different. When

O'Higgins wrote to the Senate at the end of March, for example, he stressed the importance of the capture of Valdivia to the Chilean nation, and concluded, 'the government finds itself necessary for reasons of policy, gratitude and justice to show to Lord Cochrane – the one and only author of this reconquest – due recognition that we are indebted to him for its success. He has gloriously extended himself beyond the purely naval sphere and has rendered the fatherland a truly extraordinary service'.[8] O'Higgins and his colleagues had already put their appreciation in concrete terms by doubling Cochrane's pay and prize money. Now, in addition to trumpeting his achievements, they awarded him the Chilean Order of Merit, a Gold Medal and an estate of 20,000 acres along the River Clara in the south.

Yet in spite of these clear demonstrations of government approval, Cochrane was convinced of the opposite, persuading himself that ministers were antagonistic and intriguing to get rid of him. Writing to General José de San Martin about events at the time, he claimed that 'plans and intrigues were set afoot for my dismissal from the Chilean service...for no reason other than certain influential persons of shallow understanding and petty expectations hate those who despise mean acts accomplished by low cunning'. San Martin's version of the letter includes, '...the conduct of the Senate and of Zenteno merits no other description'.[9] There is no evidence of any of this. Cochrane is never able to explain why, if they were so anxious to remove him, ministers refused to accept his many resignations. The accusation that Zenteno and his colleagues – engaged in an uncertain revolutionary struggle on which their careers and lives depended – would hamper the naval effort because of jealousy towards a foreigner defies common sense.

There were certain matters, of course, on which disagreements with the Chilean Government were inevitable. Prize money was one: not because of non-payment – Cochrane was paid his prize money promptly in spite of his later claim that he was not[10] – but because it was restricted to ships and property captured afloat or in transit. Cochrane was used to a system whereby the captors received all the booty when an enemy town was taken and expected the same to apply in Chile and Peru. The South Americans thought differently, and could not accept the idea that their cities were 'enemy' territory whose riches belonged to whoever captured them. As a result, there was no prize money following Cochrane's liberation of Valdivia and he nursed a permanent grievance.

Pay was another issue: again, not for Cochrane. Knowing his reputation, the Chileans ensured that he was paid on time and by August 1820, he had received all he was owed in pay and prize money – $37,500 (or £7500), half of which he remitted to England in bills of exchange. Despite the increased pay and share of prize money Cochrane had managed to secure from O'Higgins, his expenditure continued to run out of control and was double his income. A major cost related to the leasing of a second estate at Quintero, along the coast from Valparaiso.[11] By all accounts, Cochrane's domestic life seemed contented. Kitty was certainly enjoying herself, being the belle of many balls and gaining the admiration of John Downes, captain of the USS *Macedonian* which had relieved the *Ontario* in early 1819. She was also indulging in some adventurous travelling in the mountains and countryside of Chile. This was both exciting and dangerous, and on two occasions she was lucky to escape the attentions of footpads. In March 1820, she presented Cochrane with a baby daughter. The child was christened Elizabeth Josephine with O'Higgins standing as her godfather.

While Cochrane may have received all his pay, his men did not fare so well. The Chilean Government had difficulty producing the large sums of cash needed for the squadron now that it had returned from Callao. Thus when Cochrane returned to Valparaiso he found the men unpaid and deserting. Without delay he wrote one of the compendium letters he favoured, which complained not only about pay, but about anything else he could think of, and threatened to resign.[12] Cochrane's entourage ensured that his letter received wide circulation. Zenteno's reply, which firmly demolished many of his claims, did not.[13] Nevertheless, Cochrane's intervention helped to resolve the situation, and by 30 May the squadron had been paid.

The major preoccupation of O'Higgins and his ministers during 1820 was the organisation of the great invasion of Peru. The navy's pay demands were an unwelcome – if necessary – distraction, and they were relieved when the dispute was settled. But to their dismay, Cochrane's complaints went on and on, this time caused by personality clashes within the officer corps, which he seemed to be stirring rather than containing. Maria

Graham was later to write, 'the state of the Chilean Navy required a man of prudence as well as courage, of temper as well as firmness...and [Lord Cochrane's] gentle and courteous manner...was admirably calculated to conciliate all parties'.[14] Alas, there is no evidence that she was right. Cochrane undoubtedly exerted great personal magnetism on those immediately around him, but he seemed unable to inspire those who were not.

The situation was made worse by the followers who surrounded him. Some were excellent men, such as Robert Forster; Thomas Sackville Crosbie who would later follow him to Brazil and Greece; John Pascoe Grenfell, who became a Brazilian admiral; and William Miller of the marines who became a Peruvian general. Others were not. There was the darker influence of people such as Jackson, Dean and Stevenson; Henry Cobbett who browbeat his subordinates in Chile just as he had bullied Marryat in the *Imperieuse* in 1808; and Ford Morgell, a brave, even rash officer, but one who was notorious for his quarrelsome nature and his addiction to gambling.

At first Cochrane's social position as the son of an earl, his reputation as a fighting captain and his outstanding naval achievements gave him an unquestioned authority. But as time went on, the negative side of his character became more pronounced, until he became convinced he was being secretly criticised by disloyal subordinates. As early as December 1819, he was writing, 'I know to the marrow all who are about me; as well as the conduct and character, and the secret acts and plots, of others who little suspect it.'[15] In fact, the squadron had performed well off the coasts of Peru and the chief suspects, Captains Guise and Spry, had taken leading parts. Nevertheless, Cochrane became convinced that Guise was resentful at having lost the post of senior captain to Robert Forster and that his followers were scheming to make him the commander-in-chief. This was an astonishing allegation since the only possible alternative to Cochrane was Blanco Encalada. Martin Guise was also no conspirator. If anything he was too honest and open. Towards the end of 1819, for example, he was unwise enough to criticise the fact that Cochrane, who was acting as both commander-in-chief and captain of the *O'Higgins*, was claiming a double share of prize money.

Guise's plain speaking did him no good. Criticism was resented – and remembered – so that the *Narrative of Services* later denounces Guise for disaffection and plots. At the time, no one viewed him that way. Stevenson and Maria Graham describe him as 'a good natured, gentlemanlike man,'[16] and refused to believe he could be a villain. They preferred to take the view that Captain John Tooker Spry was his evil genius. Spry was from an obscure branch of a Cornish family who had joined the Royal Navy as a second class ship's boy in 1803, and had eventually risen to midshipman. He arrived in the West Indies in *Wolverine* in 1806 but, lacking influence, had been passed from one ship to the next without promotion. Spry's luck changed in 1810 when he was posted to the cutter *Liberty*, commanded by Lieutenant Guise. Guise made him a sub-lieutenant and encouraged him to take the lieutenant's examination and achieve promotion on 17 July 1813. From then on, Spry accepted Guise as his patron, and accompanied him to Chile in 1818.

Spry's lowly background did not endear him to the inner circle of the aristocrat Lord Cochrane. Reflecting their view, Graham (who never met him) described him as an adventurer and 'a low minded man'.[17] Likewise, Stevenson cannot restrain a sneer about his 'word of honour'.[18] Unfortunately, the republican atmosphere of Chile made Spry free with his views, and his private conversations had been reported back. The reputations of both Guise and Spry were subsequently damned in the memoirs of Cochrane and his partisans, and his animosity was soon extended to cover all the officers who served under the two men in *Lautaro* and *Galvarino*.

In the period following Valdivia, the two strands of Cochrane's obsession with his own officers and the ministers of the government came together in one small mental leap. Cochrane decided that his supposed detractors, Guise and Spry, were part of the Zenteno-inspired conspiracy to have him court-martialled. In the final version of this thesis, one biographer even writes that 'the arch-trouble maker of the Chilean Navy, Captain Spry' had gained Zenteno's ear and that it was he who was behind the plan to disgrace Cochrane for leaving Callao.[19] There is nothing to prove this. Spry was actually nowhere near Valparaiso at the time, being absent on blockade duty off Peru from September 1819 until the end of February 1820 – well after the news of Cochrane's victory at Valdivia had arrived.[20]

The situation came to a head on 11 July 1820 when Cochrane had Guise arrested and asked for a court martial. Guise was charged with 'endeavouring in…various acts of disobedience…to set at defiance and bring into contempt the authority of his superior officer, the commander-in-chief'. An examination of the papers reveals little of substance. What does become clear is that Cochrane's entourage had been watching Guise for months in order to accumulate complaints against him. These were assembled into a dozen charges, the most serious being that 'on a certain date' he had failed to report the arrest and release of an American brig; that he had been negligent in discharging a lieutenant; that he had allowed an officer ashore without reporting it; that he had been slow in sending boats to a vessel in difficulties; that he had allowed his crew to be paid before that of the *O'Higgins*; and that he had detained a ship although '*Lautaro* did not have the guard'. With Guise under arrest, Cochrane's men were able to search the *Lautaro*'s books for mistakes. This led to two more charges: failing to report deficiencies in carpenters' stores, and 'falsifying', that is, miscalculating, crew numbers.[21]

For its part, the Chilean Government were focused on the invasion of Peru and refused Cochrane's request for a court martial. Cochrane resigned but changed his mind when O'Higgins and Zenteno begged him to remain. Rumours of his proffered resignation were nevertheless received with dismay and, on 18 and 19 July, five serving captains and 15 lieutenants signed petitions of support. Significantly, four captains and eight lieutenants did not. But that was not the end of the matter. The post of flag-captain of the *O'Higgins* remained unfilled and Zenteno – probably knowing nothing of Cochrane's antipathy towards Spry – moved him into it. Cochrane was livid, and when he boarded the flagship, the unfortunate Spry was denounced by Cochrane on the quarterdeck and accused of being a spy.[22] The government bowed to Cochrane's fury and replaced him with one of his followers, a red-headed former Royal Navy lieutenant called Thomas Sackville Crosbie.

CHAPTER ELEVEN

The Liberation of Peru

BY THE CHILEAN SPRING OF 1820, the great Liberating Expedition was ready to strike against Peru. On 20 August, an army of 4500 men, with their supplies, artillery and 800 horses were embarked on 17 transports under the direction of Paul Delano, the American captain who had delivered the *Independencia* under the name *Curiato* to Chile the year before. The escort was provided by Lord Cochrane's squadron and comprised the flagship *O'Higgins* (Captain Thomas Sackville Crosbie), the frigates *San Martin* (Captain William Wilkinson), and *Lautaro* (Captain Martin Guise), the corvette *Independencia* (Captain Robert Forster), the brigs *Galvarino* (Captain John Tooker Spry), *Araucano* (Captain Thomas Carter) and *Pueyrredon* (Lieutenant William Prunier) and the schooner *Montezuma* (Lieutenant George Young). General José de San Martin was in overall command of the expedition with the title of Captain General, and it was made clear to Cochrane that he was to act under his orders. Bernardo O'Higgins knew full well that he would not take kindly to this situation and ended Cochrane's orders with the pious and flattering hope that he would do as he was told:

> It is unnecessary to recommend most earnestly to Your Lordship the most exact observance of my resolutions in all your areas of responsibility. Your Lordship has given sufficient proofs that your military conduct has followed no other course than that indicated by the Government, and I flatter myself that Your Lordship, conforming to this and to your own principles, will present yourself to the gratitude of America as the hero of its liberty...[1]

After a two-week voyage, in which Cochrane seemed to have difficulty keeping his warships and the convoy together, the expedition reached its destination and disembarked at Pisco, 100 miles south of Callao and Lima. The army secured the town, capturing useful quantities of rum and supplies, and slowly began to occupy the adjacent countryside. San Martin had made it clear from the outset that he had not come as a conqueror but as a liberator, and that the purpose of his army was to neutralise the royalist forces while the Peruvians freed themselves. He was therefore in no hurry, and believed that even without military victories, it was only a matter of time before Peru fell like a ripe plum. Indeed, soon there were signs that San Martin's strategy seemed to be working. At the end of September, the royalists sued for an armistice, although the talks broke down after a week. Then the northern province of Guayaquil declared its independence, and a month later, the Spanish Numancia Regiment deserted to the patriot side. On 28 October, the army was re-embarked and transferred to Ancon to begin operations north of Callao.

Cochrane and the squadron began to enforce a blockade of the Peruvian coast, rounding up both enemy and neutral merchant ships in the process. Protests from foreign naval commanders in the area quickly ensued. No one disputed the fact that the Chileans had the right to take such action, but a basic rule was that no blockade was legitimate unless the number of warships was adequate to the task. The Chileans had declared a blockade stretching from 21°48'S to 2°12'S − a distance of 2000 miles! Sir Thomas Hardy, Nelson's former flag captain at Trafalgar, who had replaced William Bowles as commander-in-chief of the British South America Squadron, led a wave of international protest, pointing out that Cochrane's force was too small to be able to control such a vast area, and as such the blockade could not be accepted as legitimate.[2]

This was to create real difficulties for Chile. At the end of 1818, Viceroy Pezuela had decided to improve his supply situation and revenues by allowing foreign ships and goods into Peru and by 1820, dozens of British and American ships were arriving in Peruvian waters. As far as the Chileans were concerned, all were liable to seizure. HMS *Hyperion*, HMS *Conway* and the USS *Macedonian* had been providing escorts for their merchant vessels for some time. Now the maritime powers began to increase their presence in the area. Hardy rounded the Horn in the frigate

Creole and ordered the 74-gun *Superb* to follow. The American Consul let it be known that the 74-gun *Franklin* was on its way. In January 1821 a French squadron comprising the 74-gun *Colosse*, the *Galathée* and *L'Echo* appeared. The innocent explanation that they were on a training cruise convinced no one.

As usual, Cochrane was anxious do something more spectacular than merely enforce the blockade. Determined to make up for his previous failures at Callao, he planned to lead his men into the port, attack the 40-gun frigate *Esmeralda* which was anchored within, and carry her off in true Royal Navy style. With Callao bristling with guns and defended by a squadron of warships and gunboats, it was a plan of astonishing audacity.

The attack took place during the night of 5 November 1820, and was planned with Cochrane's characteristic attention to detail. Two hundred and forty volunteers were selected, all wearing white with blue armbands to aid recognition and carrying pistols, cutlasses and boarding axes. Groups of men were allocated to take on specific tasks following the frigate's capture: topmen to release her sails, axemen to cut her anchor cable, and keepers to secure the squadron's boats. Fourteen boats were to be used in the assault, operating in two divisions. The first division, who were to board the *Esmeralda* on the starboard side, were under the command of Cochrane and Captain Crosbie, supported by Lieutenants Esmond, Brown, Morgell, Robertson and Winter of the *O'Higgins*. The second, who were to attack the frigate's port side, were under Captain Guise, seconded by Lieutenants Bell and Freeman of *Lautaro*, and Lieutenants Grenfell and Gilbert of *Independencia*.

At 10 p.m. the boats headed under muffled oars for the gap in the heavily chained boom that sealed off the harbour. They overwhelmed a guard boat on the other side, then slid silently through the black water to where the unsuspecting *Esmeralda* lay anchored. Reaching the frigate undetected, the attackers clambered up the sides and launched themselves at the startled crew. Cochrane, taking the lead as usual, was knocked back into his boat by the butt of a sentry's musket but gamely rejoined the assault. The fight was short and sharp, but the Chilean attack proved irresistible, and with the unprepared Spaniards now running below, Captain Coig was forced to surrender his ship.

Cochrane had announced that he intended to use the captured frigate

as a platform from which to attack other ships in the harbour. Whether
he seriously believed that such a feat was possible is difficult to ascertain.
At least one experienced observer, Captain Basil Hall of HMS *Conway*,
doubted it, and thought it was just rhetoric to inspire the men. In the
event, it proved an impossible ambition. Alerted by the clash of steel and
the pop of small arms, the shore batteries began to lay down a heavy fire;
and in the heat of victory, the British seamen broke into the spirit room
and – not for the first time – became dead drunk; while their Chilean
comrades concentrated on looting. Indeed, as revealed in a contemporary
account written by Lieutenant John Pascoe Grenfell, the men thought
they had done quite enough and refused all attempts by their officers to
coax them into the boats. Captain Guise, who had taken command when
Cochrane was shot in the thigh during the final stages of the struggle,
decided to cut the frigate's cable and sail her out. This he did, passing on
the way, HMS *Hyperion* and the USS *Macedonian* – the former observing
the studied neutrality which her captain's orders required; the latter
ringing with cheers and encouragement.[3] It did the Americans no good.
Next day, a boat's crew from the *Macedonian* was attacked and
murdered while ashore by a mob convinced that they had helped in
the engagement.

The cutting-out of the *Esmeralda* was another high point in Cochrane's
career. Captain Thomas Searle of the *Hyperion* called it 'a most brilliant
affair…commanded by Lord Cochrane in person, in which he carried
[*Esmeralda*] together with a gunboat, from under the batteries…in less
than half-an-hour and under sail. This was done so quick and in so
masterly a style that I had scarcely time to get out of the line of fire'.[4] San
Martin was delighted, and reported the taking of the *Esmeralda* in glowing
terms to O'Higgins, writing,

> …it is impossible for me to eulogise in proper language the daring
> enterprise of 5th of November, by which Lord Cochrane has decided
> the superiority of our naval forces, augmented the splendour and power
> of Chile and secured the success of this campaign. I doubt not that His
> Excellency the Supreme Director will render the justice due to the
> worthy chief, the officers and other individuals who have had a share in
> that successful action.[5]

Those who had taken part in the assault were euphoric – but not for long. In January 1821, San Martin decided to change the frigate's name to *Valdivia* in honour of Cochrane's capture of the Spanish stronghold.[6] Guise, who had been moved with his crew to *Esmeralda* from *Lautaro*, was disappointed by the news, and when told of it by Cochrane himself on the flagship's quarterdeck, he expressed regret that the new name did nothing to commemorate the victory that the seizure of the frigate represented. In his reply, Cochrane seemed to agree.[7]

On *Esmeralda*, the officers, too, were disappointed. On 2 February 1821, they wrote to Guise, lamenting that the new name did nothing to recognise their efforts, pointing out that half of those who had captured the frigate had not been present at Valdivia, and asking him to use his influence with Cochrane to obtain a reconsideration. Likewise, while they approved of Chilean ships being named after revolutionary heroes such as San Martin and O'Higgins, they objected to the name of Pedro de Valdivia, one of the most oppressive of Spanish conquistadors. Cochrane later claimed in his *Narrative of Services* that San Martin had proposed calling the ship *Cochrane* and that the officers wanted *Guise*.[8] There is no evidence or likelihood that either assertion is true. A letter to Cochrane was signed by all the wardroom officers: Lieutenants Robert Bell and Henry Freeman, Purser James Frew, Surgeon James Michael and Assistant Surgeon Hugh Kernan. Guise could detect nothing disrespectful in the letter. He was on cordial relations again with Cochrane, and his recollection of the Vice Admiral's response to his comments on hearing the news made him think that it would cause no problems. However, as a precaution, he asked the opinion of Colonel William Miller, an intimate of Cochrane who had overheard his conversation with the Vice Admiral on the *O'Higgins*. Miller said he could see nothing wrong either,[9] so Captain Guise sent the letter on.

But Lord Cochrane was furious. With ideas of dissent and plots still simmering beneath the surface, Cochrane saw the letter as part of a conspiracy to replace him with Guise. He ordered that the *Valdivia*'s officers be arrested and court-martialled, and when Guise protested, he was manoeuvred into resigning. Cochrane's attitude to the officers was implacable. He was unmoved by either protestations of innocence or the fact that they all had distinguished service records in Britain and Chile.

The court martial took place on 2 March 1821, and the charge was drafted so as to ensure a guilty verdict. The five officers were dismissed.

But this was not the end of the matter. John Tooker Spry had watched events with growing alarm, aware that Cochrane's antipathy made him the next target. On 22 February 1821, when *Galvarino* was ordered to sea, Spry bowed to the inevitable and asked to be replaced in command. Cochrane demanded further explanation. Spry replied that he had come to Chile under Guise's patronage, and if Guise were forced to resign, he, too, would have to go.[10] Cochrane reacted by ordering a court martial and moved the *Galvarino* under the guns of the *O'Higgins* claiming that the ship was in a state of mutiny.[11] This was untrue. Spry had handed his ship over in good order without any sign of insubordination on board.[12] Spry was court-martialled on 3 and 5 March and faced three charges – refusing to put to sea when ordered, threatening to resign in sympathy with Guise, and inciting his ship's company to protest. He was found guilty of the second charge and part of the third, and was dismissed from his command and put at the bottom of the list of captains.

Guise and the other officers tried to get themselves reinstated by appealing to San Martin, which stimulated an exchange of correspondence in which Cochrane cleverly frustrated all their efforts. Guise's last words on the subject were bitter, provoking from Cochrane the revealing accusation that Guise's behaviour had been '…stimulated by disappointment in your endeavour to force back upon the service a club of officers who have so scandalously misconducted themselves; and who vainly hoped that union would be the best means to place you, their patron, in the chief command of the squadron'.[13]

Spry fared better. Needing a naval aide-de-camp, San Martin appointed him to the post. It was only afterwards that he received Cochrane's allegations of insubordination and complaints over a further incident when the Vice Admiral had accidentally met Spry dining ashore with Colonel Miller and Major Hind. The two marines had leapt to their feet and removed their hats leaving Spry seated and defiantly covered. When challenged by Cochrane, he had walked out.[14] San Martin was embarrassed but felt unable to sack Spry without further justification. And in spite of what is said in the *Narrative of Services*, Cochrane did not object to the decision.[15]

During the course of these tumultuous events there were also changes in Cochrane's domestic life. In January 1821, HMS *Andromache* arrived in Peruvian waters carrying his wife Kitty and their three children. Lady Cochrane went ashore at Huacho on the day Colonel Miller was assembling his men before an attack and was invited to inspect the troops. As he recorded in his memoirs, Miller introduced her to the men as their new 'generala', and the sight of the young and vivacious brunette on the back of an enormous horse was greeted with cheers and wild enthusiasm. She followed this with a tour of Peru, establishing – strangely enough in view of her husband's position – warm personal relationships with the local Spanish aristocracy. Once more she enjoyed crossing mountains and deserts and swinging over precipitous ravines in rickety rope bridges. But on hearing of a plot to kidnap her and her children and hold them hostage, she made a dash for the coast, entering as she did so an area where an epidemic of fever was raging. Her baby daughter, Elizabeth, who was then less than a year old, was smitten and died. The blow increased the strain Lord Cochrane was already under. In March 1821, he wrote sadly to tell O'Higgins of the news, then made arrangements for his wife and children to avoid further danger by returning to England on the *Andromache*. Happily, they were to have company on the voyage. Also aboard was the former Vicereine of Peru, Dona Angela de la Pezuela, who was returning to Europe with servants, baggage and the silver viceregal chamber pot.

The capture of the *Esmeralda* made Lord Cochrane undisputed master of the Pacific. The Spanish frigates *Venganza* and *Prueba* were still at large, but after the affair in Callao they went entirely on the defensive, leaving Cochrane to seize blockade runners, cut more vessels out of Callao, sack Arica and raid the Peruvian coast. On land, San Martin's campaign continued to follow its slow and relentless course. Unable to bring him to action, the Spaniards began to bicker among themselves, deposing Viceroy Pezuela and replacing him with the hardliner General José de la Serna. Spanish rule continued to crumble and on 6 July 1821, they evacuated Lima and retreated to the mountains, leaving only the castles of Callao holding out. The Peruvian patriots at last stirred themselves into action, and with Royal Marines from HMS *Conway* keeping order in the city during the interim, San Martin at last entered Lima at the invitation of its citizens. Thus, he arrived as he had intended – as a liberator and not as a conqueror. On 22 July the Independence of Peru was proclaimed; and on 3 August, San Martin was installed as Protector of the new republic. Just a week later, the Spanish General Canterac led a small force to the relief of Callao, stayed a month, then evacuated the castles and the port and marched back to the mountains loaded with property and money. Cochrane urged San Martin to attack the retreating Spaniards, but the Protector merely stood aside with his army and watched. He was perfectly content for Callao to fall into his hands and for the Spaniards to withdraw without an unnecessary battle.

For Lord Cochrane, the main event of 1821 was not the dramatic cutting out of the *Esmeralda*, or the triumphant liberation of Peru – it was the feud that developed between himself and San Martin. In view of their very different personalities, a clash of wills was inevitable: inevitable, that is, given Cochrane's insubordinate streak and his inability to keep his opinions to himself. On the one hand was San Martin, a thoughtful and subtle Latin – a political cynic who believed that only authoritarian government would frustrate his countrymen's instinct for anarchy, and who saw battles as merely one means to an end. On the other was Lord Cochrane, the impulsive and opinionated Scot who saw the world in simplistic terms of black and white, a political romantic who believed in democracy, and a man who saw battles and fighting as ends in themselves. Between the two there was a total lack of understanding.

The first disagreement was over military tactics. San Martin's preference was to play for time and avoid unnecessary action. Cochrane could not comprehend this reasoning and watched with growing contempt as San Martin avoided one engagement after another. Then he objected to the way Peru was being run after liberation. In spite of giving assurances that the Peruvians would be free to choose their own government, San Martin imposed an authoritarian regime designed to prevent the internal anarchy he feared. Cochrane, who had naively assumed that the despotism of Spain would be immediately followed by a pluralistic democracy, was dismayed. And when the politicians around San Martin began to feather their nests by persecuting the old Spaniards, Cochrane wrongly concluded that San Martin was a tyrant with an insatiable thirst for power. On 7 August he felt obliged to deliver a lecture on the duties of a ruler, writing, 'no man had yet arisen, save yourself, capable of soaring aloft with eagle eye embracing the expanse of the political horizon. But if, like Icarus, you trust to waxen wings, your descent may crush the rising liberties of Peru and involve all South America in anarchy, civil war and despotism.' He added, 'flatterers are more dangerous that the most venomous serpents, and next to them are men of knowledge – if they have not the integrity or courage to oppose bad measures when formally discussed or even when casually spoken of'.[16] There were some who felt Cochrane should have applied the same principles to his own entourage.

But the final row was not about military tactics or governance. It was about money. From the beginning, San Martin had been alarmed by what was seemed to be the total inconsistency in Cochrane's demands for cash and supplies. But more alarming were the methods Cochrane began to use to get the money he needed. In early 1821, instead of arresting alleged blockade runners, Cochrane began to release them on purchase of a trading 'licence' costing 18 per cent of the value of the cargo.[17] Sir Thomas Hardy made an official protest to O'Higgins who was dismayed, complaining to San Martin, 'I have had to humiliate myself before the British commander-in-chief in order to compensate for the stupidities of this man, and have repeatedly written to him about the need for moderation'.[18] In a similar vein, when the new Peruvian Government expelled all unmarried Spanish males after confiscating half of their property, Cochrane demanded a fee before issuing a passport to leave. The amount was said to have been between $2500 and $10,000 a head (the sources are divided as to the exact amount).[18] Likewise, during the siege of Callao in August 1821, Cochrane offered surrender terms that would have permitted Governor La Mar to ship out Spanish property in the port on a cash payment amounting to 33 per cent of its value. La Mar, in fact, refused.[19] San Martin's entourage cynically assumed that much of this money was going into Cochrane's own pocket. The Protector's British aide-de-camp, James Paroissien, who referred to him as 'el metálico Lord', reflected their views when he ruefully commented, 'What a pity, that this man who does possess the elements of a hero, is so extremely avaricious'.

But the real conflict was about the squadron's pay and supplies. At first,

Cochrane had been able to cope by using equipment, gear and money taken from Spanish and neutral prizes. But now that Peru was effectively independent, this source dried up and the squadron's situation became critical. The situation was made worse by the belief among the sailors that San Martin had seized a huge treasure in Peru, and that the army was being indulged while they starved. As Protector of liberated Peru, Cochrane now expected San Martin to provide for all the squadron's needs, and at the end of July he demanded the immediate payment of $420,000. This comprised $150,000 in arrears of pay; $110,000 in prize money for the *Esmeralda*; one gratuity of $50,000 for capturing the frigate; and another of $110,000 which had been promised on the fall of Lima.[20] San Martin was astonished by Cochrane's claims and took a different stance. He accepted responsibility for the payment of the two gratuities and, indeed, explained that orders had already been given to collect the money needed, but as far as he was concerned, the pay of the squadron was the responsibility of the Chilean Government, and should be done in the normal way when it returned to Valparaiso. In regard to *Esmeralda*, he pointed out that the frigate was in the possession of the Chilean navy and that the payment of prize money was therefore its responsibility.[21]

Cochrane and San Martin met on 5 August to seek a resolution. There are conflicting accounts about what exactly took place. The Cochrane version, retailed by William Bennet Stevenson who attended as translator, depicts the Protector as triumphalist and devious, while the Vice Admiral is reasonable and honest. San Martin is alleged to have said that 'he would not pay the Chilean squadron unless it was sold to Peru, and that the payment should be part of the purchase money'. Cochrane indignantly refused, upon which San Martin, snapped his fingers in his face and said, 'Chile! Chile! I will never pay a single real to Chile! And as to the squadron you may take it where you please, and go where you choose: a couple of schooners is enough for me'.[22] San Martin's version was that he accepted the obligation to pay the bonus, but maintained that pay and prize money were a Chilean responsibility; and that he only offered to buy warships in order to help them with their financial problems.

San Martin repeated his position in writing a few days later. Cochrane brushed the letter aside, replying that unless he received pay for the squadron immediately there would be a 'tempest' of insubordination by his crews. The seamen were certainly becoming truculent over the non-appearance of pay, and during September there were disturbing messages from *O'Higgins*, *Galvarino* and *Lautaro* of sailors refusing duty. The morale of the officers was also lagging and when, on 17 August, San Martin's government began to recruit men for the fledgling Peruvian navy 13 of the squadron's 30 sea officers signed on.[23] Their numbers included five of seven captains and six of 25 lieutenants. Cochrane himself was invited to become its admiral, but indignantly refused. Guise, Spry and Freeman inevitably offered their services, but so did many others who had previously been Cochrane 'followers' such as William Prunier and John Esmond. Cochrane claimed that they were bribed to leave the Chilean service with estates and awards, but it is just as likely that they were disturbed by the flavour of the *Valdivia* court martials and by Cochrane's apparent paranoia, and decided to leave before they too incurred his displeasure. Robert Forster, who had already fallen from favour and had been excluded from the attack on the *Esmeralda* because of doubts about his courage,[24] resigned his commission and Colonel Miller transferred to the army of Peru.

Then came the final confrontation. In September, the Spaniards abandoned Callao for the interior, threatening Lima on the way. For safety, San Martin had the contents of the state treasury – amounting to $283,000 (£56,600) – loaded on to the schooner *Sacramento* and sent to Ancon for safety. Cochrane, who had been informed of the transfer by Paul Delano, now captain of *Lautaro*, promptly seized the schooner and confiscated the money. For a country which was financially exhausted and whose monthly government revenue was only $130,659 it was a devastating blow.[25]

The Peruvians demanded the return of the money, and suggested a face-saving formula whereby a commissary would come on board, pay the crews, then return to Lima with the balance. Cochrane rejected the offer. Of the total of $400,000 carried on the *Sacramento*, he agreed to return $117,000, which belonged to private individuals and the army, but the rest he kept, sending $40,000 to Valparaiso, retaining $111,382 for future expenses, and distributing the remaining $131,618 as pay and prize money. He claimed, self-righteously, that he paid himself nothing. This may be so, but he nevertheless shipped home $13,507 – the equivalent of £2700 – in coin and bullion on 14 September in HMS *Superb*.

Cochrane may have been satisfied with his actions, but in the long run they worked to his disadvantage. Zenteno, Chile's Minister of Marine, had already authorised San Martin to pay Cochrane $120,000 in prize money for the *Esmeralda* and the schooner *Aranzaza*.[26] After the affront of the *Sacramento*, the Peruvians absolutely refused to pay, leaving Cochrane with a worthless letter of credit in his pocket. Cochrane's behaviour had shocked San Martin; so did his indiscreet language. He had been surprised to receive official letters from Cochrane publicly blackguarding the Chilean Government: writing, for example, on 4 August 1821, 'to what state has the Senate brought the beautiful and fertile province of Chile…. Has not their notorious want of good faith deprived them notwithstanding the value of their rich mines…the credit necessary to obtain a single dollar in foreign countries'.[27] At the same time, Cochrane was complaining to O'Higgins about San Martin, writing about 'secret plans by the Government of Peru to get the squadron in their power' and the need to avoid letting it fall into the hands of those 'who have made themselves, in my opinion, worse enemies of Chile than the Spaniards'.[28] Then San Martin learned that Cochrane's entourage were spreading hostile rumours about his activities in Peru, and publicising their version of the interview of 5 August. On 26 September, he ordered Cochrane back to Chile. Cochrane replied with a long letter of justification and accusation, then led the squadron out of Callao in the opposite direction.

When Cochrane sailed on 6 October 1821 with *O'Higgins*, *Valdivia*, *Independencia*, *Araucano* and the *Mercedes* schooner, his ships were only three-quarters manned, with hardly any foreign seamen, only nine lieutenants and three newly promoted captains. Where he was bound was unknown, but by not heading for Valparaiso, San Martin's retinue accused Cochrane of disobeying orders. This was not Cochrane's interpretation. In his view, by becoming Protector of Peru San Martin had relinquished command of the joint expeditionary force and now had no right to tell him what to do. Indeed, Lord Cochrane regarded himself as being the sole representative of the Chilean Government and had no intention of returning to Valparaiso. After years without a refit, Cochrane's frigates were leaking like baskets, with pumps and other gear worn out. His plan was to take them north to Guayaquil for repairs, then to scour the Pacific for the last remnants of the Spanish Navy, the frigates *Venganza* and *Prueba*.

CHAPTER TWELVE

Farewell to the Pacific

COCHRANE REACHED GUAYAQUIL on 21 October 1821. He received a rapturous welcome, but there was no news of the Spanish frigates. He spent a month there, provisioning and repairing his ships the best he could while scouts were sent north to Acapulco and Panama in search of the Spanish. When Cochrane left Guayaquil with the rest of the squadron he led them north to the Equator. With the heat increasing daily, they followed the contours of the low green coastline, investigating every inlet for the elusive Spanish frigates. In mid-December, they passed the low grey volcanoes that guarded the broad entrance of the Bay of Fonseca and dropped anchor among the green islands and gleaming white beaches within. There, Cochrane's men made further repairs to the pumps, then hacked their way for miles through the lush tropical vegetation to the nearest supply of fresh water. A week later they were off again, searching the Bay of Tehuantepec with its volcanoes and buccaneering past, before heading for Acapulco in Mexico. Although famous as the destination of the Manila Galleon, Acapulco had little more to offer than a harbour, a castle, a couple of convents and a small whitewashed town nestling among dank tropical greenery. What it did not offer was any word of the enemy. Once more, Cochrane was frustrated.

At the beginning of February 1822, the Chilean squadron left Acapulco and turned south. This time the voyage was less pleasant. Heading against the prevailing winds the voyage was a tedious one, alternating between thirsty calms and violent gales which severely tested the fabric of their leaky ships. Cochrane ordered *Araucano* away to the coast of California, and *Independencia* to conduct a survey in Panamanian waters, then made once more for Guayaquil. There, his quest was at an end, for anchored safely in the roadstead was the elusive *Venganza*. But now she flew the red and white flag of Peru. Short of provisions, lacking any base, and hunted by Cochrane's squadron, the captains of the two Spanish frigates had given themselves up. *Venganza* had surrendered to San Martin's men who now had controll of Guayaquil, while *Prueba* had gone on to Callao. This time Cochrane received a frosty reception, but he was more annoyed at being denied the chance of making a capture. As far as he was concerned, the surrender of the two Spanish frigates was entirely due to his efforts and it was the squadron which should receive both credit and the prize money. Morally, he was probably right; legally, no prize court would have agreed. All he could do was to send Captain Thomas Sackville Crosbie to demand that the Chilean flag be raised jointly with the Peruvian, and to obtain an unenforceable agreement that the ship be handed over to no one without Chilean consent.

On 25 April 1822, Cochrane was back in Callao with *O'Higgins* and *Valdivia*. The situation there had changed in the six months since he had left. The royalists were making threatening moves from the interior against the southern coast. The Peruvian navy was now led by Blanco Encalada on secondment from Chile, and consisted of a frigate and a few brigs and schooners. Commanded by officers who had previously served under Cochrane, it was blockading the affected area. San Martin's government were superficially friendly, but there was an underlying atmosphere of tension. Blanco Encalada scrupulously obeyed his instructions to ignore Cochrane officially (even though, at a personal level, he was cordial) and the prize *Prueba* was packed with guns and men to make sure there was no repetition of the *Esmeralda* incident. Cochrane reciprocated in kind, refusing to go ashore, lying with his guns loaded, and even seizing the *Montezuma* which suddenly appeared off Callao under Peruvian rather than Chilean colours and sent her back to Valparaiso. This caused further annoyance since, unknown to Cochrane, O'Higgins had given the schooner to San Martin as a personal gift. The standoff lasted for two tense weeks, before he set sail and headed for Chile.

On 2 June, when the citizens of Valparaiso awoke and looked over the rainswept waters of the bay, they saw the *O'Higgins* and the *Valdivia* rolling at their anchors. Excited crowds soon filled the streets to welcome Cochrane on his victorious return. One witness to the celebrations was Mrs Maria Graham, the 37-year-old widow of the captain of HMS *Doris*. Her husband, Thomas Graham, had died three months earlier coming round Cape Horn and Maria had opted to stay on in Chile to recover her spirits. Recalling the events of the day, she recorded in her journal that:

> ...while at breakfast one of my little neighbours came running in, screaming out 'Senhora, he is come! He is come!' 'Who is it child?', I replied. 'Our admiral, our great admiral, our great and good admiral. If you come to the veranda you will see the flags in the Almedral!' Accordingly I looked, and did see the Chilean flag hoisted at every door; and two more ships in the roads than there were yesterday. The *O'Higgins* and *Valdivia* had arrived during the night, and all the inhabitants of the port and suburbs had made hasted to display their flags and their joy at Lord Cochrane's safe return.[1]

Graham was slight in build and suffered from recurrent consumption, but she was an inveterate traveller and a writer of some note. Based on previous travels abroad, she was already a published author having produced a *Journal of a Residence in India*, and *Three months Passed in the Mountains of Rome During the Year 1819*. Even now she was keeping a diary of her adventures in South America, which was to result in two detailed and colourful volumes describing life, manners and social life in Chile and Brazil. In years to come, when she had re-married to become Lady Calcott, she was to achieve greater fame as the author of the Victorian children's classic *Little Arthur's History of England*.

The Chilean Government wholeheartedly joined in the celebrations. Zenteno was now Governor of Valparaiso so it was his successor as Minister of Marine, Joaquin de Echeverria, who sent Cochrane a welcoming panegyric. It began,

> The arrival of Your Excellency in the city of Valparaiso with the squadron under your command has given the greatest of pleasure to the Supreme Director; and in those feelings of gratitude which the glory you have acquired in the late protracted campaign has excited you will find the proof of that high consideration which your heroic services so justly deserve...[2]

A second proclamation announced that O'Higgins had ordered that 'a medal be struck for the officers and men of the squadron in recognition of the national gratitude towards the worthy supporters of its maritime power'. It was a fitting tribute to Cochrane's achievements throughout the war. Captain Basil Hall put it in a nutshell when he praised 'his renown, his matchless intrepidity and his inexhaustible resources in war,' and continued, 'under his hand all things prospered and the confined naval resources of the country were turned to the greatest account with a dexterity and professional skill which astonished everyone'.[3] It was a pity that circumstances and Lord Cochrane's brooding suspicions conspired to make his last six months in Chile a sad anticlimax.

On his return to Valparaiso, Lord Cochrane was granted four months' leave and use of the schooner *Montezuma* commanded by Lieutenant John Pascoe Grenfell. Cochrane's first act was to go ashore and interview his prize agent, William Hoseason. It was not a happy meeting. Hoseason had been inefficient in handling Cochrane's financial affairs and his lack of discretion had made them the talk of the town.[4] Typically, he forgot to mention that the $120,000 bill drawn on the Government of Peru for the *Esmeralda* prize money had been rejected and was in his possession. Fortunately, Cochrane was owed $25,000 in pay and prize money – a total of £5000. He was also owed $40,812 for his share of the *Esmeralda*. This made Cochrane confident enough to send another $16,997 (£3360) back to England on the British warships *Alacrity* and *Doris*.[5]

Cochrane then spent a month in the capital, Santiago, lobbying the authorities for the payment of his men and discussing the navy's future. He also delivered the squadron's accounts for the Peruvian campaign: according to Cochrane's calculations, there was a balance in his favour of $66,000 (£13,200) which he expected to be paid. In Santiago, Cochrane found much to approve of. O'Higgins had introduced a liberal constitution which created an elected Convention, an executive headed by himself as Director, and an independent judiciary. He was also about to enact commercial regulations designed to promote manufactures and trade with the outside world. But on the flip side of the coin, the effort of liberating Peru had left Chile impoverished, and the government's coffers were empty. It was difficult to find money to pay the men and refit the ships after their long absences. In fact, only six ships remained in

service, and of these *Valdivia*, *O'Higgins* and *Lautaro* needed extensive
repairs, leaving only *Independencia*, *Galvarino* and the schooner *Montezuma*
fit for use. Now that the war at sea was over, the government doubted
whether it needed a navy at all. But there was worse news. In Santiago
Cochrane learned that San Martin's agents in Chile had submitted a
detailed 16-page complaint over his behaviour in Peru. Cochrane and his
partisans denounced San Martin's charges for being 'as frivolous as they
are base…which could be disproved from documents in O'Higgins's
possession'.[6] Disproving them, however, was not so easy, as San Martin had
backed his accusations with corroborative details and direct quotations
from Cochrane's letters. Shaken as usual by any criticism, he immediately
began to compose a bitter list of counter-accusations.[7]

At the beginning of July, there was an exciting development when
Cochrane's steamship *Rising Star* finally arrived in Valparaiso after a long
and tedious voyage from England. It was a historic moment as she was the
first vessel capable of steam power to enter the Pacific. Ordered to
conduct sea trials, Cochrane invited friends and local worthies, including
Zenteno, Captain the Honourable Fred Spencer of HMS *Alacrity* and
Maria Graham, aboard for a cruise up the coast under steam. At first, all
went well and the *Rising Star* forged ahead at a steady four miles an hour,
her tall double chimneys belching smoke. But then the machinery broke
down. Cochrane, with his usual confidence in mechanical gadgets, had
not had the sails bent to the yards before leaving, so there was an
uncomfortable and nauseous hour for the passengers amid a blustery wind
and an angry sea while that was done so that they could return under sail.
Despite this, Cochrane remained buoyantly optimistic about the new
technology. Others were not so sure. In England the engines had given
constant trouble and had caused Antonio Alvarez's successor in London to
comment that to experiment with a steamer might be appropriate for the
British Admiralty or the King of France, but for a poor state like Chile it
was a wild and imprudent gamble. The costs of *Rising Star* had risen so
steeply that it was only the intervention of Major William Cochrane
which had ensured that the vessel arrived in Chile at all. But once there,
it put the government in an embarrassing position: it was already
desperately short of money; the war had been decided without it; and the
wonder weapon did not work. Delicately it refused to accept

responsibility for either the vessel or for Cochrane's investment in it. There are no details as to her ultimate fate in the Pacific.

That done, Cochrane left for his country estate at Quintero, taking delivery of tools and seeds newly arrived from England, and discussing the machinery which engineer John Miers had brought out with him for rolling copper and stamping metal dies. The two had gone into partnership with a view to obtaining contracts for revising the coinage. And there was more excitement when a state-of-the-art lithographic press arrived – a vital tool for someone with Lord Cochrane's penchant for proclamations. Quintero was in a delightful location, set amid rolling green pastureland scattered with herds of grazing cattle against the distant backdrop of the cordilleras. Although he and his secretary, William Jackson, were busy writing his denunciation of San Martin, Cochrane was able to relax with friends, who included Miers, Stevenson and Maria Graham. Thus, present at the same time were the three people whose published memoirs were to propagate the Cochrane version of events in Chile. It is no surprise that their accounts were so similar.[8]

Some biographers have added spice to the story by suggesting that a romance developed between Cochrane and Mrs Graham. In the small expatriate community of Valparaiso it was inevitable that they would socialise – especially with Scotland, friends and a naval background in common. Indeed Graham's husband had been with Cochrane on HMS *Thetis*. But there is no evidence or likelihood that there was any kind of relationship. Nor is it borne out in Cochrane's correspondence. A more likely explanation is that the Vice Admiral's entourage were fully aware of Mrs Graham's literary reputation and decided to ensure that her books on Chile would tell the 'correct' story. Certainly, they made sure she was supplied with Cochrane's correspondence, and briefed her so successfully that her portrayals of San Martin and other Cochrane 'enemies' are, for her, untypically severe and inaccurate.

Cochrane was frequently called away from Quintero on business and with the continuing problem of getting payment for the squadron. At the end of September, he received a letter from Captain Wilkinson reporting that a story was circulating that, while his officers and men went unpaid, Cochrane was shipping home a personal fortune in gold and silver in HMS *Doris*. The rumour had to be challenged, especially as he actually had $52,000 (£10,400) in gold stored in sacks ready to take with him when he left![9] Cochrane hastened to Valparaiso to safeguard his reputation, and discovered that the story had been spread by the unruly Lieutenant Ford Morgell. A quick letter to O'Higgins put things to rights and ensured the end of Morgell's career. But by the time he described the incident in his *Narrative of Services*, Cochrane's obsessions had reached such a pitch that loose talk by a loquacious officer had been elevated to a 'plot', in which the unfortunate Zenteno was accused of being implicated.

Then the government auditors rejected the squadron's accounts. During much of the long Peruvian campaign Cochrane had been left to fend for himself in satisfying the squadron's needs. As a result his requirements had been taken from a multiplicity of sources: supplies from captured corn, rice, cordage, naval stores, clothes, hardware and rum; money from seizures, 'licences' to trade, and the local sale of prizes. His outgoings were just as complicated, covering the purchase of food, drink, clothing, naval supplies and equipment and the distribution of pay and prize money to over 1000 men. All this made the squadron's accounts excessively complicated. An accountant, skilled in the methods of the time, might have been able to keep track of all this. But the task was beyond the capabilities of Cochrane's staff – Jackson, Stevenson and Dean. As a result, there were numerous irregularities, ranging from unauthorised payments to missing receipts and faulty arithmetic. In September 1822, the Chilean Accountant General, Correa de Sa, drew attention to 80 queries and asked Cochrane to appoint a representative to go through them in detail.[10] Cochrane was deeply offended. As one of the heroes of independence, he expected his accounts to be nodded through without examination. It was a view that no auditor could accept. So Cochrane refused to reply, and the accounts remained unapproved. They would remain unapproved until 1838, when he finally attended to the questions. Meanwhile, Cochrane's partisans depicted the $66,000 balance as a 'debt' that the Chileans were refusing to repay.

On 12 October General San Martin arrived in Valparaiso on his way home, disappointed with Bolivar's refusal to co-operate in a final push against the royalists in the mountains and disillusioned with politics and accusations of despotism from the Peruvians he had helped to liberate. True to his principles, San Martin handed power to a sovereign congress and retired to become a private citizen. Now he was in Chile, explaining that he was on his way to Europe via his home in the Argentine, and had come to bathe his rheumatic arm in a well-known local spa. The arrival of the General caused some unease, but his stature as a liberator and his long service to the cause of South American independence ensured that he was received with respect and courtesy. Only Lord Cochrane was out of step. Making one of those insensitive misjudgements that studded his whole career, he wrote to O'Higgins proposing an inquiry into San Martin's conduct with himself as chief prosecutor. He was, he wrote, 'ready to prove his usurpation of the Supreme Authority in Peru...; his attempts to seduce the navy of Chile; his receiving and rewarding deserters from the Chilean service; his unjustifiable placing of the frigates *Prueba* and *Venganza* under the flag of Peru; with other demonstrations and acts of hostility towards the Republic of Chile'.[11] The Chileans tactfully ignored him.

With the destruction of Spanish sea power in the Pacific, Cochrane had worked himself out of a job, and his time in Chile was clearly coming to an end. The Chilean Government decided to demobilise its navy and began, at last, to pay off the officers and men. A bucolic existence at Quintero may have seemed attractive, but it would never have satisfied a man of Cochrane's energetic temperament. Instead he was looking for another outlet for his military talents. Towards the end of November it came in the form of a letter from the Brazilian agent in Buenos Aires, Antonio Correa da Camera. Brazil was on the brink of its war of independence against Portugal, and its Emperor, Pedro, wished to offer Cochrane command of the Brazilian navy. The rhetoric was irresistible. 'Come, My Lord', it said,

Honour invites you. Glory is calling to you. A Generous Prince and a whole Nation await you. Come, reborn Hercules, and with your honourable efforts help to tame the Hundred-Headed Hydra of a frightful Despotism. The west of America is saved by virtue of your Arm...the Sacred Standard of Independence is unfurled from the Gallapagos as far as the Cedar Isles of California! Come now and furnish our Naval Arms with the wonderful order and incomparable Discipline of Mighty Albion...![12]

For Cochrane, the offer was opportune, and was accepted forthwith. On 28 November 1822, he resigned his Chilean commission and began to prepare for the journey to Brazil. His last months had been spent at Quintero in the company of friends who – once again – included Miers, Stevenson and Graham, interrupted by occasional visits to Valparaiso to wind up his affairs. He had by this time received all his pay, totalling $40,795 (£8160) and $65,000 (£13,000) in prize money, but there remained the balance on the squadron's accounts, and the need to obtain something for the *Rising Star*. He made his preparations amidst mounting chaos. The idyll at Quintero had already been shattered when, on the night of 19 November, central Chile was struck by a series of tremendous earthquakes causing tidal waves and violent shifts in the earth. Valparaiso and other towns were wrecked and houses, churches and public buildings obliterated. Penitents prayed in the streets to avert further divine retribution, while the more practical fled inland or took refuge on the ships in the bay. The shocks continued intermittently for a month, and only petered out at the end of December. It was only then that the slow work of repair and reconstruction could begin. These natural disasters were matched by political turmoil. The hardships of life in post-independent Chile and the impoverishment of the government had steadily been bringing the euphoria of independence back down to earth. The discontent came to a head in November 1822, when Cochrane's collaborator at Talcahuana, General Freire, had raised the flag of revolt and had begun the slow march north that would end in the removal of O'Higgins. On Freire's behalf, Captain Casey tried to rally the squadron to join him, but Cochrane politely declined to become involved.

As a final flourish, on 4 January 1823 Cochrane printed three proclamations on his new press. The first was a rhetorical farewell to the Chilean people; the second, a reminder to the British merchant community of the benefits his command had brought; and the third, an expression of thanks to the officers in the Chilean navy for their loyalty and dedication. Two weeks later, the *Colonel Allen* arrived to take Cochrane to Brazil accompanied by his baggage, boxes of gold bullion worth £10,400, and five of his followers – his secretary Jackson, Captain Crosbie and Lieutenants John Pascoe Grenfell, James Shepherd and Steven Clewley. Henry Dean also wanted to come but, avoiding the unpleasant duty of dismissing him, Cochrane left him behind in the hope that he would realise his services were no longer required. Cochrane also invited Maria Graham to join the party, together with her cousin who had been temporarily invalided from HMS *Doris*. He remembered the relief he had felt when Captain William Shirreff of *Andromache* had agreed to remove Kitty from a place of danger, and felt that he could do no less for the widow of a fellow naval officer stranded so far from home.[13] On 18 January, all was ready. There was an impromptu piece of ceremonial when Lord Cochrane's flag as Vice Admiral of Chile was lowered for the last time from the mainmast of the *Montezuma*. Then, the *Colonel Allen* made sail and slowly slipped out of the bay heading for Cape Horn and Brazil.

CHAPTER THIRTEEN

First Admiral of Brazil

ON THE AFTERNOON of 12 March 1823, the *Colonel Allen* sighted
the rocky promontory of Cape Frio, the landfall for all ships heading for
Rio de Janeiro, headed west along the fringe of coastal mountains and
dropped anchor at the entrance to the Bay of Guanabara. Next day, on a
cloudy morning amid pouring rain, the brig passed between the Sugar
Loaf and the Fort of Santa Cruz and entered the sheltered waters of the
enormous bay. With its spectacular backdrop of mountains blotted out by
the weather, the brig slid past misty islands, coves and rocky outcrops
crowned with churches or forts until, passing the fortified island of
Villegagnon, she reached the city of Rio de Janeiro. A boat bearing the
port captain's representative came alongside, but on learning that Lord
Cochrane was aboard, he shouted to Captain Bartholomew Hayden to
anchor where he liked and hurried back to the shore. The news of
Cochrane's arrival spread like wildfire. The captains of the Brazilian
warships *Niterói* and *Liberal*, John Taylor and Antonio Salema Garção, came
aboard to greet their new commander. Later messengers arrived to take
Cochrane ashore to be briefed by the Chief Minister and the Emperor
Pedro himself, who had leapt into the saddle and sped over from the
Palace of São Cristovão.

The sequence of events that led to Brazilian independence had begun
16 years earlier, in 1807, when the timid and corpulent Regent of
Portugal, Dom João, had been persuaded to flee the rising tide of French
conquest in Europe by moving his government lock, stock and barrel to
Rio de Janeiro. Brazil thus became the capital of the Portuguese Empire
and prospered as a result, so much so that in 1815 the country had been
raised to the status of a kingdom – co-equal with Portugal in the Braganza
dominions. But with the conclusion of the Napoleonic Wars, King João

VI had been forced to return, leaving his son, the charismatic 23-year-old Prince Pedro, behind as Regent. Once the King was back in Lisbon, the Portuguese tried to turn the clock back and reduce Brazil once more to colonial subservience, provoking anger and widespread resistance throughout the country. The revolt was masterminded by Brazil's Chief Minister, a tough, 58-year-old scientist turned politician called José Bonifácio de Andrada e Silva, who won the impetuous young Prince over to the cause, and led the country down the path of independence. On 7 September 1822, Pedro made his historic declaration of 'Independence or Death!' and a fortnight later, he was proclaimed 'Constitutional Emperor' of Brazil.

Declaring independence was one thing: achieving it was another. In 1822, only the central region around Rio de Janeiro was under Brazilian control, the rest of the country continued to be dominated by Portuguese juntas and troops in the towns and the coastal capitals. The most significant of these were Belém, at the mouth of the Amazon; São Luis of Maranhão on the northern coast; and Salvador, capital of the state of Bahia and the site of a great naval arsenal and military garrison. Although under siege by a rag-tag Brazilian army, Salvador was seen as the springboard for Portuguese re-conquest, and reinforcements were already pouring in from Portugal.

Cochrane recognised many aspects of the Brazilian struggle for independence. As in the Pacific, sea power was the crucial factor. Only by seizing control of the sea could Brazil cut the flow of reinforcements from Portugal, blockade and expel the enemy garrisons, and make independence a reality. José Bonifácio and his Minister of Marine, a Brazilian-born naval captain called Luis da Cunha Moreira, had taken immediate steps to create a navy by seizing the dozen or so Portuguese warships stationed in Rio de Janeiro together with their crews. This provided the nucleus of armed vessels they needed, but it also presented a manpower problem since most of the officers and men were Portuguese by birth and therefore of questionable loyalty. They were also numerically inadequate for the expanded naval force the government was organising. Brazil, like Chile, was a continental country, had no sea-going population or maritime tradition, and it proved impossible to replace or even supplement them with Brazilians. So, as in Chile, the government looked overseas for the reliable men it needed. The first foreign recruits were found in Rio de Janeiro, and included two senior officers – an American captain called David Jewitt, and Lieutenant John Taylor of HMS *Blossom* who, to the fury of the Admiralty, resigned his commission to become a Brazilian captain-of-frigate. In the winter of 1822–3, the Brazilians carried out a secret recruiting campaign in London and Liverpool. Indeed, when Cochrane arrived in Rio there were already 450 sailors and 45 officers on their way to Brazil. In these circumstances, there was no problem in getting the four officers who had come with him from Chile commissioned into the Brazilian Navy and posted to the *Pedro I* with Thomas Sackville Crosbie in command.

But there were aspects of the Brazilian situation which were quite different. In Spanish South America, the independence movements had been led by republicans, who had swept away the old royalist institutions and had had to create new ones from scratch. In Brazil, the independence movement was led by the heir to the House of Braganza and was monarchical from the beginning. The machinery of government remained intact and so did the naval infrastructure – the Ministry of Marine, the Intendencia or Navy Board, the Hospital, Academy, and the Dockyard. The warships, which the government had commandeered early in the revolt, provided the necessary fighting force. Using funds from an enthusiastically supported national subscription, the government augmented its size by purchasing half a dozen brigs and schooners locally, and ordered the Brazilian agent in London, General Felisberto Brant, to buy huge quantities of munitions and naval stores.

On his second day in Rio, Cochrane was rowed out with the Emperor to inspect Brazil's new warships as they swung languidly at their anchors in the blue, sparkling water before the town. They were an impressive sight – one sturdy ship of the line, three frigates, *Piranga*, *Real Carolina* and *Niterói*, the two graceful corvettes, *Maria da Glória* and *Liberal*, three workmanlike two-masted brigs and brigantines and a small number of schooners. Three ships particularly caught Cochrane's eye. There was the two-decker *Pedro I*, fresh from the dockyard and newly painted black with white bands along the gundecks and round the stem in modern fashion. She had had a thorough refit and possessed all the requirements of a flagship, including a handsome stern cabin upholstered in green morocco leather. Then there was the *Piranga*, a teak-built frigate of the newest and largest type, carrying 62 guns with 24-pounders on the main deck. Finally, there was the big corvette *Maria da Glória*. Clearly built for speed, her lines were familiar. American-built, she had originally been the *Horatio*, sister-ship to the *Independencia* which Cochrane had known in Chile. He was impressed with the physical condition of the Brazilian ships, but was struck by the poor quality of the sailors. All the captains complained of the difficulty of finding men and, as Cochrane noted with surprise, most were Portuguese. He was also puzzled when the Emperor described the enemy in his speeches as the 'Portuguese parliamentary forces' as if to imply that it was only one faction and not Portugal as a whole against which Brazil was fighting.[1]

Cochrane visited the Minister of Marine to finalise the details of his appointment. What exactly happened at the meeting will never be known. The only surviving account is that given by Cochrane himself, but the *Narrative of Services* is unreliable and it is difficult to believe that Cochrane actually treated the worthy and dedicated Cunha Moreira with the rudeness and sarcasm described in the book.[2] What is clear is that although Cochrane accepted the rank of Admiral, the pay was rejected as being too low. The outcome is that it was agreed that the pay would be the same as he had received in Chile.[3] Only Cochrane knew what his Chilean pay had actually been, and there can be no doubt he tricked the Brazilians into believing that it was considerably greater than the actual figure. If in Brazil he had received the equivalent of his total Chilean emoluments of $10,000 per annum, he would have been paid 9600 Brazilian milreis. Instead, he was paid 17,290 milreis – the equivalent of $17,960. Cochrane's insistence in having his terms spelled out in his commission gives the game away.[4]

Cochrane knew exactly what he was doing. Indeed, the financial claims he was to make against Chile and Brazil in the 1840s stated explicitly that his basic pay in each state had not been the same but had been $6000 and $12,000 respectively.[5] However, when they produced the *Narrative of Services*, his ghost writers spotted the discrepancy and tried to explain it away by claiming that Cochrane's pay in Chile had been '$8000 per annum, with permission...to appropriate another $4000 from the Government moiety of captures made'.[6] There is no truth in this. His pay was never $8000, and there was never any thought of quantifying a prize money expectation and adding it to his emoluments. But the Brazilians had no choice but to accept Cochrane's word. As a result, in Brazil he was paid over 75 per cent more than he had actually received in Chile – a sum which was three times more than any other Brazilian flag officer, and £500 a year more than he would have received as a British admiral!

The issue of pay resolved, Cochrane then learned that there were already two admirals in the Brazilian navy. He refused to serve unless he was given clear overall authority. Once more, the government agreed and created the special rank of First Admiral especially for him. This was acceptable and, on 21 March 1823, to the thunder of gun salutes, Cochrane hoisted his flag in the *Pedro I* and took command of the nine ships that were to be called 'the Squadron of Independence' – the frigates *Piranga*, *Real Carolina* and *Niterói*, the corvettes *Maria da Glória* and *Liberal*, the brig *Guarani*, and the schooners *Leopoldina* and *Real*. On the same day, Cochrane received his commission. It reflected his terms exactly and read,

> Being well known the valour, intelligence, activity and other qualities that are to be found in Admiral Lord Cochrane, which have been demonstrated in the different services with which he has been charged, each of which has provided proofs of the greatest bravery and daring; and acknowledging that it is to the advantage of the Empire to profit from the recognised worth of such a distinguished officer: it is judged well to confer upon him the patent of First Admiral of the National and Imperial Navy receiving an annual salary of 11,520 milreis whether on land or sea; and an allowance for subsistence of 5,770 milreis when embarked, *being the same emoluments as he received when in Chile* [author's italics]; no other admiral in the navy having the right to occupy the post...which is created uniquely on this occasion from the particular consideration of the above mentioned Admiral Lord Cochrane.[7]

While Cochrane was negotiating these advantageous terms of service, there was another stroke of good fortune. In the last week of March, the merchantmen *Lapwing* and *Lindsays* arrived in Rio de Janeiro with six officers and 170 men recruited in England. The crews of the warships were immediately reshuffled and the British sailors allocated to the

Pedro I and the three frigates. The men were signed on, allowed ashore and within a few hours were gloriously drunk. When some officers complained to the Empress, it is said she laughed and said, 'Oh, 'tis the custom of the north where brave men come from. The sailors are under my protection; I spread my mantle over them!'[8] The Brazilians received the officers with equal relief. Their leader, Captain James Thompson, was given command of the *Real Carolina* with Commander Benjamin Kelmare as his first officer. Lieutenants Sam Chester and Francis Clare were posted to the *Niterói* under John Taylor, and Lieutenant Vincent Crofton and James Nicol were appointed to the *Guarani* and *Piranga*. William Parker, one of the mates of the *Lindsays* and nephew of the owner, also volunteered and was posted to the *Pedro I* as a midshipman.[9]

Expressed in one simple paragraph Cochrane's orders were to blockade Salvador, destroy any Portuguese forces he might meet, and collaborate with the army in the capture of the city. They were exactly the kind of instructions he relished. At dawn on 1 April, the squadron set sail on a voyage that was to decide the independence of Brazil. To the crowds who had risen early to witness the squadron's departure, the scene was dramatic as well as historic. Maria Graham confided in her journal that 'as the fort began to salute, the sun broke from behind a cloud and a bright yellow flood of light descended behind the ships to the sea where they seemed to swim in a sea of glory'.[10] At 9 a.m. the Emperor left the flagship for the State Barge, standing to acknowledge the cheers of each ship's company as they passed. An hour later, Cochrane headed east to his first rendezvous.

On the voyage to Bahia, Cochrane and his captains began to drill their ships and men into some semblance of order. It was not easy. The sails and much of the gear were of inferior material, and the crews were made up of Englishmen who spoke no Portuguese, of Brazilians who were ignorant of the sea, and of sullen Portuguese. The Brazilian marines were no better: most were freed slaves who refused to clean their quarters and knew nothing of small arms or the ships guns. As the voyage progressed, Cochrane used the social life of the flagship to get to know his subordinates. The British officers were comfortable in the monarchical regime of Brazil, and found the routines of its navy familiar. Cochrane did not surround himself with a group of outsiders as he had in Chile. William

Jackson remained as secretary, but other staff work was done by 'regulars' of the Brazilian navy.

The squadron did not make orderly progress. Cochrane was more concerned with reaching Salvador than with keeping his assorted ships in formation. But by the end of April they began to snap up enemy supply ships and merchantmen. On 3 May the coast of Bahia at last came into sight as a blue smear on the north-western horizon. Cochrane tacked and, with ships thrashing to windward, stood out to sea and maintained course until nightfall. Next morning, sailing westwards once more, they sighted the Portuguese squadron, which had been sent from Salvador to see them off – 11 frigates and armed ships steering north in line with the 74-gun *Joao VI* in the centre. With a bravery bordering on recklessness, Cochrane led his tiny force straight towards them, meaning to cut the Portuguese line in true Nelson fashion. Accordingly, when the two sides came into contact and began to exchange broadsides, *Pedro I* swept through the line ahead of the eighth ship, the *Princeza Real*, while Jewitt's *Piranga* and Taylor's *Niterói*, engaged from windward.[11] The attack did not go as planned. A well-drilled 74 would have left the *Princeza Real* a shattered wreck; the *Pedro I* left her hardly damaged. Not only did the discipline of the flagship falter, but disgruntled Portuguese seamen were actually preventing the flow of powder from the magazine until dragged on deck by Lieutenant John Pascoe Grenfell. Likewise, on *Guarani* and *Real*, the crews were so unreliable that their captains kept well clear of the enemy.

By nightfall, the Portuguese van had joined the action and Cochrane, recognising that the situation had become desperate, retreated in haste to a small harbour called Morro de São Paulo some 30 miles to the south. From there he sent a damning letter to José Bonifácio, writing,

From the defective sailing and manning of the squadron it seems to me that the *Pedro I* is the only one that can assail the enemy's ships of war, or act in the face of a superior force so as not to compromise the interest of the Empire and the character of the officers commanding. Even this ship is so ill-equipped as to be much less efficient than she could be...our cartridges are all unfit for service...the guns are without locks...the sails of this ship are all rotten...the head of the mortar

I received on board was crushed on the first fire, being entirely rotten…and the Portuguese sailors on board have been so prejudicial to the success of the expedition…that to tell Your Excellency the truth, one half of the squadron is needed to watch the other half!

But Cochrane was not indulging in recriminations. He continued,

I am aware of the difficulties under which a new government labours and am ready to do all in my power under the circumstances. What I would request of you, is that you will do me the justice to feel that the predicament in which I am now placed is somewhat analogous to your own and that if I cannot accomplish all I would wish the deficiency arises from causes beyond my control.[12]

Cochrane's official report was short, giving only a bare outline of the action and of his plans. The battle had been a disappointment, but with typical resilience he was already deciding his next move. If the squadron could not meet the Portuguese at sea, he would blockade Salvador with his fastest vessels manned by the pick of his crews and rely on fireships to attack the enemy fleet. The reorganisation was quickly put into effect. The British and Brazilian officers and men were transferred to *Pedro I* and *Maria da Glória*, and the some of *Piranga*'s heavy guns were transferred to the flagship. In company with the newly arrived frigate *Real Carolina* he put to sea once more, intent on blockading a port defended by a naval squadron so much greater than his own. It was an astonishing piece of bravado even by Cochrane's standards.

Cochrane's blockading tactics were audacious, but they created legal problems which were to catch up with him later. International rules laid down that a blockade was only legitimate if it was enforced by a superior force. The fact that Cochrane had fewer warships than the Portuguese caused an immediate technical difficulty. Sir Thomas Hardy pondered the problem, and ruled that as far as Britain was concerned, the legal beginning of the blockade was not the time of Cochrane's arrival but the date on which the Portuguese squadron had returned permanently to Salvador – that is, 2 June 1823. Any ship taken before that date was a 'bad' prize and would occasion a vigorous protest before any prize court.[13]

With the city surrounded by the Brazilian army on land, the cutting of Salvador's lifeline by sea reduced the Portuguese to despair. Then, at dusk on 12 June, Cochrane's three ships slipped silently into the Bay of Bahia intending to launch a surprise attack on the anchored fleet.[14] At first all went well. But when they came within striking distance, the sea breeze faltered and disappeared. Windless and in the middle of a hostile harbour, Cochrane abandoned the plan and was forced to drift out to sea again with the tide. But Cochrane's show of daring was the last straw. Indeed, the supply situation in Salvador became so bad that on 20 June, Military Governor Madeira de Melo decided to evacuate the city. Outside the bay, Cochrane waited with the *Pedro I*, *Real Carolina*, *Niterói*, *Maria da Glória* and the brig-of-war *Bahia*, which had just arrived. She had originally been the *Colonel Allen* which had brought Cochrane from Peru, but in its quest for ships, the Brazilian Government had bought the brig, commissioned her captain Bartholomew Hayden – who had resigned as Second Master of HMS *Conway* to follow his fortunes in South America – as a commander in the Brazilian navy, and sent her to reinforce Cochrane carrying the latest contingent of over 100 seamen from England. Also on board was Henry Dean, who had clearly not taken the hint when Cochrane left him behind in Chile.

On 2 July 1823 the Portuguese evacuated Salvador in a massive convoy of 17 warships and 75 merchantmen loaded with the contents of the dockyard, the arsenal and the warehouses, packed with troops, and carrying all Portuguese citizens who wished to escape. An advanced guard of the Imperial army immediately occupied the city and by noon, the green and yellow flag of Brazil was flying over the forts. The war in Bahia was at an end.

CHAPTER FOURTEEN

The Liberation of the North

As THE PORTUGUESE CONVOY laboriously assembled outside the Bay of Bahia, Cochrane wrote his official report. 'I have the satisfaction to acquaint Your Excellency', he began, 'that the enemy have this day evacuated Bahia, their resources by sea being no longer available'.[1] Then he attended to his correspondence, for the *Bahia* and HMS *Creole*, encountered at sea the day before, had delivered letters. From one he learned the good news that Lady Cochrane had disembarked in Rio de Janeiro from the merchantman *Sesostris*, accompanied by a new baby daughter called Katherine Elizabeth (nicknamed Lizzie). She had hired all the passenger accommodation on the vessel at a cost of £1200 and had come with half a dozen servants and two gentlemen, one a distant relation of Cochrane called George Sutton who had come on the understanding that he would get a job on his staff. He was to be disappointed. There were also letters and copies of newspapers updating him on events in Chile. One was from Accountant General Correa de Sa, repeating his request that Cochrane appoint a representative to settle his final accounts. Cochrane ignored it.

Cochrane then issued his orders to the squadron. The object of the ensuing chase, he emphasised, was to drive the Portuguese out of Brazilian waters, prevent a landing in the north of Brazil and, to make the triumph complete, seize as many troopships and as much military equipment as possible. The registers and logs of all prizes were to be retained, but to avoid weakening the ships' complements, prize crews were to be kept to a minimum: instead, ships were to be left with only enough water to reach port and their rigging was to be so dismembered that they could only sail before the wind. Captain Thompson of the *Real Carolina* was ordered to maintain the chase for some days and then to return to Salvador to take command of the naval station. Hayden in the *Bahia* was to accompany the *Pedro I* to the latitude of Recife. Taylor in the *Niterói* was given the duty of chasing the convoy as far as the coast of Portugal itself.[2]

On 3 July, Cochrane's five ships set off in pursuit of the unwieldy Portuguese convoy, which quickly became scattered. Racing along under a press of canvas, the Brazilians swooped on transports, which the men-of-war were unable to protect, capturing 16 ships and over 2000 troops in the first week. *Real Carolina* and *Bahia* then turned south, shepherding flocks of prizes to Salvador and Recife. Commander Hayden carried letters from Lord Cochrane to the local junta announcing the liberation of Bahia and asking for the recruitment of seamen. 'We must have sailors to end the war', he had written. 'I do not mean Portuguese seamen who are enemies; but those of any other nation, and I need scarcely say that…I should prefer British seamen to all others'.[3] The appearance of the letter in the *Diario do Governo* caused panic. British Consul-General Henry Chamberlain in Rio issued a strong protest, fearing wholesale desertions from British merchant ships; and even Hardy ordered his captains to be extra vigilant in the face of such temptation.[4]

The convoy straggled northwards, its ships now dispersed over miles of ocean with the *Pedro I*, *Niterói* and *Maria da Glória* still in pursuit. On 9 July two more transports were taken, and escorted to Recife by the corvette's captain, Commander Teodoro Beaurepaire, who was ordered to assemble the prizes there and escort them to Rio for adjudication. *Pedro I* and *Niterói* were left to follow the convoy alone past the grey rocky peak that marks the island of Fernando Noronha and into the tropical zone. Cochrane was not content merely to shadow it out of Brazilian waters. Employing his legendary ingenuity, he kept the Portuguese in a state of constant alarm, mounting surprise attacks in the *Pedro I*, and releasing empty casks filled with gunpowder at night to drift down on the enemy where they exploded amid a gratifying amount of panic. A more sophisticated design was produced by adding a sail and a lantern.[5] After two weeks, the convoy had crossed the Equator and was clearly bound for home. Although his orders did not require it, Cochrane realised that the liberation of the north of Brazil was the next priority. So, leaving Taylor in the *Niterói* to harry the convoy as far as Portugal, Cochrane headed west for the lush topical coasts of Maranhão.

On 26 July 1823 the *Pedro I* sighted the whitewashed houses and churches of the capital, São Luis. Cochrane's plan for the capture of Maranhão was a typical piece of cunning and bravery. Flying the red ensign, and making sure that vessels in the vicinity were visited by an ostentatiously English boarding party, he approached São Luis posing as a British ship coming to aid the Portuguese cause.[6] The local authorities were fooled and even sent out the brig *Infante Dom Miguel* with a message of welcome. But as soon as the town was in range of *Pedro I's* broadsides, the British colours were replaced by the green and yellow of Brazil. Exploiting the shock, Cochrane sent in letters. With the air of a weary conqueror wishing to conserve energy, he announced that Bahia had been liberated, implied that he had a vast fleet and army ready for action just over the horizon, and concluded,

> …the naval and military forces under my command leave me no room to doubt the success of the enterprise in which I am about to engage, namely, to liberate Maranhão from foreign oppression and to allow the people to choose their system of government… It is for you to decide whether the inhabitants of these countries shall be further exasperated by a resistance which appears to me to be unavailing.'[7]

Cochrane's bluff succeeded. Faced with an apparently overwhelming force, and under the guns of the biggest warship ever seen off São Luis, the Portuguese authorities agreed to join the cause of Independence.

Cochrane's arrival in São Luis was opportune. At first, Maranhão had remained fiercely loyal to Portugal and had remained aloof from what was going on in the south. But uprisings in the interior of neighbouring states created a chain reaction: Brazilian militia units rallied in support, and an army of irregulars eventually crossed the border into Maranhão. The story was repeated: one by one the cities of the interior surrendered until, by July 1823, only São Luis remained in Portuguese hands. In the town, news of the patriot successes brought despondency and the will to fight evaporated. The municipal council met on 14 July 1823 in an atmosphere of gloom to decide whether the city should declare for Brazil or continue to resist. It was only the arrival of a Portuguese schooner and six troop transports from the Bahia convoy, which had somehow slipped past

Cochrane, that enabled the military commander, General Agostinho de Faria, to dissolve the meeting and insist that São Luis fight on.

The town's resolve lasted a fortnight until Cochrane's arrival. Stunned by news of the fall of Salvador and faced with Cochrane's implied threat, the authorities capitulated. Accordingly, on 28 July 1823, independence was solemnly proclaimed in São Luis and, to the ringing of church bells, Brazilian colours were hoisted on the city, the forts and the ships of war in the harbour. Cochrane immediately shipped General de Faria and his men back to Portugal before their suspicions could be aroused by the non-appearance of the imaginary Brazilian fleet and army. That done, a new provincial junta took up office with Miguel Freire Bruce, a local lawyer of Scottish descent, as President. But for many Brazilians, independence meant more than a new flag and a change of allegiance. Old scores were settled, officials were replaced, and Portuguese merchants were insulted in the streets. Rival political factions within the city began to struggle for power with Bruce filling the public offices with his supporters and using loyal troops to enforce his will. A failed *coup* was followed by widespread violence and arrests. Cochrane tried to blunt these excesses, but his efforts had little effect.

Cochrane's political views may have been moderate, but on other matters they were uncompromising. As far as he was concerned, São Luis was an enemy city captured by force of arms whose wealth now belonged to the conquerors. No sooner had the independence ceremonies ended than he wrote to the junta asking for detailed lists of all public property and debts, of cash in the customs house and the treasury, and of ships in the port together with their cargoes.[8] Henry Dean was sent ashore to receive and check the information. Then the seizures began. First, Cochrane took possession of the *Infante Dom Miguel* (renamed *Maranhão* and sent off under John Pascoe Grenfell to demand the surrender of Pará), the schooner *Emilia*, eight gunboats together with the slaves who manned them, and 16 merchant vessels in the harbour on the grounds that existing prize rules awarded their total value to the captors. Next he laid claim to the monies in the provincial treasury and the customs house; the munitions and gunpowder in the forts; and the goods in the government storehouses, arguing that it was all enemy property and now belonged to the captors. According to the information provided to Henry Dean, the total value of this booty was 309 contos of reis, or £62,000 sterling.[9]

The junta was appalled by Cochrane's actions. A far as they were concerned, São Luis had always been a Brazilian city and the ownership of public funds had been automatically transferred from the old junta to the new. There was no question of capture or prize. It was the same argument that Cochrane had heard in Chile following the capture of Valdivia. But this time he had the whip hand and was adamant, though offering to accept one third of the amount demanded if it was paid within two weeks. Next he turned his attention to private property, demanding a list of all Portuguese-owned goods and decreeing the confiscation of two thirds of their value. Cochrane ignored the resulting uproar and began to seize ships and property, shipping tons of merchandise to Rio de Janeiro in the prize *Pombinha* for adjudication by the prize courts.

Cochrane was well aware that the same rules would not apply to Portuguese private property in Maranhão, which was valued at 170 contos (£34,000). However, knowing that the Emperor had issued a decree on 11 December 1822 permitting the confiscation of enemy property, he used it to justify his claims, arguing that 'such property had been wholly awarded to the captors' by this decree which had been 'promulgated to attract foreign seamen into the Brazilian service'.[10] This was twisting the facts. The decree had not awarded confiscated property to the takers, and it had nothing whatever to do with the recruitment of seamen.

In late August 1823, emissaries from the Brazilian irregular army occupying the interior entered the town to congratulate him on the adhesion of São Luis and to demand money for the troops. Realising that these men posed a serious danger unless they were paid off and sent home, Cochrane agreed, and allowed the junta to send them 100 contos (£20,000). He stressed, however, that this was a loan from prize money and that repayment was expected in full.

The settlement of that problem coincided with excellent news from the Amazonian province of Pará. Although Cochrane had never set foot there, he had managed to secure its liberation by using the same *ruse de guerre* he had employed in São Luis.[11] The task had been entrusted to Commander Grenfell and the crew of the brig *Maranhão* who had sailed up the Amazon and arrived off the capital, Belém, as dusk fell on 10 August. Next morning, to the astonishment of the townspeople, Grenfell raised the green and yellow flag of Brazil, fired a salute and delivered letters from Cochrane to the local Portuguese authorities claiming that the First Admiral was at the mouth of the river at the head of a huge Brazilian force.

Deceived by Cochrane's letters, the Portuguese surrendered and handed over power to a new Brazilian junta. But, as in Maranhão, the patriot camp was immediately torn by a struggle between the extremists who favoured the seizure of Portuguese jobs and property, and the moderates who favoured harmony and reconciliation. In the ensuing disorder, Grenfell himself was stabbed in the ribs, although the wound was not deep. In the crackdown that followed, 150 conspirators were rounded up and deported. Nevertheless, with the liberation of Pará, Grenfell had successfully carried out the first part of Cochrane's orders.[12] Now he busied himself with the second, seizing a dozen vessels and gunboats, then taking possession of a 50-gun frigate which had recently been completed in the dockyard, renaming her *Imperatriz* and fitting her out with masts, rigging and stores.

Cochrane's task in the north was now complete. São Luis had been liberated, the Portuguese troops were on their way home, and the states of Pará and Maranhão had declared their adherence to the Brazilian Empire. Only the political infighting continued to cause problems and this, he hoped, would be settled by the forthcoming elections. So, at the end of September 1823, Cochrane said his farewells and sailed in the *Pedro I* bound for Rio de Janeiro.

CHAPTER FIFTEEN

Politics, Prize Money and Rebellion

ON 9 NOVEMBER 1823, a triumphant Lord Cochrane returned to
Rio de Janeiro. He was greeted at the harbour mouth by the Emperor
himself who bestowed upon him the title of Marquis of Maranhão.
Others honours followed – the Grand Cross of the Cruzeiro de Sul, a vote
of thanks from the Assembly, membership of the Privy Council. The
honour and glory that Cochrane so richly deserved were his. In a
campaign of only six months he had driven a Portuguese army and a
greatly superior naval squadron from Bahia, had harried them out of
Brazilian waters and chased them across the Atlantic. He had forced the
Portuguese to evacuate Maranhão and Pará leaving those provinces free
to adhere to the Empire. In Rio, the news of Cochrane's triumphs had
been received with joy and acclaim. There were days of rejoicing, the city
was illuminated by night and gala performances were held at the theatre.

All these events were chronicled by Maria Graham. For six months
Graham had been installed in a house in Rio near to a childhood friend,
William May, and his wife. May was a partner in the local firm of May &
Ludkin which acted as Lord Cochrane's agent. Unable to return to
England because of illness, Graham had made the most of her time in
Brazil, making friends in the British community, renewing acquaintances
with officers of the Royal Navy's South America Squadron and taking a
modest place in Brazilian society. She was a frequent visitor to the
Imperial Court where she met Lady Cochrane and formed a friendship
with the Empress Leopoldina. Graham was also writing another book
describing, in delightful and colourful terms, the society, politics, manners,
food and social habits of the new Brazilian Empire.[1] With an intellectual
curiosity which more than compensated for her poor physical health, she

investigated every aspect of life, indefatigably visiting the commercial quarter, the warehouses, the arsenal, the dockyard, the foundling hospital, the botanical gardens, the library, the theatre, the forts and the churches as well as the Indian settlements and farms of the interior. Inevitably, she had been to the slave market and the plantations, and had returned horrified by the experience. Her book was also to give details of Cochrane's successes in the north. For, as in Chile, the First Admiral and his followers had sent her long letters and copies of despatches to ensure that her story was the 'correct' one. But there was to be no reunion. On 23 October 1823, she had sailed for England in the packet *Chichester*, her major regret being that she would miss Lord Cochrane on his jubilant return.

During Cochrane's absence there had been significant political changes in the capital. As independence had become a reality, the Assembly had split into two factions. Both supported independence, but the 'patriots', made up of the Brazilian aristocracy and the rural population, favoured an anti-Portuguese line; while the 'moderates', comprising Portuguese adherents and the urban elite, wanted national reconciliation and the restoration of friendly relations with Portugal. Initially, Chief Minister José Bonifácio de Andrada e Silva had ignored both factions, but in July 1823 they had forced his resignation. He promptly became leader of the patriot group whose rhetoric became increasingly anti-monarchical as well as anti-Portuguese. After three months, the Emperor had had enough. On 12 November 1823, he dissolved the Assembly, surrounded the building with troops and artillery and ordered the delegates to disperse. After a final session, which lasted for over 24 tense and exhausting hours, the members filed wearily out between the bayonets. José Bonifácio's brother, Antônio Carlos, bowed towards the guns and expressed the feelings of them all. 'I obey the sovereign of the world', he said, 'His Majesty the cannon'. The leaders of the 'patriot' party were arrested without delay and Emperor Pedro appointed a government from the moderates. His next act was to draw up a new constitution, which, he was sure, would be more liberal than anything Brazil's unruly politicians could devise. Cochrane was sympathetic, although – as was his way – he felt obliged to deliver a long written lecture on the role of a constitutional monarch.

The ministers who formed the new Brazilian Government were

competent but uninspiring. José Severiano Maciel da Costa became Chief Minister, Luis de Carvalho e Melo – a friend of Maria Graham – Minister of Foreign Affairs, and Francisco Villela Barbosa Minister of Marine. The new government was plunged straight into difficulties. Internally, the 'patriot' party remained a powerful force; while externally, Britain and Austria were exerting pressure in favour of peace. Thus, the government was faced with conflicting demands: on the one hand, for the continuation of the war and the seizure of enemy prizes; on the other, for the suspension of hostilities, the restoration of confiscated property and, even, the dismissal of its British naval officers.[2]

Up to this time, Lord Cochrane's relations with the Brazilian Government had been cordial. In private letters he had praised the 'utmost confidence and candour' with which he had been treated and had expressed satisfaction at the freedom of action his orders had given him.[3] In an attempt to keep his confidence, on 24 November 1823, Villela Barbosa, who had been Minister of Marine for only five days, visited the First Admiral to offer his respects and assure him that action on prizes would soon be taken. He then ordered the courts to act speedily so that the prizes could be sent to the Supreme Military Council for final judgement.[4]

From a prize as well as a military point of view, the independence campaign had been brilliantly successful: Cochrane's men had blockaded one port, achieved the surrender of two others, and pursued a heavily laden convoy for hundreds of miles. In all, the squadron had taken some 78 merchant vessels, three warships including a brand new frigate, eight gunboats and huge amounts of public and private property. Its total value was estimated to be 1260 contos of reis (or £252,000 at the prevailing rate of exchange).[5] By January 1824, 24 ships and cargoes worth 600 contos of reis (£120,000) were already in Rio, and Cochrane was looking forward to their speedy condemnation by the prize courts according to local law, which as he knew, awarded one eighth of the value to the commander-in-chief.

Cochrane's expectations regarding prize money were soon to be frustrated. The restoration of captured Portuguese property was a basic plank in the government's policy of peace and reconciliation, and the size of Cochrane's victory caused a problem. First, lawyers had to rule on whether a conflict between two equal kingdoms under the Portuguese crown was a 'war' in the accepted sense. Then they had to decide what prize laws Brazil should apply. And when the prize courts eventually got down to business, they seemed to be more concerned with the political need to restore Portuguese property than with any law or with Cochrane's expectations. Thus a decision that no vessel taken in port or within two leagues of the coast was a lawful prize secured the release of most of the merchantmen; the squadron's claims to captured warships were dismissed on the grounds that they were *droits* of the Crown; and Cochrane's claims to public property seized in Maranhão and Pará were disallowed on the familiar argument that these provinces had not been enemy territory, but had merely been under temporary Portuguese administration. Further disputes arose due to a host of technical infringements. The prize laws laid down, for example, that cargoes were to be left untouched and that all papers and two officers from each captured ship were to be detained to give evidence. During the chase of the Portuguese convoy out of Salvador and the capture of São Luis, Cochrane had failed to do this. Some prizes had arrived in Brazilian ports without officers, some without prize crews, some loaded with merchandise which did not belong to them and, when Cochrane had run short of men in Maranhão, he had sold the goods he could not remove and kept the cash. The result of all this was that by February 1824, the Superior Prize Court had dismissed the squadron's claims to almost all the ships and property it had taken.

Cochrane was incensed. The confidence he had placed in the Brazilian Government was replaced by deep and morbid suspicion. Adamant of the justice of his claims, he became convinced that the denial of his prize money was due to double-dealing. Unable to appreciate the subtleties of Brazilian politics, he sprang to the conclusion that the ministry was pro-Portuguese, was following anti-Brazilian policies, and was actually hoping for the dismemberment of the country. Once this suspicion had taken hold of Cochrane's mind, the Brazilian Government could do nothing right. 'It would be wearisome to enter into the details of the arrogance and injury now systematised by the Portuguese faction in the administration', he writes in the *Narrative of Services*.[6] Unfortunately, he then did so, finding sinister motives for even the most banal events.

Cochrane persuaded himself that the 'Portuguese faction' was trying to weaken the navy by undermining his authority and driving away its officers with harsh treatment and the denial of prize money. Cochrane did not, however, include the Emperor in his complaints, preferring to believe that Pedro was a vigorous and patriotic monarch who was ready to intervene on his behalf to frustrate the 'plots' of his ministers. As in Chile, it was Cochrane's immediate superior, the Minister of Marine, who bore the brunt of his hostility. Temperamentally, apart from the fact that neither suffered fools gladly, the two men were as different as chalk and cheese. Cochrane's formal education had been haphazard; he was impulsive and driven by sentiment rather than logic, with a romantic belief in democracy. Villela Barbosa, on the other hand, was a trained mathematician, educated like many of the Brazilian elite at the University of Coimbra. By training and temperament he was cold, calculating and authoritarian. He was also a highly efficient administrator and, under his leadership, the Brazilian navy was to become the largest in the Americas.

By February 1824, Cochrane had become so disenchanted that he wrote a long letter to the Emperor listing his services, protesting at his treatment and offering his resignation. Inevitably the open complaints of its commander-in-chief and the unaccountable release of prizes led to a drop in the navy's morale. Pay was another problem. There was no grievance about its speed or regularity, but with the amount. The officers found that they were worse off in Brazil than they had been led to believe, and many of the men had actually been cheated. The Brazilian agent in Liverpool had dishonestly promised inflated rates to the sailors recruited there which, on their arrival, the government refused to pay. And when Cochrane protested on their behalf, he was told that the men should accept the normal rate or go.[7] Many of them did just that, and by March over 100 sailors had left the service. The spectre of a manpower shortage once again raised its head, and Cochrane reported that it would get worse unless the navy's claims for pay and prize money were resolved.

The growing dissatisfaction of Lord Cochrane and his men was a matter of deep concern. Ministers may have been trying to encourage peace, but they were equally determined to maintain an effective navy in order to frustrate any Portuguese attempt at re-conquest, and to preserve the unity of their vast, sprawling country. However tiresome Cochrane might have seemed, they were reluctant to lose his incomparable talents, and were concerned that he might offer them to a potential enemy.[8] The problem was thrashed out at a meeting of the Council of State on 12 February 1824. It was decided that the answer lay in compromise: the policy of returning Portuguese property would continue but to appease Cochrane and his men, the Treasury would pay them the value of all prizes whether they were condemned or not, and would meet claims for damages from aggrieved owners. It was also agreed to distribute 40 contos of reis (£8000) immediately on account. These concessions represented an enormous financial commitment for the Brazilian Government. Not only was it desperately short of revenue but the amount involved – 1260 contos or £252,000 – was the same as the cost of the navy for a whole year.[9]

A week later, as a further indication of their goodwill, Cochrane's title, which had hitherto been referred to in official documents as 'commander-in-chief of the Imperial Squadron in this port', was changed to 'commander-in-chief of the naval forces of this Empire'. Cochrane welcomed the extension of his authority, although he objected to the wording of the decree limiting his service to '…the duration of the present war'.[10] By March, morale was restored to the extent that a squadron under John Taylor's command sailed to blockade Pernambuco which was seething with rebellion.

The agreement of 12 February coincided with a change in Cochrane's personal circumstances. Lady Cochrane had not enjoyed her time in Brazil. She had found the Imperial Court trying, had suffered during the heat and humidity of the Brazilian summer, and was now pregnant with their third son, Arthur Auckland Leopold Pedro. Cochrane arranged for her to return to England in the packet *Marchioness of Salisbury* on 17 February with her baby daughter and servants. He was left alone to ruminate on his grievances. Cochrane was taciturn when meeting strangers at the best of times; now he became tense and withdrawn, seeing enemies all around. One neutral observer, Captain Kotzebue of the Russian navy, who was looking forward to meeting the hero in Rio de Janeiro, was puzzled and disappointed by the encounter. He was later to describe Cochrane at this time as a man whose 'appearance and manners are off-putting, and who in conversation never does more than express himself in monosyllables so that it is difficult to detect the intelligence and experience beneath….Tall, thin and round shouldered, his eyes are always downcast; he never looks to the front or at the person to which he is speaking.'[11]

The Brazilian authorities nevertheless continued to treat Cochrane with all the respect his position as commander-in-chief required. His opinion was sought and valued on all maritime matters whether broad issues of national defence or technical details such as the design of steamships or the availability of anchors or cables. At the same time, the normal procedures of naval administration continued to be observed, every order to the squadron and its personnel being scrupulously passed through Lord Cochrane.[12] There were instructions for victualling, paying off, naval movements, transfers, promotions, pensions, prizes and pay.

But Cochrane's festering mistrust of the government occasionally broke to the surface. On 20 March 1824, he submitted his resignation once more. On 30 March, he wrote a long letter to the Chief Minister. It was the compendium list of grievances in which Cochrane specialised. He complained about the squadron's lack of repairs, the irregularity in payments, the looting of prizes, and the penalties being imposed for infringing the prize laws; he mocked the need to legally confirm the existence of a war; and ended sarcastically, 'it is certainly a hardship for the Portuguese gentlemen in the Court of Admiralty to be under the necessity of condemning property belonging to their countrymen, friends and relations'.[13] Da Costa replied in a tone which could not disguise the government's growing weariness with Cochrane's continual complaints, writing,

…the intentions of HIM and the members of his Council are, and always have been, to do pleasure to Your Excellency, and the proof of this is that the misunderstandings…have always been decided in a manner favourable to Your Excellency. The difficulties surrounding the question of the prizes have origins so well known that it is melancholy to see them attributed to the ill-will of the Council of HIM who have already dismissed two judges because they were not endowed with the requisite activity… As to the ideas that the difficulties that you have met with in the arsenal and in other offices, were commanded, or at least tolerated

by the Ministry, I believe them to be totally imaginary... For the rest, let
Your Excellency reflect for a moment and it will be found that the
Government of HIM, simply and entirely to do pleasure to Your
Excellency, have incurred an enormous financial liability in the
engagements made with you. It is unfortunate that in the place of thanks
and satisfaction, Your Excellency should think it right to reply by
recriminations both bitter and violent. For myself...I do not know in
what manner we can content you; and do believe that your official
correspondence, once made public, would prove it.[14]

Cochrane would not be mollified. 'I am battling the watch here with the
same kind of people I left on the other side', he wrote to his brother, 'an
ignorant, obstinate, narrow minded gang: the Emperor however is my
friend'.[15] On 3 May he replied to the Chief Minister at even greater
length. On 12 June he listed his complaints to the Minster of Marine, this
time making three demands; that Brazil should adopt British naval
regulations, that Portuguese-born members of the prize courts should be
dismissed, and that 200 contos of reis (£40,000) should be paid to the
squadron as an advance on prize money. By June, Cochrane was
conducting a vitriolic and anonymous correspondence in the newspapers
with Villela Barbosa – the latter writing under the synonym of 'Curioso'.

In May, John Pascoe Grenfell arrived back in Rio from his success at
Bélem with the *Imperatriz*. While he was ashore, the authorities removed
40,000 milreis in prize money from the frigate and ordered an inquiry
into complaints made by the junta of Pará. This was followed by a
contrived denunciation of his activities in the newspaper *A Estrella
Brasileira*. Grenfell went into semi-hiding, but eventually gave himself up
and was acquitted of all charges. Cochrane, worried that the same tactic
would be used to seize the 77,000 milreis in prize money he had brought
from Maranhão and hidden on the *Pedro I*, tried to send a large sum back
to England through a local merchant called John London. Although he
was assured it was money from Chile, London refused to oblige, fearing
that it might compromise his position with the Brazilian authorities.[16] In
June 1824, Cochrane was warned by Madame Bompland, the wife of a
resident French naturalist, that the authorities intended to use the excuse
of a naval review to remove the money from the *Pedro I*. In a farcical

interlude, Cochrane rode to the Palace of São Cristovão in the dead of night, interviewed the Emperor still clad in his nightshirt, and secured the abandonment of the plan.

In reality, the Brazilian Government had more important things to attend to than Cochrane's grievances. Reports from Europe told of massive Portuguese preparations for re-conquest. In response, troops were raised and fortifications rebuilt; the blockade of Pernambuco was abandoned, and Villela Barbosa began to expand Brazil's naval forces, buying some of Cochrane's prizes and ordering another recruiting campaign in London. To pacify the complaints of those already in the service, he raised the pay of officers and men, and advanced the 200 contos in prize money Cochrane had demanded for distribution among the squadron. Finally, on 27 July the minister settled another of Cochrane's complaints by issuing a decree, which permitted him to continue as commander-in-chief for as long as he wished, with an entitlement to receive half pay after he chose to retire.

During July, however, there was encouraging news from Portugal, where Pedro's vicious younger brother, Miguel, had seized power from his father. The situation was confused, but it was clear that an invasion of Brazil was now out of the question. This enabled the Brazilian Government to throw its full weight against the rebellion in the north-east, where Pernambuco, under the leadership of a wily and unscrupulous politician called Manuel de Carvalho, had allied itself with four adjacent provinces to declare a separate republic called the 'Confederation of the Equator'. De Carvalho had himself written the constitution of the new state, based on that of Colombia but with strong American influence, which was hardly surprising for a man who had spent years of exile in the United States and whose three daughters had been baptised Carolina, Philadelphia and Pennsylvania. Throughout the north-east, the green and yellow of Brazil had been replaced with a sky blue flag bearing a white circle containing the words 'Religion Independence Union Liberty', and emblazoned with branches of coffee and sugar, numerous white stars, a scarlet cross, a hand and the eye of Providence. The Confederation had formed an army and a small navy and had gone on to the offensive against Imperial positions to the south. The blockade of Recife was immediately re-imposed and, on 2 August, an expeditionary force of 1200 troops

under the command of Brigadier Francisco Lima e Silva sailed to crush
the rising. The escort was provided by a flotilla led by Cochrane in the
Pedro I. His instructions were to act under Lima e Silva's orders in
restoring order to the state of Pernambuco, then to bring the other
rebellious provinces back to Brazilian allegiance.

On 13 August, the army disembarked at Alagoas, the nearest deep-water
port in Imperial hands to Pernambuco, where it gathered horses, guns and
local militia units. While Lima e Silva pushed northwards in a series of
forced marches, Cochrane went on ahead to take command of the
blockade of Recife. His first act on arrival – to the consternation of
foreign residents – was to threaten to bombard the town. Then he tried
negotiation, using his old acquaintance, Maria Graham, as an
intermediary. Graham had arrived on the packet from Falmouth on her
way to Rio de Janeiro where she was to act as governess to the Emperor's
daughter, the Princess Maria da Glória. But these negotiations were
abruptly broken off when de Carvalho – who knew Cochrane's
reputation all too well – offered him a bribe of 400 contos (£80,000) to
change sides! Deeply offended, Cochrane sent in two schooners to
bombard the town. But the demonstration was a failure and, uninterested
in a tedious period of blockade duty, Cochrane sailed away to look for the
Brazilian army. He found it on 4 September 1824, marching northwards
along the coast. Lima e Silva, who was convinced the rebel regime was
fragile and would collapse at the first blow, was keen to attack the capital
by land and sea at the first opportunity. Cochrane, who took the opposite
view, ignored the Brigadier's request for a meeting,[17] and disappeared over
the horizon. He had business in Bahia.

Lima e Silva's rapid advance threw the rebel forces into total confusion,
and at nightfall on 11 September, the army reached Recife, swept aside all
resistance and seized one of the two islands on which the city was built.
De Carvalho, who had been caught up in the panic, fled on a fishing raft
and sought refuge on HMS *Tweed*. The American David Jewitt, now a
commodore, reached Recife the same day with a reinforcement of
warships. There was no sign of Cochrane, so it was Jewitt who co-
ordinated plans with Lima e Silva for a combined assault on the city.
Accordingly, on the night of 16 September, 400 men from the squadron
under the command of Captain James Norton were rowed silently ashore

in the rear of the enemy positions. At dawn, while the army launched a frontal assault, the naval division attacked from the seaward side. The pincer movement was a complete success. The army overwhelmed the defenders while Norton's men captured the forts guarding the approaches and took possession of the shipping in the port.[18] With Recife secured, Lima e Silva pursued the retreating rebels northwards towards the old capital of Olinda. At 8 a.m. the Imperial troops began to fight their way into the city and by noon it was all over.

News that Recife had been captured and the rebellion crushed was received with acclaim in Rio de Janeiro. But the absence of Cochrane at the moment of the assault was noted with displeasure.[19] While Lima e Silva and Jewitt had been fighting their way into Recife, Cochrane had been in Bahia with Dean paying out prize money.[20] When he returned to Recife on 25 September 1824, he was therefore surprised to find the city in Lima e Silva's hands. There were fulsome congratulations, but relations between the two were cool and awkward, and disagreements were never far from the surface. But with Pernambuco back under Imperial control, Cochrane was ready to follow his instructions to pacify the other rebel provinces. Accordingly he headed for Rio Grande do Norte and Ceará. The latter had been a hotbed of insurrection, but news of the collapse of Pernambuco and the threatening guns of *Pedro I* and *Piranga* were enough to persuade the rebel authorities to have a change of heart. Hard-core units in the interior continued to resist, but by the end of the November, the province was under Imperial control and Cochrane set sail for Maranhão. The province had played no part in the Confederation of the Equator, but Cochrane had unfinished business there.

CHAPTER SIXTEEN

Goodbye to All That

LORD COCHRANE arrived in Maranhão to find anarchy and open warfare between the President, Miguel Freire Bruce, and the opposition factions. In other words nothing had changed since he had left it a year earlier. His first act was to restore order by appointing Commodore David Jewitt as military commander of the province and sending him ashore with a party of armed seamen. A hail of petitions, letters from foreign consuls, and Jewitt's own enquiries, revealed that the tyrannical behaviour of the President was the cause of the trouble. Within a week Jewitt's men had taken control and had disarmed the troops Bruce had recruited from freed slaves and the dregs of the population to impose a reign of terror in the capital. Even then the situation remained dangerous. On 10 December 1824 spies reported that the negro units had been secretly re-armed and that there was a plot to murder Cochrane and the loyalists backing him. When confronted with the evidence, Bruce did not even attempt to deny it. The rebel troops were rounded up, and Bruce was taken with his family to Rio de Janeiro. After two months, Maranhão was uneasily at peace, with Cochrane's nominee, Antônio Teles Lobo, acting as President. The Imperial government wrote warmly to approve Cochrane's actions and to inform him that on 4 December they had anticipated his actions by dismissing Bruce and replacing him with a new man called Pedro da Costa Barros.

Cochrane's nerves were beginning to be affected by his exertions and by continual brooding on his supposed injustices. In December 1824, Cochrane wrote to his wife complaining of persecution by the 'Portuguese faction' and saying that he could never return to Rio de Janeiro as he was now liable for huge prize court damages. On 1 January 1825, he celebrated the New Year by writing yet again to the Emperor repeating his grievances and submitting his resignation (which was rejected). At the end of the month, another catalogue of complaints was on its way to the Chief Minister.[1]

Cochrane's behaviour clearly showed that his obsession with persecution by an 'anti-Brazilian' administration had not changed one iota. In fact, private letters from Maria Graham confirmed his worst suspicions. As governess to the six-year-old Princess Maria da Glória, Graham had taken up residence at the Palace of São Cristovão. But far from being welcoming, the Palace was a nest of intrigue and gossip, controlled by a group of Portuguese-born chamberlains and domestics who made life as difficult as possible for her. After a series of confrontations, which came to a head over the shocking and improper – to Graham – Brazilian practice of bathing the princess naked in front of servants, she resigned and moved out.

The British community's reaction to Graham's tribulations was mixed. Some rallied round; others were unsympathetic. Her position was made worse by her outspoken support for Cochrane whose activities were by now a source of concern. But her access to the gossip of the Portuguese domestics in the Palace prompted her to warn Lord Cochrane that his 'enemies' were secretly intriguing against him, and were even talking of dismissing the navy's British officers.[2]

Cochrane's arrival in Maranhão had been motivated by more than just the restoration of public order. On 11 January 1825 he showed his hand in a letter to the Provincial President in which, ignoring the rulings of the prize courts, the wishes of the government and, indeed, the agreement of 10 February 1824, he demanded payment of the prize money he had claimed following the capture of São Luis in 1823. The total was 424 contos (or £85,000), although Cochrane offered to accept a mere 106 contos (£21,100) if it were handed over within 30 days.[3] As the embodiment of Imperial power, backed up by a 74-gun warship, the junta had no choice but to agree to Cochrane's demands.

All seemed to be going in Cochrane's favour, but on 5 February 1825, the *Animo Grande* dropped anchor in São Luis carrying the new Provincial President, Pedro da Costa Barros. Cochrane had no intention of having his plans spoilt by the substitution of the pliable Antônio Teles Lobo by a new man who was in the confidence of the Rio government.

When Costa Barros began to ask questions, Cochrane used the
technicality that he carried no Imperial Patent to prevent Cochrane from
carrying out his functions. When supporters protested, the First Admiral
accused Costa Barros of fomenting public disorder and on 11 March
shipped him off to Belém at the mouth of the Amazon.[4]

Emboldened by Costa Barros's presence, on 10 March the junta had
reneged on the prize payments. Cochrane confronted the members four
days later and, with the fate of Costa Barros fresh in their minds, they
agreed once more to his original terms. The first instalment of 33 contos
of reis (£6600) was handed over in silver and letters of credit two days
later, and within two months the whole of the 106 contos was in his
hands.[5] As the money came in, Secretary Jackson, added it to what
remained of the 200 contos received in Rio de Janeiro and paid it out
again in prize money and bonuses. Unfortunately, Cochrane's haphazard
way of dealing with financial matters meant that the only people who
benefited were members of his immediate entourage and the crews of
ships lucky enough to put into São Luis. John Taylor and his men, for
example, now back in Rio, received nothing for their efforts. Cochrane,
of course, received both his pay and his one-eighth share of prize money
and was able to buy £28,000 worth of cotton and send it back to England
in four merchant ships.[6]

Cochrane had no qualms about his behaviour in Maranhão. Indeed, on
16 March he wrote to the Minister of Marine justifying what he had
done.[7] On 22 March, however, he addressed a private letter to Luis
Carvalho e Melo, the one minister he regarded as a friend, saying that his
'action in Maranhão will be represented as an outrageous robbery' and
adding, 'it is not from the Portuguese faction in Rio that I expect either
credit or justice: their object is sufficiently clear – namely the expulsion
of every foreign officer from the service by means of privation or insult'.[8]
Cochrane had certainly taken the law into his own hands, and his
subordinates were becoming worried by his actions. Jewitt, who had
always been coldly critical of the commander-in-chief, secretly reported
that Cochrane had 'the most horrible intentions against the interests of
HIM' and had even suggested that the squadron should blockade Rio de
Janeiro until its prize money were paid.[9]

Once Cochrane had achieved his objective he prepared to leave. First he manoeuvred Jewitt into a position where he could not interfere with his plans. At the end of March 1825, Jewitt and his officers were transferred to the *Pedro I* and ordered back to Bahia while Crosbie and his most trusted lieutenants moved with Cochrane to the *Piranga*. Next he tried to make his peace with the British authorities. Writing to Consul-General Henry Chamberlain, he presented his actions in Brazil in the best possible light, stressing that the police actions the Brazilian navy had carried out in the north had been of enormous value to British trade, and that commercial relations were now at an 'unprecedented' level. Furthermore, he assured Chamberlain that as a patriot it had always been his intention to act in such a manner. Likewise, although he had held 'the destiny of Brazil and of South America in my hands', he had acted responsibly and with honour. In his opinion he deserved credit for his efforts but so far had received only injustice from the Brazilian authorities. As the representative of a great and friendly power he felt that Chamberlain should be made aware of the truth. On a more personal note, Cochrane had been alarmed to hear that Maria Graham's loudly expressed support had caused trouble with the Consul-General. He sought to distance himself from Graham's well-meaning activities, stressing that his only association with her was his natural sympathy for a naval widow, and confiding that Chamberlain's good judgement would enable him to put things in perspective.[10] Finally, Cochrane wrote to the Ministry of Marine, explaining that his officers and crews had been debilitated by the heat and humidity of the northern coast and that he intended to put to sea in order to restore their health.[11]

With Cochrane's exit strategy now in place, on 20 May 1825 he weighed anchor in the *Piranga* and headed north apparently taking the quickest – though longest – passage to Rio de Janeiro by working the frigate across the equatorial zone, picking up the trade winds and then sailing a clockwise route north-east to the Azores, then south to the Canaries and the Cape Verde Islands. It was similar to the route he had followed on his first return from Maranhão in 1823. But as the frigate approached the Azores, Cochrane discovered – no doubt as he intended – that the *Piranga*'s running rigging was rotten, her main topmast was sprung and her spare spars so useless that it was necessary to put into the nearest friendly port. For political reasons France and Spain were out of

the question; so he set course for England. A month later, *Piranga* entered
the Channel and sighted the Lizard. Ignoring the haven of Plymouth the
frigate sailed boldly on, passing Bolt Head, Portland Bill and St
Catherine's Point on the Isle of Wight. At last, on 27 June 1825, Cochrane
brought the *Piranga* to anchor in Spithead and, in a historic moment, the
Brazilian flag was formally saluted for the first time by a European power
in its own waters.

Chapter Seventeen

Home and Away

LORD COCHRANE'S return to Britain was greeted with enthusiasm by lovers of freedom and romantic liberals alike. Wearing the laurels won in the liberation struggles of Latin America he was cheered in the streets by excited crowds and fêted by radical friends. In Edinburgh, when a reference to South America was inserted into a play Lord and Lady Cochrane were attending, the whole audience turned to the box where the two of them were sitting and broke into prolonged and spontaneous applause. Lady Cochrane promptly fainted. Sir Walter Scott, who was equally overcome, extemporised an emotional but mediocre poem, which was published in *The Morning Post*.

Not everyone was overjoyed. Foreign Secretary George Canning may have been following liberal policies overseas, but the attitude of the Tory government to internal affairs was firmly reactionary. To Lord Liverpool, the Duke of Wellington and the Cabinet, the return of a radical hero such as Cochrane was highly unwelcome. Many regarded him as a demagogue and a trickster. In fact, so sharp was the animosity that ministers took legal advice on whether he was liable for prosecution under the Foreign Enlistment Act. This had been passed in 1819 to stem the flow of volunteers who were rushing to serve in overseas wars in which Britain wished to remain strictly neutral. Cochrane's service in Chile had started before the law had been passed; but he was prima facie guilty of breaking it by serving in Brazil. Manuel Gameiro Pessoa, who was acting as Brazilian agent in London during General Felisberto Brant's absence in Rio attending the recently opened Portuguese–Brazilian peace negotiations, was horrified when he heard, feeling that prosecution of an Imperial officer would be a serious blow to national honour.[1]

Cochrane's appearance in London also caused a flurry of international concern. Peace negotiations between Portugal and Brazil were in progress and, in January 1825, to give impetus to the proceedings, the Emperor Pedro had played his trump card and threatened to send the Brazilian navy to attack the coasts of Portugal.[2] Now, Lord Cochrane had suddenly arrived in European waters with a big Brazilian frigate! Alarming conclusions were drawn. It took time to establish that his arrival was purely accidental. In the Brazilian Legation in London, Gameiro Pessoa was equally surprised by the appearance of *Piranga* at Spithead. Nevertheless, he acted quickly. With some difficulty he was able to find £2065 to cover arrears of pay, and £2291 in prize money for the crew. His financial problems were eased when Cochrane made a contribution of £2000 towards these expenses from the money he had taken in Maranhão. The British Government may have been prepared to salute the Brazilian flag, but they refused to have a warship belonging to an unrecognised foreign power – however friendly – repaired in Portsmouth dockyard. Fortunately, the works needed by *Piranga* were only minor and Gameiro Pessoa was able to arrange for them to be done in a private yard so that Cochrane and the frigate could return to Brazil without delay.

Lord Cochrane, however, had no intention of going back. When Gameiro Pessoa managed to run him to ground in Tunbridge Wells, where he had been reunited with his family, he was told vaguely that Cochrane intended to stay in England until the peace negotiations between Brazil and Portugal had been concluded.[3] In reality, Cochrane was playing for time. In 1825 the attention of liberal England had focused on the Greek struggle for freedom from Turkey. The study of the classics and of ancient Greece, which formed the basis of the education of all European gentlemen, made them fervent partisans of the Greek cause. Stories of Turkish cruelty and of massacres inspired them further and committees were formed in every European capital to raise funds and provide support. The London Committee was 80 strong and included a number of Cochrane's political friends, such as Sir Francis Burdett and John Cam Hobhouse who had succeeded him as Member of Parliament for Westminster. All were convinced that the noble cause of Greece should be the next beneficiary of Cochrane's military talents, and no sooner had he arrived back in England than they offered him command of the Greek navy. Cochrane was interested, but he was determined to ensure that his pay would be adequate and that he would have the means at his disposal to achieve victory. His demanded a colossal salary of £57,000, £37,000 of which was to be paid in advance, and the construction of six armed steamships and two heavy frigates. With his usual blithe disregard for the technical problems involved, he announced that with steam vessels at his disposal, he would easily be able to destroy the whole Turkish navy. The members of the London Committee were quick to accept Cochrane's terms. They had already been looking for armed steamships at the suggestion of Captain Frank Abney Hastings, a former Royal Navy officer who had fought at Trafalgar and had devoted himself to the Greek cause since 1822. He had suggested that it would be easier and quicker to buy and adapt existing steam vessels rather than start them from scratch. Cochrane dismissed the idea out of hand.

These discussions created a dilemma. Cochrane did not want to go back to Brazil, but could not formally accept the Greek offer until his Brazilian service had come to an end. Yet he was unwilling to resign his position as First Admiral lest it weaken his claims against the Imperial government. For months Cochrane managed to avoid the issue, but when news of his Greek appointment was carried openly in the newspapers, an increasingly desperate Gameiro Pessoa demanded to be told the First Admiral's intentions in writing.[4] Cochrane, who had disappeared to visit friends and relatives in Scotland, replied on 24 August with a masterpiece of evasion, saying that he had not refused the Greek offer but that he would not leave the Brazilian service until his work was completed. Gameiro Pessoa's translator failed to capture the nuances of the First Admiral's ambiguity and the letter was interpreted as confirmation that he had decided to leave the Imperial service. And when Gameiro Pessoa acknowledged the apparent resignation with a glowing tribute to his contribution to Brazilian independence, Cochrane was forced to reply in haste from Edinburgh to disabuse him.[5]

In Rio de Janeiro the consternation created by Cochrane's poor performance in Pernambuco in August 1824, when he had deserted Francisco Lima e Silva, had been partly alleviated by his pacification of the northern provinces. But his activities in Maranhão had caused alarm. And when, in June 1825, the arrival of his own despatches confirmed that Cochrane had deposed President Costa Barros, had ignored the rulings of the prize court and was effectively holding Maranhão to ransom, the government felt obliged to act. On 27 June the Minister of Marine had sent an order of recall but, as Consul-General Henry Chamberlain reported, no one from the Emperor downwards expected him to return.[6] It took over two months for a copy of Villela Barbosa's order to arrive in London. And when it reached Lord Cochrane at the end of September, it only inspired another evasive reply.

Gameiro Pessoa was now determined that even if Cochrane refused to return to Brazil, the *Piranga* would sail without further delay. Repairs had been completed, the expenses of maintaining the frigate were mounting, and her English crew were beginning to desert. On arrival at Portsmouth, Captain Crosbie had resigned his Brazilian commission and was in London preparing to accompany Cochrane to Greece, so command of the *Piranga* devolved upon the frigate's erstwhile first lieutenant, James Shepherd. On 8 October 1825 Gameiro Pessoa demanded that Captain Shepherd put himself under his orders and prepare *Piranga* for an immediate return to Rio de Janeiro. Gameiro Pessoa brutally pointed out that if he valued his future in the Imperial navy, he had better do as he was told. Shepherd refused and reported the whole incident to Cochrane in a private letter.[7] In desperation Gameiro Pessoa tried to persuade the British authorities to seize the frigate. When this failed, he cut off all pay and supplies to the *Piranga* and, on 7 November, informed Shepherd that they would not be resumed until he put the frigate at the disposal of the Legation and declared he was no longer under Cochrane's orders.

In the beginning of September 1825, Cochrane had received news that his Greek appointment had been formalised in a letter of invitation from Alexander Mavrocordatos, Secretary of the National Assembly. He went back to London a month later to check on the progress being made on the engines for the steamships being built for Greece. Their manufacturer, Alexander Galloway, who had been selected personally by Cochrane for the job in spite of his poor performance over the *Rising Star*, was already showing signs of the incompetence that would eventually compromise the whole project. In his house in Regent Street, Cochrane and Jackson began to settle their Brazilian accounts. His 30 months in Brazil had been profitable. In total he had received 39,587 milreis (£7910) – being his pay and allowances up to 30 September 1825 – and another 65,100 milreis

(£13,020) in prize money. On a more pleasant note, Cochrane received a call from Maria Graham who was back from Rio de Janeiro. Less agreeable was a reunion with Henry Dean, who had sailed from Bahia on hearing the news of Cochrane's whereabouts with a demand for £1653 which, he claimed, Cochrane owed him for his prize work.

At the end of October, Cochrane learned that the British Government had decided to prosecute him under the Foreign Enlistment Act. Instant flight to the European continent until his Greek arrangements could be finalised seemed the only possible course of action. But how could he terminate his service with Brazil without putting himself in the wrong by formally resigning? The timely confirmation that the peace negotiations had been successful and Portugal had recognised Brazilian independence gave Cochrane the excuse he needed. On 5 November 1825, two days *before* Gameiro Pessoa's ultimatum to Shepherd, Cochrane wrote a courteous letter to the Minister of Marine telling him that the *Piranga* was about to return, congratulating the Imperial government on the conclusion of peace and finishing, 'I have confidently to express my hope that HIM will feel satisfied that I have faithfully performed my duty during the period to which he was pleased by decree of the 28 February 1824 to limit my command of His Majesty's Forces, and which period has now expired.'[8]

In other words, Cochrane justified his departure from the Brazilian service by quoting the decree of 28 February 1824 which, by restricting his period of service to the end of the war, had effectively discharged him on the coming of peace. The fact that this decree had been superseded – at his own insistence – by another dated 27 July 1824 which allowed him to remain in the Imperial navy until he chose to resign was conveniently overlooked. So, ending his service in Brazil with a piece of deception almost as great as that which had begun it, Cochrane accepted the offer of the Greek command. On 9 November 1825, Lord Cochrane and his family embarked hurriedly on a steamer at Tower Hill bound for France.

Across the Atlantic in Rio de Janeiro, Villela Barbosa had been watching Cochrane's antics through the medium of Gameiro Pessoa's despatches with escalating annoyance. On 20 August 1825, he ordered Cochrane once again to return to Brazil. On 30 December he repeated the instruction. These despatches reached Cochrane months later in Brussels.

From there, he wrote two letters to the Minister of Marine on 10 February and 16 March 1826, in which he repeated his interpretation of the decree of 28 February 1824 and asked for the payment of the final instalment of his salary up to 10 November 1825 when news of peace had arrived. For good measure he added a claim for £1000 to cover the cost of Lady Cochrane's trip to Brazil in the *Sesostris*, which he said the Emperor had promised to refund![9] Villela Barbosa sent another order of recall on 9 June 1826. This stimulated another infuriatingly courteous reply in which Cochrane expressed his deep desire to return to Rio but regretted that the 28 February decree made it impossible.[10]

The Minister of Marine was forced to give up. On 10 April 1827, Lord Cochrane was formally dismissed from the Brazilian navy in a decree that was as terse as the original invitation had been fulsome. In the period between these two documents, Cochrane had probably made a greater contribution to Brazilian independence than any other single individual apart from José Bonifácio and the Emperor himself. Unfortunately, as so often occurred in his career, astonishing achievements were followed by contention and controversy.

CHAPTER EIGHTEEN

———

In the Cause of Greece

FRESH FROM SOUTH AMERICA and without the benefits of a formal classical education, Lord Cochrane had little knowledge of Greece, either ancient or modern, and so he began to immerse himself in the subject. John Cam Hobhouse provided him with a library of some 60 books, and Frank Abney Hastings gave him a pithy description of the major personalities and warlords involved in the fight for independence.

The Greek revolt against Turkish rule had begun in 1821 and had made good progress in the Peloponnese, where the Greek naval commander, Andreas Miaoulis, was able to dominate the coast and the islands. But the campaign had been marked by bloodletting on a monstrous scale. Both sides brutally massacred or enslaved the populations of captured towns, murdering men, women and children indiscriminately; and the Greek effort had been fractured as individual warlords vied with each other for political supremacy.

The Greek struggle had received help through propaganda and fund raising by the London Committee, and the hundreds of philhellenes who arrived, often at their own expense, to offer their services. They were a mixed bunch. At one extreme, they included representatives of the best families, schools and regiments; and at the other humble artisans and seamen. But they all tended to be individualistic, radical, adventurous and enthusiastic; many convinced they were fighting for the glory of Ancient Greece against Turkish oppression. What they found on the ground was altogether different. Their disillusionment was brought to a head in April 1825, with the death of the most famous philhellene of all, Lord Byron, who had emerged not only as a romantic but as a practical figurehead round which the various Greek factions could gather. The next 12 months saw demoralisation set in. Many volunteers went home lamenting that modern Greeks were unworthy of their great heritage; others were sucked into local feuds; more than a few committed suicide.

The Committee in London came to the conclusion that Greek independence would not be gained by guerrilla warfare and piracy but by the creation of disciplined forces on land and sea. It was this thinking that brought about the recruitment not only of Lord Cochrane but of General Sir Richard Church to command the army. Church was a good choice. He had gained his first experience of the eastern Mediterranean when he had served in the expedition against the French in Egypt in 1801 – at exactly the same time as Cochrane was making his reputation in *Speedy*. Seven years later, Church had participated in the British invasion of the Ionian islands, and he had subsequently raised and, for many years, commanded a regiment called the Duke of York's Greek Light Infantry. He had gained a sound knowledge of the Greek method of fighting and knew what they were capable of and, more significantly, what they were not capable of. Indeed, his appointment was greeted with the joyful declaration, 'Our father is at last come! We only have to obey him and our liberty is secured'.

In Turkey, Sultan Mahmoud had realised that his forces could not restore the situation in Greece unaided, and had decided to call in the Albanian-born Viceroy of Egypt, Mehemet Ali, and his formidable son, Ibrahim Pasha, to secure victory. At the beginning of 1825 Ibrahim invaded the Peloponnese with a huge army and a navy of 130 vessels of all types, and by the time Cochrane accepted the offer of the Greek command, Ibrahim was in the process of taking Greek towns and strongholds one by one and brutally subduing the countryside. In the west, Missolonghi was under siege, and in the east, Athens. The revolt was within an ace of collapse.

It did not take Cochrane long to grasp the essentials of the situation. Fame and reputation would not be enough, and to yield to the arguments of his philhellene friends and hasten to Greece without the means of ensuring naval supremacy would mean disaster for both the Greek cause and his own reputation. For this reason he determined to stay in Europe until the construction of the vessels he had demanded as part of his terms of service was complete. These comprised six 42-

horsepower steamships, armed with heavy guns at the bow and the stern, costing £25,000 each, and two heavy 60-gun frigates of the largest size, 1728 tons in burden, 177 feet in length and armed with thirty-two 32-pounders on the main deck – the same calibre of gun that HMS *Victory* had carried at Trafalgar. The two frigates were to be built in the United States, each costing £75,000. Work on the steamships in England, however, began to go wrong. Cochrane's reputation and strength of character had initially overawed the Greek Committee who had accepted his demands that the steamers be built rather than bought, and that they should be fitted with over-complicated high-pressure engines. And the incompetence of Galloway caused the project to suffer delay after delay. The bankers J. and S. Ricardo wrote in frustration to Cochrane that Galloway was 'the evil genius that pursues us everywhere…his presumption is only equalled by his incompetency. Whatever he has to do is deficient. We do not think his misconduct is intentional, but it has proved most fatal to the interests of Greece'.[1]

In France Cochrane had taken up residence with his family in Boulogne – practical for England but out of the reach of the law should the government decide to charge him under the Foreign Enlistment Act. But even France became too hot for him when angry owners took out a prosecution for his detention of the *Gazelle* in at Guanbacho in 1819. To avoid arrest, Cochrane moved on to Brussels. It was there, in May 1826, that news arrived that the first steamship, *Perseverance*, was ready to leave with Hastings in command and a crew of British officers and men, and that the second and third steamers, *Enterprise* and *Irresistible*, would be completed in a month. Cochrane hastily embarked at Flushing in his new schooner *Unicorn*, purchased in London by the Committee for his use, and headed across the Channel to Weymouth. Travelling discreetly up to London, he visited Galloway's engine works at Greenwich to check on progress and receive more promises, then had final talks with the Greek Committee. That done, he sailed for the Mediterranean – only to spend nine months aimlessly waiting for the rest of the force to arrive. The time was not entirely wasted. Stopping in Marseilles, he was able to meet Hobhouse for a briefing on affairs in England, and make contact with members of the French Philhellene Committee. He formed a friendship with one of its leading members, the Swiss doctor Louis-André Gosse, who was the driving force behind a decision to supply him with a brig-of-war called *Sauveur*, and who later travelled to Greece to become the navy's commissary general.

At the beginning of 1827, however, it was becoming painfully clear to Cochrane that his plan to give Greece overwhelming superiority by providing a flotilla of armed steamers was unravelling. *Perseverance* was the only vessel that had been completed, and she was held up on the way to the Mediterranean by boiler trouble and delays in the delivery of her guns. Likewise, the cost of the American frigates had so escalated that only one – the *Hellas* – actually arrived. The second had to be sold to the government to raise the extra money needed and became the USS *Hudson*.[2] In their place Cochrane had to make do with the brig *Sauveur*, commanded by a Royal Navy veteran George Thomas, the corvette *Hydra*, and Hastings' steamship *Perseverance* which on arrival was renamed *Kartería*. It was with this scratch force that Cochrane, against all his instincts, yielded to pressure and headed for Greece.

Cochrane's *Unicorn* entered the glittering blue waters of the Aegean in March 1827, and at noon on the 17th the island of Hydra came into view, the white houses of the town scattered over the slopes of the mountains, which were brown and tree-less except for splashes of green from the odd garden or olive grove. He headed for the port of Poros, taking a deliberate detour to bring him within sight of Athens. Passing by at sunset, he was able to admire the rose-tinted marvel of the Acropolis hill with the occasional dwelling and cypress, but regret that the sky was smeared with the smoke of the cooking fires of the besieging army and the scene itself occasionally lit up with the detonation of Turkish mortars.

Next day, Cochrane arrived at Poros. Moored in the deep waters of the port, he announced his arrival with a proclamation, calling on the Greeks to unite and quoting the words of Demosthenes. Greece's leading men hastened to the island to offer their services and Admiral Miaoulis immediately relinquished his post and offered to serve as commander of the frigate *Hellas*. Cochrane was at the height of his fame and reputation, and his presence had a salutary effect on the warring factions. At Cochrane's insistence, and because both his appointment and that of General Church as commander of the army seemed to signify British official support, local rivalries were put aside. At last, it was possible to call the Greek factions together in a single National Assembly. Meeting outdoors in a lemon grove on the mainland, the deputies elected Corfu-born Count John Capodistrias as President and confirmed Cochrane and Church in their positions. The election of the influential Capodistrias had an overtly political slant for, although in his youth he had been a Greek freedom fighter, in middle age he had served as a minister in the government of Imperial Russia. With the army and naval commands going to the British, his appointment was an acknowledgement of the importance of the Tsar's influence and of the need to satisfy the pro-Russian faction in the country.

With the two military commanders came a new group of philhellenes. Hastings had brought Captain John Hane, Lieutenant William Scanlon, an East India Company surgeon called Dr Howe, George Finlay – already a veteran of Greece independence and later to be its historian – and his brother Kirkman. Cochrane's party had a distinctly Scots flavour and consisted of his nephew George, who acted as secretary, Edward Masson his translator, Charles and David Urquhart, and another military veteran of the wars, Colonel Thomas Gordon. Church's entourage, by contrast, was made up of Captains Charles O'Fallon, Francis Castle, Francis Kirkpatrick and Gibbon FitzGibbon – all Irishmen like himself.

Cochrane took up his duties with the attitude of Christ cleansing the Temple. He began the offensive in his usual style by issuing a proclamation. 'To arms! To arms!' he wrote,

> One simultaneous effort and Greece is free. Discord, the deadly foe you have most to fear is conquered. The task that now remains is easy. The Youth everywhere fly to arms... Let the young seamen of the islands emulate the glory that awaits your military force. Let them hasten to join the national ships and, if denied your independence and rights, blockade the Hellespont, thus carrying the war into the enemy's country. Then the fate of the cruel Sultan, the destroyer of his subjects, the tyrant taskmaster of a Christian shall be sealed.... Then shall the sacred banner of the Cross once more wave on the dome of Saint Sophia. Then shall the Grecian people live secure under just laws. Then shall cities rise from their ruins, and the splendours of future times rival the days that are past.[3]

Those who had witnessed the disorder of the previous six years read it with wry cynicism. Cochrane, who never seemed to doubt the power of the printed word or of his own rhetoric, then issued a long and repetitive proclamation designed to intimidate the Turks and Egyptians. In it he called on Mehemet Ali to 'quit the classic sacred soil of Greece'; to stop 'the flayings, burnings and impalings…the ripping up of pregnant women and the hewing of their infant babies, and other acts yet worse than these – too horrid to relate'; and to concentrate on promoting 'industry, the arts and science' at home![4]

Missolonghi, after a bloody and brutal year-long siege, had fallen in April 1826. Athens had continued to hold out, defended by a small garrison under French General Charles Fabvier. To raise this siege was a major objective, both psychologically and strategically, and Cochrane was determined to justify his reputation and get to work. Greek armies were already assembled on both sides of Piraeus, one under General Karaiskakis the other commanded by the able and experienced Colonel Thomas Gordon, but their route to relieve the Acropolis was blocked by a Turkish outpost in the monastery of Saint Spiridion. Cochrane threw all his energies into the challenge and effectively took control of the campaign, appearing with dramatic effect in the Greek camp carrying a blue and white flag of his own design with an owl in the centre, and promising a thousand dollars to the man who unfurled it above the Acropolis. His plan was to send his own men to take the monastery, then to move Karaiskakis's troops nearer by water so that they could march on Athens while other Greek units made a diversion to distract the Turkish besiegers. Hastings was sent off to destroy the ships that were supplying the Turkish army then, on the night of 24 April, the marines were landed under Major Charles Urquhart. Next morning, Cochrane launched a spirited assault on the earthworks around the monastery, leading an attack in typical style armed with nothing more lethal than a telescope. The garrison of Saint Spiridion was astonished and, when the big guns of the *Hellas* began to smash the monastery's walls to pieces, it surrendered. But the situation quickly began to deteriorate, and Cochrane and the other horrified British officers were forced to watch impotently while the Turkish troops were massacred as they left the monastery.

This was followed by a disaster. Generals Church and Karaiskakis, who knew full well the fighting attributes of their men and were short of supplies and entrenching tools, were reluctant to make the rapid advance on Athens that Cochrane had planned. But the Admiral was hungry for victory and determined to raise the siege. So against his better judgement Church ordered his men forward. Tragically, the advance was carried out so slowly, and with such caution, that the Greek forces were caught in the open by a Turkish cavalry force and totally destroyed. Historians have been highly critical of Cochrane's role in this fiasco;[5] Colonel Gordon later called it 'an insane scheme'.[6] Cochrane's supporters tried to defend him by claiming that the scheme was, in fact practical – all the Greeks had to do was to ensure that the movements of their units were co-ordinated and the troops were able to repel cavalry through disciplined drill and bayonets. Unfortunately the Greeks were able to do neither. The best that can be said is that Cochrane's plan may have been theoretically sound, but it was doomed by his impatience and his ignorance of the capabilities of those who were to execute it.

When the Acropolis did fall at the beginning of June 1827, Cochrane was not there to see it. In the words of one historian, he had 'sailed away contemptuously indifferent to the catastrophe he had precipitated.'[7] While Athens was being taken by the triumphant Turkish army, he was in Egyptian waters in the *Hellas*, leading an attack by 14 brigs and eight fireships on the enemy base of Alexandria. That was also a fiasco. First, there was a lack of volunteers so that only two fireships could be manned and released into the harbour. Then, when Cochrane prepared to take advantage of the confusion by leading the squadron past the fort at the narrow entrance and into the circular bay around which the white minarets, houses and warehouses of the town were built, his Greek crews misinterpreted the panic-stricken movements of the Egyptians within as an attack and fled over the horizon.

Cochrane was by now 52 years old. George Finlay described him as

>...tall and commanding in person, lively and winning in manner, prompt in counsel, and daring but cool in action. Endowed by nature both with strength of character and military genius, versed in naval science both by study and experience, and acquainted with seamen in every clime and country... Unfortunately, accident and his eagerness to gain some

desired object engaged him more than once in enterprises which money
rather than honour appeared to be the end he sought.[8]

It was not an unfamiliar portrait. Cochrane may have been at the peak of
his powers but the chaotic situation in Greece was quite unsuited to his
style and abilities. In Britain – and in Chile and Brazil, whose navies
closely followed British practices – discipline and patriotism had ensured
that the men would follow his leadership. But here it was different. The
Greeks had no discipline; stirring appeals to patriotism and quotations
from Demosthenes made no impression; and the consequence of failure
was so horrific for them that they were unwilling to take on the Turks
unless in greatly superior numbers. Experienced foreign leaders, such as
Church, Finlay, Gordon and Hastings, understood this and tailored their
operations and expectations accordingly. Cochrane, who complained that
his men were 'wild and frantic savages whose acts are guided by
momentary impulses or avidity to grasp some pecuniary advantage',[9] who
had to use a combination of personality and fists to keep discipline, and
who walked the deck with a pistol in his waistband,[10] was perfectly aware
of this. Yet in action, he made no allowances and applied exactly the same
methods he had used elsewhere. In Greece, they did not work. His usually
unnerving proclamations became empty bombast; and the moustachioed
ruffians he led regarded his attacks against superior numbers as foolhardy
gambles and his personal bravery as sheer madness. But Cochrane learned
his lesson and, following the failure at Alexandria, restricted himself to
single-ship actions, commerce raiding, and assaults on isolated forts using
the few vessels and commanders on whom he could rely.

In the event, Greek independence was not secured by Cochrane's ships
or Church's army but by the intervention of the Great Powers. London
and St Petersburg had watched the progress of the revolt with growing
alarm: Russia could not allow the Greeks to be subdued for reasons of
blood and religion, while Britain could not tolerate the destruction of the
Ottoman Empire lest it left a power vacuum into which Russia could
move. As early as April 1826, they had sensibly decided on a co-ordinated
approach, and in July 1827 – when Cochrane was retreating in haste from
Alexandria – they agreed with France to impose a compromise whereby
Greece would achieve independence but under continued Turkish

sovereignty. They also threatened armed intervention if an armistice was not agreed within one month. The British squadron in the eastern Mediterranean, now commanded by Vice Admiral Sir Edward Codrington, was joined by Russian and French forces under Rear Admirals Louis de Heiden and Henri de Rigny and began to enforce a truce by preventing the ships of either Cochrane or Ibrahim from taking offensive action.

Alas, Frank Abney Hasting knew nothing of this. Operating independently in the Gulf of Lepanto with *Kartería* and *Sauveur*, he was busy demonstrating the superiority of armed steamers by destroying a Turkish flotilla and a dozen coasters sheltering under the guns of Salona. Ibrahim put to sea to avenge the outrage, only to be intercepted and shepherded back to his base by the allies. On 20 October 1827, Ibrahim's fleet of 82 ships was anchored in a half-circle in the Bay of Navarino, when 25 British, French and Russian vessels came round the headland and took up parallel positions. The atmosphere was charged with tension and resentment and at 2 p.m., a discharge of musketry acted like a spark in a tinderbox and triggered a general engagement. The slogging match lasted all day, with the broadsides of the disciplined and better-equipped allies soon smashing down any resistance. Dawn broke next day to reveal the air thick with the smoke of burning Egyptian ships, and the waters littered with Egyptian dead. The naval force on which Ibrahim's operations in Greece depended had been annihilated.[11]

With a forced settlement now on the horizon, the two sides began a scramble for territory. The allies did not intervene as long as the lands and islands being taken over respectively by the Greeks and Turks conformed to the realities of what would clearly be the post-independence map. Thus they allowed the Ottomans to be driven from the Peloponnese – indeed hastened it through the landing of a French force – but permitted them to consolidate their control over Albania and the islands. Chios was attacked by Cochrane and Crete by Charles Urquhart, who lost his life in the attempt. Cochrane was anxious to play his part and assist in this expansion; but for him it was not a happy time. From the beginning he had been dogged by problems of supply, lack of discipline and desertion, and he scornfully denounced the Greek crews for refusing to serve unless paid in advance. But the situation worsened after Navarino. With Turkish naval power crippled, Greek seamen turned back to the more profitable fields of privateering and piracy, and when *Enterprise*, the second steamship, arrived under the command of his former South American follower, Thomas Sackville Crosbie, who had been left behind to spur Galloway into action, it proved totally impossible to man her. Cochrane became exasperated, especially since the allies held him responsible for the deprivations of the Greek ships. His letters to Kitty, now enjoying the social whirl in Paris, became increasingly despondent. She tried to revive his spirits, writing somewhat ingenuously, 'I cannot understand your state of mind or feeling: what is it you dread? There is no fighting now in Greece. You cannot be well or such vile blue devils would not hold you so tight. I would strongly advise you to look on the bright side and leave that sad train of thoughts', and to take up 'reading, writing, walking…in fact anything or you will addle your brain and you will look so old'.[12]

In January 1828, Cochrane left for London and Paris in the *Unicorn*, leaving Hastings and Church to carry out the Greek policy of pre-independence expansion. His aim was to make a desperate last attempt to get the rest of his steamer force to sea manned by reliable mercenary seamen. But he was unsuccessful. The Greek Committees in London and Paris had become disillusioned with the struggle, the recruitment of men for an obviously armed struggle was out of the question, and the money had run out. Indeed, critics even suggested that by returning Cochrane had deserted his post and should have refunded the £37,000 already paid.

Even more dejected, Cochrane returned to Greece in September with nothing to show for his efforts except for a new, armed steamer, *Irresistible*, which, on arrival, was re-christened *Hermes*. But things had changed. Ypsilanti had marched troops west through Attica and was besieging Athens. Church had led his army across the Peloponnese, and with Hastings' help had crossed the Gulf of Corinth to attack Missolonghi and the string of forts that stretched as far as the Gulf of Arta. Sadly, Hastings had lost an arm during the campaign and had died. President Capodistrias was getting a grip on the internal anarchy. He was a diplomat and an administrator and, to his tidy mind, the value of the uncoordinated efforts of individual philhellenes was dubious. It was clear to Capodistrias that the independence and the future of Greece depended on the Great Powers and not on the efforts of a collection of foreign enthusiasts. As a result, he was relieved when Cochrane not only submitted his resignation but offered to make over his final salary instalment of £20,000 and all his prizes to the Greek State.[13] Capodistrias replied with thanks, delicately confirming that 'the provisional government can engage in no warlike operations worthy of your talents and your station'. That done, in December 1828, Cochrane lay down his command, pleased to be able to shake the soil of Greece from his shoes or, as he phrased it in a letter to Gosse, 'glad shall I be when the tops of these mountains shall sink below the horizon'.[14]

Now that the burden was being lifted from his shoulders, Cochrane reverted to form and began to complain of ingratitude and injustice, beginning with the 'privations and insults' to which he had been exposed by the captain and crew of the brig in which he had left Greece. No doubt these rough and ready Greeks failed to treat him as he expected – as a celebrity, a peer and an admiral. Admiral Heiden, whose opinion of the Greeks was as low as Cochrane's, thought the same and provided a passage to Malta with all the honours of his rank in the Russian corvette *Grimachi*. There, his old ally in the Basque Roads affair, Sir Pulteney Malcolm, now an admiral, put HMS *Racer* at his disposal to take him to Naples.

Cochrane reached Paris in March 1829, to be reunited with Kitty and the children. But he was still profoundly troubled. Financially he had done well and had made a huge profit on his £37,000 salary advance which he had invested in the Greek Funds, but on a personal level his brother Archibald had died the previous August, and Kitty had suffered a dreadful miscarriage. However, it was his lack of success in Greece that played most on his mind and brought him close to a nervous breakdown.

CHAPTER NINETEEN

Return and Rehabilitation

THE CONCLUSION of the struggle for Greek independence marked the end of Lord Cochrane's career as an active naval commander, but his fighting days were not over. The loss of honour and position that had followed his conviction for the Stock Exchange fraud had never left his mind and he was to dedicate the rest of his long life to a crusade for personal justice. Cochrane maintained that he had been guiltless of any fraud and, unable to accept the weight of circumstantial evidence against him, pursued the idea that he had been the innocent victim of a political and legal conspiracy. In the years that followed, he was to devote all his energy first to obtaining a review of the Stock Exchange affair which, he believed, would easily establish his innocence, and then to securing his re-admission to the navy and the restoration of his knighthood.

A petition in 1828 to George III's second son, the Duke of Clarence, who had been trained as a naval officer and was now briefly Lord High Admiral, achieved nothing. The Tories were still in power and the petition was curtly rejected by the Prime Minister, the Duke of Wellington. So Cochrane remained abroad in France and Italy, nursing Kitty back to health and restoring his own battered self-confidence. His spirits slowly improved. Charles Greville, the aristocratic diarist, met him in Florence in 1830, and had long talks about the political crisis developing in Britain and his desire to visit Algiers to observe a French attack that was being planned against the city. Reflecting on their differing circumstances, Greville remarked on the profit of £100,000 Cochrane had made on his Greek bonds, and concluded wistfully after an al fresco dinner party in his garden, 'It is a pity he ever committed a robbery: he is such a fine fellow, and so shrewd and good humoured'.[1]

By 1830 the political scene in Britain had changed in Cochrane's favour. The fair-minded, if rough and ready, Duke of Clarence had become King, and the turmoil in the Commons was reaching its climax. In the early 1820s, it had looked as if the enlightened politics of William Huskisson at the Board of Trade and George Canning at the Foreign Office would usher in a new progressive style of Toryism, which could ride the rising tide of radical protest and middle-class impatience with outdated institutions. But by 1827, both were dead and the Tory government had returned to its former stance under the Duke of Wellington. Irrepressible protest forced him to repeal the Test Acts, which had restricted public office to Anglicans, and to enact Catholic Emancipation; but on reform of the Parliamentary system he refused to budge. Seizing their opportunity, the Whigs placed themselves at the head of the reform movement, courted middle-class opinion and forced a vote of confidence in November 1830. Betrayed by the Tory right in revenge for Catholic Emancipation and deserted by the left wing 'Canningites'; Wellington's government fell. The Whigs, under Lord Grey, took office and began to prepare the great Reform Bill, which would sweep away the political corruption and rotten boroughs against which Cochrane had so energetically campaigned. With his political allies and sympathisers in power, Cochrane returned to Britain with his family determined to restore his honour and position.

Cochrane's personal position also changed. In July 1831, his father died in Paris, and Cochrane was raised to the 10th Earl of Dundonald. His eldest son, Thomas, now became known as 'Lord Cochrane' (although for convenience this book will continue to describe the new Earl by his original and more familiar title). In terms of reversing the Stock Exchange verdict, however, things did not go smoothly. Henry Brougham, one of Cochrane's defence team at the trial, and now Lord Chancellor, warned him that he would have a fight on his hands. Opinion in the nation, the navy and the Cabinet was divided as to his innocence or guilt. Some felt strongly about the issue; but the majority probably shared the view of the Prime Minister, Lord Grey, who could not deny the evidence that there had been some involvement, but felt that Cochrane was more likely to have been the innocent dupe of his uncle than a major conspirator, and that it was wrong for his outstanding naval achievements to be ignored because of a financial peccadillo.

Cochrane maintained the pressure. Under its liberal editor John Delane, *The Times* was supportive, as were Brougham, Lord John Russell, Lord Lansdowne and Lord Auckland, the last a close friend, particularly – so it was rumoured – of Lady Cochrane. The Memorials were written and strings were pulled; Sir Francis Burdett raised parliamentary support; and Kitty was brought in to assist, securing a dramatic and tearful audience with the King at the Royal Pavilion in Brighton. In the end, the campaign proved irresistible and, in May 1832, the Privy Council granted Lord Cochrane a Royal Pardon and restored him to his original position in the Royal Navy List next to the Honourable George Dundas who had been promoted to captain on the same date in 1801. And as the escalator which was the Captain's List had now inexorably moved on, Cochrane found himself to be a Rear Admiral of the Blue! By its very nature, the Pardon gave no ringing endorsement of Cochrane's innocence in the Stock Exchange fraud, and merely served to draw a veil over the past. But it provided the springboard he now needed to press for the restoration of his Knighthood of the Bath.

Circumstances once more favoured Cochrane's campaign. Times had changed, and the accession of Queen Victoria to the throne in 1837 symbolised it. The rumbustious days of the Regency with its bucks and blades, prize fighters, cavalry sabres and lax morals were replaced by a new and more serious era of economists, steam engines, a civilian police force, family values and duty. At 62 years old, Cochrane was seen as one of the heroic survivors of the Napoleonic Wars; a man whose political struggles for Parliamentary reform had been vindicated; and a fighter in fashionable foreign struggles of liberation. There was a spate of literature to reinforce the image. In the late 1820s, three books appeared which touched on his activities in South America – Maria Graham's *Journal of a Residence in Chile*, John Miers' *Travels in Chile and La Plata* and William Bennet Stevenson's *Historical and Descriptive Narrative of 20 Years Residence in South America*. All three authors had been intimates of Cochrane, and each repeated the Admiral's highly partisan version of his activities. In the 1830s the novels *Frank Mildmay* and *Peter Simple* by Cochrane's former midshipman Frederick Marryat were published. Semi-autobiographical in nature, these books included detailed accounts of the operations of the *Imperieuse* and heroic descriptions of a thinly-disguised Captain Lord Cochrane.

Nor was Cochrane backward in broadcasting his own version of his career. Aided and abetted by William Jackson, between 1837 and 1857 he published a mass of pamphlets, petitions and memorials recording his services and listing his complaints against the governments of Britain, Chile and Brazil.[2] They included the genesis of his later autobiographies in an 1847 production called *Observations on Naval Affairs…including Instances of Injustice experienced by the Author*. Published as a small book, it provided a compendium account of the activities and grievances of his career to date, focusing on the Napoleonic Wars and the early Victorian period but touching also on his services in South America. They were to be refined and elaborated at length in the years to come. But for the first time the book revealed that Cochrane considered that the governments of Britain, Chile and Brazil owed him a total of £225,000!

The location of the adventures he describes may have been different, but whether set in Britain, Chile or Brazil, the underlying pattern was the same – namely, incredible deeds by the author followed by betrayal by subordinates and persecution by superiors. By the middle of the nineteenth century, Cochrane had outlived most of his British antagonists and evidence from South America was inaccessible, so there was no one to counteract his prejudices or cast doubt on his story. Not that anyone wanted to. The Victorian period was one of gross sentimentality, and the saga of the warrior hero performing prodigies of valour while being betrayed by lesser men – mostly foreigners – had deep appeal. Likewise, the Victorian admiration for the aristocracy and the cult of the gentleman were reaching new heights and – as everyone knew – a feature of both was an inability to speak anything but the truth. Thus, Cochrane's story was swallowed whole, even though in justifying himself Cochrane felt it necessary to remorselessly savage the reputations of his contemporaries both great and humble.

Queen Victoria and Prince Albert were as emotionally affected as anyone else by Cochrane's story of suffering. In 1841 he reached the rank of Vice Admiral and was given a pension for 'good and meritorious service'. And when the dismissal of the Tories and the arrival of a Whig government under Lord John Russell in 1846 gave Cochrane the opportunity to press his case once more, the Queen personally intervened and decided that the next vacancy in the Order of the Bath would be his.

It came the following year. He was actually promoted within the Order, becoming a Knight Grand Cross. Cochrane was able to wear his star and ribbon at the Queen's Birthday Drawing Room in St James's Palace on 27 May 1847, and in July he was formally installed in Westminster Abbey with the unfortunate son of Lord Chief Justice Ellenborough being prevailed upon by Prince Albert to act as his sponsor. Commenting on these events, Cochrane noted with satisfaction, 'Her Majesty has had a conversation with me as to the justice of some further atonement for the injuries that have been inflicted on me and...said it was a subject of regret that such was not in her power; but should the subject be entertained by her advisers, her concurrence would not be wanting.'[3] By 'further atonement', Cochrane meant being given Royal Navy back pay from 1814.

The First Lord of the Admiralty in the new Whig administration was Cochrane's friend and political sympathiser Lord Auckland. The major strategic preoccupation he inherited was the naval rivalry with France, which had already triggered a number of invasion scares and had been given urgency by a think-piece on naval doctrine written by the Prince de Joinville. Cochrane used the opportunity to resurrect the secret plan he had devised in 1811 to overwhelm French coastal fortresses with explosion vessels and poison gas. The result was the same: it was referred to a committee of experts who shelved it once more as being too risky and too ungentlemanly. Auckland had also taken over the challenge of developing steam and screw propulsion, and was faced with the question of how to make an effective fighting force by integrating line-of-battle ships, which had the fire power but were dependent on wind and tide, with small steam vessels, which carried few guns but were largely wind- and tide-proof. Auckland welcomed innovative thinking on both counts and respected Cochrane's ideas on both the development of steamships and the new tactics that would be required to use them.

Auckland was a great admirer of Cochrane's professional abilities and was convinced that he would hold high command if there was ever a war with France or, indeed, the United States which was emerging as a threat to Britain's possessions in the Caribbean. In January 1848 he appointed him commander-in-chief of the North America and West Indies station. Among the mountain of congratulatory letters upon his appointment was one from his predecessor on the station, Vice Admiral Sir Francis Austen, the eldest of Jane Austen's naval brothers. Austen had been an evangelical and a follower of Lord Gambier, so it was remarkable that his letter also expressed support for Cochrane over the Basque Roads affair and criticised his erstwhile patron for excessive caution.[4] In reporting the correspondence, Cochrane – who continued to dwell on the rights and wrongs of the long-forgotten business and was still accusing the Admiralty of falsifying charts and refusing access to them – mistakenly assumed that Austen had been present at the Basque Roads himself.

Cochrane's new command extended from the icy waters of Labrador in the north to the tropical forests of the Brazilian border in the south. But it was not a time of war and his force only consisted of his flagship, the two-decker *Wellesley*, and a dozen frigates, sloops and survey vessels. Even so, there was plenty for him to do. In addition to dealing with the squadron's normal administration, he had to see that it was deployed around the various trouble spots – protecting the Newfoundland fisheries, suppressing the Cuban slave trade, attempting to control the expansionist ambitions of the United States in the Caribbean, and generally defending British interests. For Cochrane to be able to walk a British quarterdeck and experience the familiar routines of the Royal Navy once more must have been a tonic for his spirits. His son Arthur came along as his flag-lieutenant, and was quickly promoted into the sloop *Sappho*. Under Cochrane's command the squadron was subjected to a more rigorous regime than in Austen's time with inspections and drills aimed at efficiency and battle readiness. But his egalitarian manner and his prohibition of flogging pleased the men, who referred to him as 'Dad' and were thrilled by stories of the old hero's exploits against the French and the Spanish.

Social and professional rehabilitation apart, the 1840s was a bad decade for Cochrane: as shall be discussed in the next chapter, his marriage was in difficulty and his children had numerous financial and personal problems, while his inventions were running into trouble and swallowing money. His three-year term as commander-in-chief enabled him to escape from his worries and to revive his intellectual curiosity and scientific interests. Nothing escaped his attention. With Auckland's encouragement he reported on a mass of issues – the collapse of the West Indian economy following the abolition of slavery; the location of military hospitals; the state of the fishing industry; the reorganisation of

Bermuda dockyards; the mines of Nova Scotia; the drainage of malarial swamps; and the destitution of the black population. But when Auckland died suddenly in December 1848 to be replaced by the less interested Sir Francis Baring, Cochrane turned to more personal areas of study such as the topography and geology of the Caribbean. His inventive flair was also stimulated by the sight of the great Trinidad pitch lake, and he began to devise schemes for the commercial use of bitumen.

Cochrane returned to Britain in 1851 to find the country basking in peace and prosperity, and showing its technical self-confidence and optimism for the future in a Great Exhibition in Hyde Park. But it was not to last. The Eastern Question loomed once more. The Tsar had always considered Turkey to be a Russian sphere of influence and had been poised to take advantage of the steady disintegration of the Ottoman Empire. In 1853, Russia invaded the Danube provinces and destroyed the Turkish fleet in the Black Sea. An ultimatum from Britain and France was ignored, and the following year the two powers declared war on Russia. Cochrane offered his services as commander of the Baltic Fleet in what was to be called the Crimean War. But his offer was declined. As the First Lord, Sir James Graham, explained in a note to the Queen, while Cochrane's zeal and ability could not be doubted, the government feared that his well-known impetuosity and disregard of orders might get them into trouble. 'Lord Dundonald is seventy nine years of age', he wrote,

> ...and although his energies and faculties are unbroken, and although, with his accustomed courage, he volunteers for the service, yet, on the whole, there is reason to apprehend that he might deeply commit the force under his command to some desperate enterprise, where the chance of success would not countervail the risk of failure and of the fatal consequences. Age has not abated the adventurous spirit of this gallant officer, which no authority could restrain; and being uncontrollable it might lead to most unfortunate results. The Cabinet, on the most careful review of the entire question, decided that the appointment of Lord Dundonald was not expedient.[5]

It was a disappointing response but an astonishing tribute to his vigour.

In fact there had been a misunderstanding. As he explained in a letter
to *The Times* on 10 March, Cochrane had offered his services in the Baltic
on the assumption that he would be permitted to implement his 'secret
plan' for chemical warfare – this time aimed not at the French but at the
Russian strongholds of Kronstadt and Sebastopol. He was uninterested in
a naval command on any other terms and, indeed, as he explained in a
letter to John Pascoe Grenfell – now a Brazilian Vice Admiral and Consul-
General in Liverpool – doubted whether the expedition had been
adequately mounted and whether he was physically up to the job.[6]
Nevertheless, in spite of the rebuff Cochrane began to exert pressure for
the revival of his 'secret war plan' for the reduction of enemy fortresses by
bombardment, smoke screens and poison gas. The idea, as Cochrane
explained in August 1854, was simple:

Red hot shot and missiles being now generally used in maritime
fortifications, it is manifest that attacking ships are infinitely more
endangered than formerly when cold shot were the only missiles.... To
avert this peril, it is proposed that iron vessels containing large masses of
combustible materials (bituminous coal or other matter) shall be kindled
at a proper distance to windward of the fortification or batteries to be
attacked so that dense vapours – more obscure than the darkest night –
shall conceal the ships from the batteries, until they arrive at a position
to (fire?).

If the assailing force, as there is great reason to believe, is still endangered
by incendiary missiles, sulphur vessels may be conducted to appropriate
positions, the fumes from which will expel artillery men from the
strongest casements, and drive them from their guns, wherever situated,
within a mile of the burning sulphur carried down by the breeze.

The works at Kronstadt are particularly exposed to this mode of
attack – being partly isolated and partly situated on a long sea wall
running in the usual course of the prevailing wind, whereby one or two
smoke and sulphur vessels would clear the whole range.[7]

The plans were dusted down and scrutinised as they had been in 1811 and
1846 by a high powered technical committee, this time consisting of the
veteran Admiral of the Fleet, Sir Byam Martin, Admiral Sir William

Parker, commander-in-chief Plymouth, Admiral Berkeley, a Lord of the Admiralty and General Sir John Burgoyne, Inspector General of Fortifications. The reaction was the same – flattering tributes to Cochrane's ingenuity, concern at the technical problems revealed by experts such as Professor Michael Faraday, and unease at the brutal aspects of what was being proposed.[8] Once more, it was shelved. When the disasters in the Crimea led to the fall of Lord Aberdeen's government in 1855, the new Prime Minister, Henry Palmerston, was sorely tempted to try Cochrane's plan, but eventually decided against it.

The debate over Cochrane's secret weapon was carried out in the strictest secrecy, but news inevitably leaked out. Indeed, in May 1855, *Punch* carried an enigmatic *Ode to Lord Dundonald* which began:

DUNDONALD, much neglected man
What is the nature of your plan,
the Russians to destroy
Whether balloon, or monster shell
I do not know I cannot tell
What agent to employ

It then went on to argue that the beastly behaviour of the Russians justified any response, and ended:

But if its sole demerit be
Its mischievous enormity
As I, indeed, have heard
For Mercy's sake, I say
Let us that scruple cast away
So empty and absurd

Is it a fact? We should inquire
Then – poison fumes or liquid fire –
Whatever be your plan
No measures with them let us keep,
But simply to perdition sweep
As many as we can.[9]

Cochrane had always been unhappy that he had received no more than a pardon for the Stock Exchange conviction, but successive governments had refused to reopen the case because of the passage of time. But his pleas of innocence were enhanced in the 1850s by a succession of legal biographies by leading Whig lawyers who, in passing, accused Lord Chief Justice Ellenborough of misleading the jury by asserting Cochrane's guilt in his summing-up. The most significant of these was Lord Justice Campbell's *Lives of the Chief Justices* published in the 1850s. As a lawyer, it was natural that Campbell would concentrate on procedural matters, but the fact that the conduct of the trial might have been flawed did not of course mean that Cochrane was innocent. Indeed, the weight of circumstantial evidence against him was so strong that it is by no means certain that the jury would have acquitted him even if Ellenborough had maintained studied neutrality. The resulting controversy was fuelled by accusations of legal incompetence, which Cochrane made against his legal team in his *Autobiography of a Seaman*. This led the *Law Magazine and Review* to mount a detailed study of the case in 1861, which concluded that,

...though Lord Cochrane took no part in the particular fraud of which de Berenger was the agent, yet he was probably aware that Cochrane-Johnstone was concocting some trick intended to effect their speculation in the funds. How far Lord Cochrane was cognisant of what was going on, and acquiesced in his uncle's scheme – whether Cochrane-Johnstone made him a confidant to any extent, found him a willing tool...or contrived artfully to fix a deeper stain of complicity upon him than was just – we do not pretend to determine. We wish we could come to another conclusion upon the evidence, and believe that Lord Cochrane was as entirely innocent as he so frequently and vehemently protested he was. It is repugnant to one's moral sense to associate mean trickery and pecuniary baseness with such personal chivalry and gallant qualities as Lord Cochrane possessed. We sympathise with the desire to prove that it is untrue that a man stamped with the true marks of nobility, genius and greatness has ever...sunk to petty aspirations and ambiguous dealing... Yet history, experience, and even the consideration of the nature of the human mind, forbid us to deny the possibility, even the high probability, of such a conflict of character and repugnant conduct.[10]

The continuing debate was not helped by Cochrane's insistence of his integrity and his refusal to offer any explanation. But Henry Brougham, who had been one of his defence team, hinted on more than one occasion that Cochrane had probably known about the fraud but had not blown the whistle on his clearly guilty uncle out of family loyalty. It was a view that later letters between Cochrane-Johnson's daughter and Cochrane seem to support. Notably too, relatives such as Sir Alexander Cochrane maintained a studied silence over the affair. But whatever the rights and wrongs of the matter, it triggered a series of printed accusations and counter accusations between the descendants of Cochrane and Ellenborough that lasted well into the twentieth century.[11]

In naval matters Cochrane's career continued to flourish. He was already the recipient of a host of British and foreign decorations and, in 1857, the Chileans restored him to the rank of Admiral on full pay. In Britain, articles on his career were featured in the newspapers; he reached the rank of Admiral of the Red in the Royal Navy; was nominated by the Prince Regent as an Elder Brother of Trinity House; and appointed to the honorific post of Rear Admiral of England. By the late 1850s, Cochrane had not only achieved full rehabilitation – he had become a national institution.

CHAPTER TWENTY

Family and Inventions

WHEN COCHRANE AND KITTY returned to London after twelve years of overseas wandering, they bought Hanover Lodge, a large, square, white-stuccoed villa in Regents Park, as their main residence. It was there in 1832, after Cochrane's reinstatement in the navy that Kitty celebrated in typical style by organising a sumptuous reception, buffet dinner and dance (with illuminated garden) which lasted from 3 p.m. to midnight and was attended by a glittering throng of guests which included one Prince, one Marquis, three Dukes, ten Earls and innumerable knights and lesser grandees. Kitty adored parties and managed to persuade herself that they were necessary parts of Cochrane's campaign for social rehabilitation. United at last and living together in England, their family comprised three sons and one daughter – Thomas, aged 18, who was about to be launched on a military career, Horace, aged 14, who was at Eton and later to go to Sandhurst, Lizzie, aged 10, and Arthur, aged 8, who was at Westminster School. A fourth son – named in typical style after Cochrane's current political hero as Ernest Grey Lampton – was born in 1834.

Cochrane was not interested in the social whirl that Kitty so obviously enjoyed, and while he waited for his campaign for the restoration of honours to gather momentum, he concentrated on his inventions. Even before his return to London, he had begun working out solutions to the boiler and pressure problems he had encountered in the *Rising Star* and had been corresponding with a number of engineering firms on the subject of rotary stream engines for steamships.[1] Now in London, he patented another idea – a process for using compressed air in underground excavations – which was to solve problems being encountered by the engineers who were tunnelling under the Thames at

Rotherhithe and also under the Hudson River in the United States.[2] In 1834, he turned his attention to the design of a steam locomotive which would have a smooth enough transmission system to enable it to pass over the viaducts of the London and Greenwich Railway without shaking them to pieces. Cochrane warned the railway company that modifications to both track and carriages would be needed; but they were never made and the initiative ended in disappointment and legal disputes.

By the end of the 1830s, however, relations between Cochrane and his wife had reached crisis point. Kitty resented his preoccupation with inventions and the way they were eating up money. Cochrane, for his part, was impatient with her socialising, annoyed by the cavalier way she spent money and by the steep rise in her entertainment budget. For Kitty, the glamour of marriage to a romantic hero 20 years her senior was rapidly eroded by the realities of permanently living with him. In 1839, they decided to separate, Kitty moving to Boulogne with a generous financial settlement made up of French Bonds purchased with the three-fold profits made by the Greek stock that Cochrane had bought with his pay of £37,000. They would never live together again, and on Kitty's infrequent visits to London she kept her distance, staying in expensive Mayfair while Cochrane made do with modest Pimlico.

Cochrane's family problems did not end there. To his alarm his eldest children seemed to be going off the rails. It may have been due to the insecurity of their early lives as they were moved continuously from place to place, or to the fact that their father was physically absent from 1821 to 1829 – except for the 12-month interlude following his return from Brazil in 1825 – but all were having difficulties in adulthood. Thomas, who returned from service in Canada in 1836 as an officer in the 66th of Foot, was in financial trouble, obtaining money on false pretences, drawing bills under false names, and borrowing at vast interest from a money-lender called Kelly to whom he quickly worked up a debt to the sum of £5000. Cochrane offered Kelly terms for a settlement and in 1842 made arrangements to get Thomas out of the way and sent on a five-year posting as Assistant Quartermaster General in Hong Kong. Horace's position was worse. He had made a good start serving with the 92nd Regiment in Malta, but on his return in 1841 he had gone rapidly downhill. Addicted to gambling, and living a life of total extravagance, he too had borrowed from Kelly, had been forced to resign his commission, and was living under an assumed name to escape his creditors. Lizzie had – against all advice – contracted a marriage in 1840, of which neither family approved, with one John Fleming of Stoneham Park, Hertfordshire. Only Arthur, who entered the navy as a midshipman in 1841, seemed to stick to the straight and narrow path of prudence and responsibility. Cochrane recognised this, advised total abstinence from drink and tobacco in his letters and warned the 17-year-old that the ruination of his brothers meant that he was the family's only hope!

Hanover Lodge had to be sold – at a loss – and Cochrane moved into bachelor accommodation in unfashionable Victoria Square, Pimlico. As a relief from his family worries he buried himself in his inventions, working on a new design for the screw propeller, developing his rotary engine and high pressure boilers, and expounding a novel design theory for steamships based on a series of interlocking parabolic curves to minimise underwater resistance. He had also concluded that the advent of steam required drastic changes in traditional naval tactics. Steam power was clearly not yet reliable or efficient enough to power the fleet's heavy line-of-battle ships, although he argued that this was a priority in the long term. What was needed in the short term was what he called a 'mosquito fleet' of small steamships armed with a few heavy guns. 'Give me a good fast steamer', he wrote, 'with a heavy long range gun in the bow and another in the hold to fall back on, and I would not hesitate to attack the largest ship afloat'.[3] Parliament was ready to listen to his ideas. Contrary to popular legend, the Admiralty was not resisting the advent of steam in order to protect its superiority in wooden battleships, but was actively seeking to solve the technical problems encountered by steam-powered vessels. Sir George Cockburn, First Naval Lord in the Tory government of 1841 to 1846 – who dominated the thinking of his department and of his political chief, First Lord of the Admiralty Lord Haddington – had begun to realise that large ships need less power per ton that small ones, and that many of the problems encountered in the 1830s, when the average steamer was of less than 450 tons and 95 horsepower, were due to the fact that the ships were too small. The result was that ships increased sharply in size. The launch in 1843 of the steam paddle frigate *Retribution*, of 1641 tons and 800 horsepower, was the shape of things to come.[4]

Cockburn also wanted to encourage experimentation, and invited the two leading exponents of steam power, Lord Cochrane and Sir Charles Napier – both political opponents - to submit designs. The result was that between 1844 and 1846 the navy built two experimental paddle steamers to their specifications: HMS *Janus*, of 763 tons and 200 horsepower, to Cochrane's; and HMS *Sidon*, of 1316 tons and 560 horsepower to Napier's. Cochrane devoted much time and money to the project, and there were encouraging reports of his engine's performance.[5] But in any experiments there are winners and losers. Napier won, and Cochrane lost. *Janus's* final trials in 1847 were a disaster, due, so Cochrane claimed, to shoddy work by the manufacturer. The vessel's draught had been miscalculated and the engine blew up. But there was more to it than that. The experimentation of the 1840s had suggested that screw propulsion was the thing of the future and the tug-of-war between the paddle steamer *Alecto* and the screw-powered *Rattler* in April 1845 had confirmed it. Indeed, in 1846 the first scew frigate *Amphion* and the first screw line-of-battle ships *Ajax* and *Blenheim* had been launched. Cochrane's design was obsolete. Inevitably he claimed that the Admiralty's refusal to go any further with his design was due to political intrigue.[6]

By the late 1840s Cochrane was taking pleasure in his reinstatement in the Order of the Bath, basking in royal favour, and enjoying a slight improvement in his family circumstances. His eldest son and heir, Thomas, returned from Hong Kong a changed man, married Louisa, the daughter of the wealthy head of the clan McKinnan, and settled down to become a responsible and sober citizen. The naval career of the conscientious Arthur continued to prosper in the Mediterranean and South America stations, and he had been joined in the service by his younger brother, Ernest. Horace, unfortunately, remained incorrigible, piling up debts, unable to hold down a job, and hiding from his creditors. Lizzie had also thrown discretion to the wind and had deserted her husband to run off abroad with another man. John Fleming, however, seemed relieved, and even settled £600 on her on the sole condition she did not come back!

Cochrane's appointment as commander-in-chief of the North America and West India station provided a three-year respite from his family woes.

In 1851 he was back in England. Having no residence of his own, he lived first with his brother William in Albany Street, then took lodgings at 12 Bedford Road. Little had changed during his absence. Horace's financial ruin was complete and he was living in Holland to avoid the repayment of debts, which now totalled £8000. Lizzie was in Florence, shunned by respectable society and allegedly being involved with a series of men. Thomas remained a solid citizen, keeping aloof from the family tumult by living in Auchintoul House in distant Banff. Arthur and Ernest prospered in their naval careers, the first commanding the steam sloop *Niger* in the Far East, the second on the North America station. They both served with distinction in the Crimean War. Kitty remained in France enjoying – as far as she could – a glittering social round in company with a distant relation, the Duc de Gramont, in Paris, Cannes and then Rome after the Duke became French Ambassador there.

Cochrane paid his wife a visit in 1854, when they went together to pay their respects to Prince Albert who was visiting Napoleon III and the Empress Eugene in a chateau near Boulogne. Cochrane was almost 80 years old and Kitty claimed that she had to help the old man to dress, to cut his nails, clean up his red ribbon and his clothes, and generally make him respectable. From then on she depicted Cochrane as a 'dotard' whose physical and mental powers were in decline and whose scientific pursuits with pitch and engines were ruining the family. Cochrane for his part maintained a dignified silence, refusing to criticise either his wife's behaviour or her extravagance. Kitty had no such inhibitions. For years she had been writing letters which demanded money and sowed dissension in the family. Now they took on an even more strident tone. She lambasted Cochrane for bad investments; denounced the character of his advisers, notably Jackson; and sneered at him for carrying on an unseemly relationship with his housekeeper.

Cochrane was ageing and was certainly deaf, but there was no sign of any diminution in mental vigour or curiosity. In 1852, he produced his exhaustive *Notes on Mineralogy, Government and Condition of the British West Indian Islands and the North American Maritime Colonies.* Between 1854 and 1856 he was busily pressing his 'secret war plan' on the Cabinet for use in the Crimea. Work on inventions also continued apace. The Admiralty may have rejected his engines and boilers, but civilian lines were interested, and a French company decided to place his machines in three of its ships. Likewise, inspired by what he had seen in the Trinidad pitch lake, he began to develop his ideas for the use of bitumen as a surface for roads, as a way of insulating cables and pipes, as a waterproof lining for tunnels and canals and as part of a visionary scheme to build an embankment along the Thames. Profits from the bitumen process and from a new plough designed to dig trenches were settled on Horace who, in 1852, was sent to New York to take out the appropriate patents. The benefits of most of his other inventions were given to Thomas.

Not only did these inventions take up much of Cochrane's time, they also, to Kitty's annoyance, began to swallow up his income, already reduced by the allowances he was paying to his children and their debtors. Writing to her son Arthur, she begged him never to 'imbue your hands in that hateful pitch and dirt'. She went on,

> For forty years and more, I have been your father's wife and I have seen two noble fortunes spent and not one penny of money *ever returned*: £10,000 lost in Lamp concerns, nearly as much in copper rolling machinery, then came the fatal *Janus* of ruined memory and now these dreadful pitch affairs. Oh Arthur, it is fearful – to say nothing of £70,000 spent in two elections in younger days, our little place sold at Holly Hill for which he paid £13,600 was sold for £8,000. The house at Hanover Lodge cost £16,000 besides £5000 laid out in it, was sold to pay for the outlays of that hateful *Janus*.

Some of Kitty's criticisms of her husband may have been excessive, but some had a strong ring of truth, as when she concluded her letter to Arthur with the exclamation:

> Look at the result – see what wretchedness this most fearful and most unprofitable line of life has led to! I do not believe a more miserable man breathes upon earth, dissatisfied with himself and everybody else, he moans over the years that are past in perfect uselessness, money squandered [and] without any real friends or supporters he is left to end a life that might have been the brightest that mortal man ever had a chance of possessing.[7]

In 1855, as Cochrane passed into his eighties, the *Illustrated Times* described him as,

> ...a broad-built Scotsman, rather seared than conquered by age, with hair of snowy white, and a face in which intellect still beams through traces of struggle and sorrow, and the marks of eighty years of active life. A slight stoop takes away from a height that is almost commanding. Add to these a vision of good old-fashioned courtesy colouring the whole man, his gestures and speech, and you have some idea of the Earl of Dundonald in the present year of 1855.[8]

Lord Cochrane was not finished yet. Indeed, he was about to throw his efforts into the production of four volumes of detailed and contentious autobiography. This was to be the climax of a 20-year campaign designed to demonstrate that he had been right in all his innumerable quarrels and that the governments of Britain, Chile and Brazil owed him vast sums of money. It was also written to ensure that the last word on his long and controversial career would be his.

CHAPTER TWENTY-ONE

Settling Accounts

A FIXATION WITH MONEY was one of the most consistent features of Cochrane's reputation and, indeed, performance during his lifetime. Prize money was a major motivating factor for all naval officers and Cochrane's interest in it was not unusual; but it went further than that. In Chile and Greece his haggling over pay was remorseless and, in Brazil, it was dishonest. In Peru he rapidly acquired the nickname 'el metálico Lord'; in Pernambuco the rebels assumed that the best way to secure his loyalty was by a bribe; and in 1846, when the British Cabinet was persuaded to re-examine his 'secret war plans', their initial reaction was to ask what 'remuneration' he expected. But his desire to increase his income was balanced by an inability to control his expenditure. Cochrane received huge sums of pay and prize money in Britain, South America and Greece, but most of it slipped through his fingers.

When Cochrane returned to London following the Greece campaign in 1831, he was a comparatively rich man who was well able to afford the £21,000 needed to buy and renovate Hanover Lodge. For the first few years, he aimed to live on no more than £4000 a year, £455 of which came from his half pay as a rear admiral, the rest from investments. His accounts show that he was able to manage this, although the special allowance he was paying to Kitty steadily increased until it reached £750 a year.

The first of Cochrane's financial problems arrived when various South American chickens came home to roost. First he was sued by his Brazilian agents May & Ludkin, then he was taken to court by William Hoseason and Henry Dean who claimed that he owed them £10,000 each.[1] Prize-taking was a risky business, and commanders were liable for damages if they made seizures later ruled illegal. For Cochrane, the blockades he had operated in Peru and Brazil had broken the fundamental principle that the ships of the blockading squadron must be numerous enough for the task, and be present in greater force than the enemy. As a result Cochrane found himself being sued by the owners of the French and British merchant ships he had seized in both theatres. According to him, adverse judgements in these actions cost him £14,000.[2] His financial situation was further weakened by the terms of the separation agreement with Kitty by which he paid her £100,000 in French bonds. Then, there were the debts of his sons to be paid off, and the development costs of his inventions, including those of the *Janus* which soaked up at least £25,000.[3]

As Cochrane's financial situation deteriorated, so he began to look round for other sources of money. In 1839, he put in a claim for £4000 being the half-pay he should have been paid in the Royal Navy between 1814 and 1832, disregarding the fact that he had been earning vast sums while serving other countries during this period. But to Cochrane the logic was inescapable: he had suffered financially and psychologically as a result of the Stock Exchange conviction, and now that it had been proved to be unjust, he expected full restitution of what he had lost. Indeed, in reply to the Cabinet's question in 1846 about what price he had in mind for his secret war plan, he said that he wanted nothing but hinted menacingly that he expected compensation for the 'collateral deprivations and losses' he had suffered. In the event, he only asked for repayment of the £1000 fine, but he certainly toyed with the idea of reclaiming the total cost of the trial plus compensation of £40,000 for a lost legacy from Uncle Basil Cochrane and £50,000 for the loss of the Culross Estate![4]

Once Cochrane realised that there was little chance of getting more out of the British Government, he pinned his hopes on South America and on the huge debts which, he was convinced, were owed to him by Chile and Brazil. In actual fact, he left Chile with the whole of his pay and a substantial amount of prize money. But behind him he had left two acknowledged debts – the balance on his accounts for the Peruvian campaign which he estimated to be $66,000 (or £13,200), and his share of the *Esmeralda* prize money. Cochrane had been pursuing these claims in a desultory way through a local agent called Caldclough, but in 1837 he initiated a more concentrated campaign by producing a *Petition to the President and Congress of Chile*, which described his services during the war

of independence and detailed his financial claims. Two years later, Foreign
Secretary Lord Aberdeen was prevailed upon to order the British Consul-
General in Santiago, Colonel John Walpole, to exert pressure on
Cochrane's behalf; and in the early 1840s, Arthur, then serving with the
navy's South America squadron, was sent a power of attorney and told to
add his weight.

They were actually pushing on a half-open door. The Chilean
Government had put money aside in anticipation of such a claim,
although nothing had been possible at an earlier date because of
Cochrane's refusal to answer the audit queries on the squadron's
accounts.[5] As soon as he agreed to do so – and the size of the balance was
reduced accordingly – the Chileans offered him £6000 in settlement.
Walpole, who had seen all the figures and arguments, thought the sum
'not unreasonable'. Cochrane indignantly rejected it and in 1845
produced a second memorial. He had been busy elaborating his claims,
which had now risen to $297,000 (or £60,000), but this time the claims
had nothing to do with real debts. Cochrane had managed to convince
himself that his emoluments as Vice Admiral of Chile were only designed
to covered his routine duties, and that bonuses were payable for 'extra-
official services' – that is, for doing anything else. On the basis of this novel
idea, he now demanded a series of additional payments: $50,000 for
taking Valdivia (without orders), $30,000 for leading the attack on
Esmeralda in person, $10,000 for refusing San Martin's offer to lead the
Peruvian navy, $30,000 for raiding the coast of Peru during the blockade
and for chasing *Venganza* and *Prueba*, plus, of course, 21 years' half-pay at
$3000 a year.[6] The Chileans remained tactfully silent in the face of these
shameless demands and it was not until 1852 that Cochrane saw sense and
accepted the money on offer.

Next, Cochrane set his sights on Brazil. In 1847 he appointed the
Liverpool firm of Bramley Moore & Co. and its Rio subsidiary, James
Moore & Co., to act as his agent, and began his campaign with a *Petition
to the Emperor Pedro II*. The negotations went quiet while Cochrane served
his time on the North America and West India station. With a Vice
Admiral's annual pay and allowances of £2550, the proceeds of 'freight' –
that is, money – transported by the squadron, and a useful legacy of
£3000, his finances improved. But the costs of developing the bitumen

process on his return once more put his bank balance under strain.[7] Cochrane and his assistants dusted down his Brazilian claims and began to bombard the Imperial government with memorials and petitions detailing his financial demands. They were originally comparatively simple – 30 years' half-pay and a one-eighth share of the prize money payments agreed on 12 February 1824. Since the final tally of vessels captured was calculated at 126, worth 2000 contos, his share would have been 250 contos, or £28,000 at the current rate of exchange. Cochrane of course disregarded the huge amounts of prize money he had already been paid. In March 1854, a new round of lobbying began with the production of a detailed *Description of Services*, followed a year later by a *Memorial to the Legislature of Brazil* and a second *Petition to the Emperor*, both supplemented with an annex of quotations from selected documents. John Pascoe Grenfell in Liverpool gave invaluable advice on tactics and helped with translations.[8] These documents included a detailed account of Cochrane's operations during the war of independence and in the pacification of the northern provinces. They also enumerated his financial claims. Yet again Cochrane resorted to deception. In 1825, he had justified his leaving the Brazilian navy by quoting the decree of 28 February 1824, which had limited his services to the duration of the war. Now he claimed that the London agent, Manuel Gameiro Pessoa, had effectively dismissed him and invoked the decree of 27 July 1824 which had authorised him to remain in the service until he chose to resign and retire on half pay. And since he had never actually resigned but had been illegally dismissed – so he now argued – he was entitled to 31 years' *full* pay, a total of £70,000![9]

Cochrane's account of his operations in Brazil arrived just in time for the debate on the subject in the Senate scheduled for 26, 27 and 28 July 1855. It had enormous impact. The Brazilians were impressed, but refused to swallow the dismissal story. Nevertheless, in the middle of August, James Moore were able to report that the government had accepted his claim in principle, and had agreed to pay Cochrane the small amount still owing on his salary and a half-pay pension for the 30 years since 1825. However, not all the news was good. There had been no mention of interest on Cochrane's back pension, and it looked as if payment would be made at the current rate of exchange and not that agreed in 1823.[10]

Cochrane reacted in anger. Not only would a settlement on these terms reduce the payments to a quarter of what he had in mind, but a Ministry of Marine report submitted during the debate had contained criticisms of his behaviour. He and his supporters returned to the attack. In June 1856 a new 'Exposition' was on its way to Rio followed by a third Petition to the Emperor, this time delivered personally by the incoming British Minister, Mr Scarlett. In it, Cochrane referred mildly to his bid for full pay, but concentrated his arguments on the question of exchange rates. He pointed out that his letter of appointment had explicitly stated that he was to receive 'the same emoluments he had received when in Chile'. His interpretation of this was that any payments should be calculated in strong Chilean pesos rather than weak Brazilian milreis which had fallen in value heavily since the 1820s.

Emperor Pedro gave the judgement of Solomon and eventually agreed that the Admiral should receive his 30 years' half pay, but that it should be converted at the advantageous Chilean rate. The implementation of the decision was delayed due to an outbreak of yellow fever, which sent the population of Rio de Janeiro heading for the hills, but on 23 February 1857, James Moore and Co. triumphantly remitted bills of exchange to Lord Cochrane worth £34,000, being the whole of his back-pay plus half-pay calculated at $6000 a year. From that date until he died, the Admiral received a payment of £310 promptly every quarter; and his widow, Kitty, Lady Dundonald, continued to receive it until she died in Boulogne five years later.

The prize money issue was more difficult. The Brazilian Government had taken the initiative in 1855 by voting 250 contos to settle outstanding claims from the independence campaign. Under new regulations, Cochrane was entitled to a fifth of this as commander-in-chief. But it was years before the Brazilians could sort out the complications, and by this time Cochrane had elaborated his claims. He insisted, for example, that he had been awarded an estate in Maranhão to match his title, which had then been confiscated; that the £2000 he had given to Gameiro Pessoa in London to pay off the *Piranga* had been a loan, and that the Emperor had promised in 1823 to pay the $66,000 owed by Chile for the balance on his acounts.[11] There was not a scrap of truth in any of these claims. Indeed many of them had never appeared before 1859. The Brazilians were not convinced, but in 1865 they agreed to settle Cochrane's prize claims by awarding him 84 contos, or £9450 at the going rate of exchange. Alas, the judgement came too late to benefit Lord Cochrane who had died five years previously; and both the money and the fight to get more was inherited by his son, Thomas Barnes Cochrane, 11th Earl of Dundonald, who returned to the offensive in true Cochrane style. In 1874 the Brazilians, anxious to arrive at a settlement lest the embarrassing dispute dragged on for another 30 years, decided to go to international arbitration. The findings of the arbitrators were unanimous.[12] They found no evidence of 'harsh and cruel' treatment as Dundonald claimed, and confirmed that Lord Cochrane had been treated with 'indulgence and generosity' throughout. They agreed with Cochrane's estimates of the prize money due under the 10 February agreement, and recommended an award of £46,000. The Brazilian Government accepted the judgement and, having made an adjustment for monies already handed over, in December 1874, honourably paid Dundonald £40,298 5s 9d in final settlement.[13]

In 1855, with a mass of documents at his disposal, a team of eager confederates and the bones of his story already available in a mass of petitions and memorials, Cochrane decided to write the story of his life in the way he wanted it remembered. The first two books appeared in 1859 under the title *Narrative of Services in the Liberation of Chile, Peru and Brazil*. They were joined the following year by the *Autobiography of a Seaman* which recounted, in two further volumes, his adventures and feuds during the Napoleonic Wars. Cochrane never wrote an account of his adventures in Greece, but they were described in 1869, when the 11th Earl of Dundonald produced a two-volume *Life of Lord Cochrane* which completed his father's story and covered his subsequent campaigns for rehabilitation in England.

Cochrane was 84 years old when the two *Narrative of Services* were published, and although he had contributed half-remembered reminiscences, they were really the work of a professional author called G. P. Earp, aided and abetted by William Jackson. Earp later declared that his method of working was to write the story from documents, then to refer the text to Lord Cochrane for his reactions and corrections. This apparent objectivity was compromised by a second declared purpose, namely to vindicate Cochrane, to prove that he had been right in his every one of his quarrels, and to justify his financial claims. Indeed, Earp was promised a percentage of any payments the book might stimulate. It is therefore hardly surprising to find that these autobiographies are filled with inaccuracies and present a travesty of the truth.

The quality of the books varies considerably. *The Autobiography of a Seaman* is the best. When Earp wrote it, he had plenty of books, newspaper accounts, parliamentary reports and memoirs on which to draw, as well as masses of Cochrane's own papers. Despite the obvious bias, the books are colourful, detailed and atmospheric. When he came to write the Chilean volume of *Narrative of Services*, Earp had a much greater problem. Material from Chilean and Peruvian sources in South America was inaccessible and much was in Spanish. As a result, he was forced to rely on what Jackson chose to provide from Cochrane's extensive archives. On the positive side, Earp had access to the books already published by Maria Graham, John Miers and William Bennet Stevenson, and this enabled him to get the framework of events more or less correct. But in terms of balance, all three sources were blatantly partisan and, rather than help to correct the old Admiral's distorted and even paranoid memories of events, they reinforced them. The Brazilian volume of the *Narrative of Services* posed the greatest challenge. Here – apart from Maria Graham's memoirs, which only covered a six-month period in 1823 – there were no books or background material. Earp had to rely exclusively on Jackson's highly inaccurate diary, a handful of carefully chosen documents, and Cochrane's vivdly recalled grievances. It is small wonder that this volume is the most unreliable of all. There are glaring errors as to dates and geography and an excessive concentration on his financial transactions; documents which did not support his claims are deliberately omitted; his achievements are quite unnecessarily exaggerated; and many of the complaints were thought up well after the event.

Cochrane's books were read avidly and uncritically in Britain. The dramatic quality of his story, the nobility of the causes for which he fought and, indeed, the element of betrayal by lesser men, confirmed Cochrane as the archetypal Victorian warrior-hero. They have also provided easily accessible material for innumerable biographies. Even up to the present day, Cochrane's blatantly prejudiced version of his life has been repeated by biographers again and again. Inevitably too, the Cochrane story has stimulated a host of supporting legends and myths, such as the story that Napoleon had referred to Cochrane as 'the Sea Wolf' and that, in the Pacific, his fearful enemies had called him 'El Diablo'. There is no evidence for either claim. Likewise, loose words from Kitty resulted in a ridiculous fable that Cochrane actually planned to rescue Napoleon from St Helena and crown him as Emperor of South America!

Lord Cochrane spent the last years of his life in the home of his son and heir Thomas, at Queen's Gate, Kensington. In October 1860, he underwent an operation for the stone and died, just short of his 85th birthday. He was buried on 14 November with all the elaborate ceremonial of a Victorian funeral – an ornate hearse drawn by six black, plumed horses, eight carriages of mourners, silent crowds lining the route of the procession, and the press filled with eulogies. Repeating faithfully the Cochrane version, *The Times* lamented:

One of the great characters of the past generation has just departed. After attaining to an age beyond man's ordinary lot; after outliving envy, obloquy and malice, after suffering much, doing more, and triumphing at last, Lord DUNDONALD has closed in peace and honour the days of his eventful life. History can produce few examples either of such a man or of such achievements. There have been greater heroes because there have been heroes with greater opportunities, but no soldier or sailor of modern times ever displayed a more extraordinary capacity than the man who now lies dead. He not only never knew fear, but he never knew perplexity, and was invariable found master of the circumstances in which he was placed. Nothing can exceed the audacity of his designs or the singularity of his successes although, owing to the jealousy or spite of his superiors, his exploits were usually confined to spheres comparatively unimportant or remote. We need be at no pains to recapitulate the incidents of his wonderful career. Lord DUNDONALD had told the story of his own life so recently and so well, and we have since repeated it...fully in our columns.[14]

As befitted a giant of the age and one of the great names of the

Napoleonic Wars, Cochrane was laid to rest in Westminster Abbey before a distinguished civil and naval congregation which included the Chilean and Brazilian ambassadors, Henry Brougham, his comrade in the Basque Roads, Admiral Sir George Seymour, and his loyal follower in the South American Wars, Admiral John Pascoe Grenfell of the Brazilian navy. The memorial on his tomb was adorned with the arms of Brazil, Chile, Peru and Greece, listed his titles and summarised the features of his astonishing career:

Here rests in his 85th year
Thomas Cochrane
Tenth Earl of Dundonald
Baron Cochrane of Dundonald
Of Paisley and Ochiltree
In the Peerage of Scotland
Marquess of Maranham in the
Empire of Brazil
GCB and Admiral of the Fleet
who by the confidence which his genius
his science and his extraordinary daring
inspired, by his heroic exertions in the
cause of freedom and his splendid
services alike to his own country
Greece Brazil Chili and Peru
Achieved a name illustrious throughout
the world for courage patriotism
and chivalry

It was appropriate that even in death the description on the tombstone exaggerated his achievements, referring to him as Admiral of the Fleet, a rank he never achieved. Cochrane would have approved of that.

CHAPTER TWENTY-TWO

Epilogue

LORD COCHRANE was undoubtedly a great man. By the time of his death, he had acquired legendary status on account of his accomplishments during the Napoleonic Wars and the liberation struggles in South America and Greece. In charge of a single ship with an independent remit, Cochrane was indomitable. The challenges of keeping a coast in uproar by amphibious landings and sudden raids from the sea as in Catalonia or Peru, subduing isolated ports such as Port Vendres or São Luis, attacking strongholds such as Valdivia or Callao, or defending others such as Rosas were ideally suited to his tactical flair and ingenuity. They also showed his courage and extraordinary powers of personal leadership. In later life when he was in command of whole squadrons, he was less comfortable, so much so that in Chile and Brazil he often preferred to act with his flagship alone. Commanding a fleet, enforcing a blockade or escorting a convoy made him bored and impatient, and the weight of responsibility depressed his spirits, leaving him stressed and irascible.

Cochrane was a master of tactics, but not of strategy. His idea that the French effort in the Peninsular War would have been crippled had he been deployed to harry the highway to Spain was fanciful at best. In South America, he failed spectacularly to understand either the strategic situation in Peru or the realities of a post-independent Brazil. As a result, his assessment of San Martin was way off the mark and his criticism of his military objectives was misconceived. His understanding of the politics of Brazil was crude to the point of caricature. For an experienced naval commander, he also seemed strangely insensitive to the risks involved in prize-taking and, in South America, seized merchant ships with reckless abandon. He paid the price when he was subsequently sued for damages by irate owners and faced with a number of expensive adverse judgements. Likewise, the single-minded energy that made Cochrane such an asset in wartime turned him into a quarrelsome nuisance in peace. Seeing the world in terms of black and white, the subtleties of political reality were beyond him and the intuitive genius and superb planning which marked his conduct at sea were replaced by a series of catastrophic misjudgements.

Cochrane saw humanity in the same simplistic terms. There were no half measures: people were either friends or enemies. To be classified as an enemy was not difficult – all a person had to do was to express contrary views, offer criticism or oppose his wishes, especially when they involved money. And once a person had been so identified, there was no remission. Cochrane was remorseless in pursuing supposed enemies and in using his autobiographies to eternally tarnish the memories of otherwise hard-working and dedicated people who were unfortunate enough to incur his displeasure. The reputations of great men such as St Vincent and San Martin were strong enough to be impervious to these accusations, but those of lesser-known adversaries such as Zenteno, Villela Barbosa, Croker and Guise were not.

Both heredity and environment played their part in the formation of Cochrane's contradictory personality. As the child of social privilege, and one who had never been subjected to the constraints of formal education, it is not surprising that Cochrane emerged an individualist and a loner. He had few friends and was not a sociable or 'clubbable' man, as he told the United Services Club in the 1850s when it offered him membership. He was never comfortable amid the camaraderie of the wardroom of a ship-of-war – unless, as in his early days, it was filled with relatives. His background and boundless self-confidence turned him into a natural leader, but it also made him an impossible subordinate. His failures of judgement with Lord Gambier over the Basque Roads, with San Martin in Peru, and with Lima e Silva at the siege of Recife – were all rooted in his unease at being under command. It also led to a life-long reputation for insubordination. From his earliest years in *Barfleur* and *Speedy* to the time of the Crimean War he developed a tendency for disregarding orders and embarking on schemes of his own. The results were sometimes spectacularly successful – as in Valdivia or Maranhão – but it made his superiors uneasy. Arrogance and self-righteousness were never far from the surface. His tendency to lecture everyone, from heads of state down, can hardly have been endearing. And whether justified or not, Cochrane had a high opinion of his abilities and seemed to expect privileged treatment. He was uninterested in humdrum but important naval chores such as convoy work or the protection of Britain's vital whale fisheries, and was resentful if he was not employed in front-line campaigns or on destructive, but lucrative, commerce raiding expeditions.

By any standard, Cochrane's career was brilliantly successful. He was a master of naval warfare, the scourge of the French, the liberator of South America, a talented inventor, and a fearless fighter for radical causes. But he was not a happy man, and the older he got, the more bitter he became. The personal trials and tribulations he suffered as a result of his estrangement from an increasingly acerbic Kitty and the feckless and dishonourable behaviour of his children had something to do with this. Much of it was due to his own insecure and troubled personality. Here again, his upbringing left its mark. The death of his mother and the indifference of his father left him hungry for recognition and reassurance. He was quick to attribute the lack of continual congratulations from an Admiralty replete with naval victories as a sign of hostility. Regarding politicians with cynicism and deeply mistrustful of the Establishment, he was convinced that he was naturally surrounded by betrayal and double-dealing and ignored all evidence to the contrary. The Admiralty, for example, openly recognised his talents and kept him fully employed, often in areas filled with opportunities for glory and prize-taking. Yet he persuaded himself that it was hostile and full of enemies. In South America, where he was awarded both the highest honours and substantial amounts of money, he still became obsessed with supposed ingratitude and poor treatment. He paid the politicians back in kind, even resorting to deception in his dealings over pay and prize money. And he brooded. The supposed injustices he had suffered – notably relating to the Stock Exchange affair – rankled with him for years. Indeed, he appeared to enjoy the role of the betrayed and persecuted hero. In public he seemed incapable of admitting mistakes, but in private he was excessively self-critical, and supposed failure – as in the *King George* affair or the campaigns off Callao and in Greece – threw him into deep depressions.

Cochrane's personality was filled with contradictions. In private life, or at ease with his friends or trusted subordinates, he was amiable, modest, affable and courteous. His treatment of even the most inept followers was marked by tolerance and forbearance. Yet with people he did not know, or with those identified as enemies, he was aloof, prickly, suspicious to the point of paranoia, and implacable in his hostility. Cochrane's career shows how heavily great and busy men were dependent on their staffs for both the competent discharge of business and their relationships with the outside world. In Chile, in particular, he was poorly served by an entourage who were not only inefficient in handling his affairs but who encouraged the negative side of his personality and muffled the positive. This was unfortunate since, while he was clearly able to exert great personal magnetism on those immediately around him, he found it difficult to inspire those who were not. Likewise, while he was touchingly supportive of his children and of Kitty in the face of severe provocation in old age, he seemed unaware of the damage that his single-minded obsessions and the dissipation of his fortune on inventions were doing to his family. His attitude to money matters showed the same contradictions. His memories of being an aristocrat with social rank but no cash, and his penny-pinching youth at Culross Abbey, left their mark. He was notorious throughout his life for the pursuit of money: he hounded the governments of Chile and Brazil remorselessly for the payment of debts, many of which were imaginary, and too many of his associates − such as Earp, May & Ludkin, Hoseason and the unfortunate Dean − had to go to law to get their dues. But he deliberately gave up a fortune from his uncle in order to marry for love, and however single-minded he may have been in acquiring money, he could never control his expenditure and the vast sums of money he acquired throughout his life were, to the despair of his wife, lost on handouts, unwise investments and inventions. Indeed, the chaotic nature of his accounts must have made it difficult for him to know what his cash flow actually was.

Cochrane was also a mixture of originality and inflexibility. He had an insatiable technical curiosity, even if few of his mechanical inventions achieved perfection or commercial success. As an officer in the navy of Britain, and of those of Chile and Brazil, which were run on similar principles, his tactics were a model of ingenuity and of the unexpected. But in Greece, where the context and discipline was alien, he seemed unable to adapt, and the techniques he had used so effectively elsewhere fell embarrassingly flat. Likewise, once he had jumped to a conclusion about individuals or events – such as the Basque Roads court martial, or the Stock Exchange affair, or the campaign and politics of South America – his ideas became fixed and unchangeable. And his mind quickly adapted all evidence to suit previously-arrived-at conclusions rather than *vice versa*.

Many of Cochrane's political attitudes, like his ideas on steam propulsion and naval tactics, were certainly in advance of his time. He was hostile to the Georgian Establishment and to the system of patronage which underpinned it and, as a naval hero whose patriotism could not be doubted, became an important radical figurehead. This was particularly evident during the turbulent years following the Napoleonic Wars when he provided the means through which working-class petitions and protest could penetrate the walls of an un-reformed Parliament. But his refusal to toe any party line caused suspicion among his fellow radicals who suspected that his political attitudes were rooted in personal grievances and a feeling of exclusion rather than being grounded in principle. This was reinforced by the fact that, beyond the reform issue, he had a personal agenda dominated by naval abuses. Here again he was in trouble. His wide-ranging attacks on the Admiralty could only be effective if the navy was demonstrably failing to deliver, whereas it was, in fact, delivering one victory after another. And when the defeats of individual ships in the American War gave him the opportunity, he misjudged the situation, overplayed his hand and was humiliated.

There is also the question of how effective Cochrane was as a public speaker. The chunks of speeches quoted in his *Autobiography of a Seaman* and his known performance at the hustings give the impression that he was a silver-tongued orator. Yet almost every personal description says that he was a poor communicator, seldom saying anything in company and often conversing in awkward monosyllables. He certainly seemed to prefer working on paper and, with the untiring aid of Jackson, began more and more to write his complaints and justifications and, indeed, to publish them in print. With the passage of time, they became increasingly lengthy and more tedious. He also morbidly analysed incoming letters, frequently detected hostility and criticism where none was intended.

Cochrane's liberalism was to be of a theoretical, rather distant kind. His relationships with his crews and with his Westminster constituents were certainly open and relaxed – 'condescending' is the word most frequently used – but his attitude seemed to have been rooted in a well-meaning paternalism in which the lower orders were seen as a vague group rather than individuals. In the City of London tavern meeting, he showed himself insensitive to the real, rather than the theoretical impact of poverty, and his papers contain numerous enquiries from anxious working-class parents asking about the whereabouts of sons who had joined the Brazilian navy which he clearly could not be bothered to get his secretary to answer. Likewise, Cochrane had little patience with the lower orders when they failed to play their expected roles as loyal and unthinking supporters. He was contemptuous of both the hesitation and lack of deference shown by the sailors of Greece, and in Chile, he was openly hostile to the British seamen who were under the command – and therefore presumably the influence – of Captains Guise and Spry.

Cochrane was undoubtedly a political radical but not all his attitudes were liberal or progressive. Some have assumed that his onslaughts on privilege and placemen in Parliament, and his efforts to get his subordinates promoted showed that he favoured merit rather than influence. There is no evidence to support this notion. In the system of patronage that underpinned Georgian society, patrons were expected to advance the careers of energetic aides and followers. And throughout his life, Cochrane benefited from a network of family and political 'influence' and used it to the full when he had the chance. His entry into the navy through his uncle, Sir Alexander Cochrane, was normal procedure and there were plenty of influential people pulling strings on his behalf with the Admiralty in the years that followed. His early progress in the service, particularly his vital promotion to commander over the heads of humbler men, was due to his membership of the navy's Scottish mafia and to the patronage of its leader, Lord Keith. And during his subsequent fight for rehabilitation, he exploited to the full the privileged access which his position as an earl gave to government and royalty. Nor were Cochrane's views on political freedom and liberty universally applied. When he accepted command of the Brazilian navy he was careful to satisfy himself that the cause was in keeping with his liberal principles.

But the fact that Brazil was the world's leading slave state passed unnoticed. Indeed a number of the prizes to which he laid claim were slave ships, and the Portuguese property he seized in Maranhão and Pará included slaves. In disposing of them, Cochrane and his prize agents were actually involved in the trade, yet there is no evidence that his principles were in any way stirred. None of this is to suggest that Lord Cochrane was a hypocrite or behaved improperly. It merely demonstrates that he was a man of his time who knew how the world worked and behaved accordingly. He may have been a radical in his views on Parliamentary reform but to claim, as some biographers have done, that he was a progressive on all social issues is inaccurate.

There is, however, one area in which Cochrane was in advance of his time. These days we expect that governments will 'spin' information and that individuals will produce slanted autobiographies that put them in as good a light as possible. Cochrane must have been one of the first to realise that if History was to tell the story as he wanted it told, then he had to control the information on which it was based – indeed, to write it. Time has shown that he was right. Since his death, it is his version of events that has become accepted as the truth. In South America, Cochrane's memoirs have been accepted at face value and have had a baneful influence on the way the naval wars of independence have been recorded in Chile, Brazil and Spain. And in Britain, innumerable biographers have uncritically repeated his self-portrait as the betrayed and persecuted hero. In the interests of truth and accuracy, it is time that the Cochrane version of his dramatic and controversial life was revised in the light of contemporary documents and objective evidence. This book has attempted in a small way to do just that.

Notes

Abbreviations used
AN   Arquivo National
NAS   National Archives of Scotland
NA   National Archives (PRO)
NMM National Maritime Museum
NRS   Navy Records Society
SNR   Society for Nautical Research

CHAPTER ONE **Roots and Relations**
1. See John Sugden, 'Archibald, 9th Earl of Dundonald: an Eighteenth Century Entrepreneur', *Scottish Economic and Social History* (Spring 1988).
2. Lord Cochrane's *Autobiography of a Seaman* (London 2000 reprint) is filled with entertaining insights into his youth at Culross.
3. For details of Cochrane's family and of the careers of its members see Donald Cochrane, *The Fighting Cochranes* (Edinburgh, 1983).
4. Muster Books of *Caroline* and *Sophie*, NA Kew, Adm 36/9762 and /9869.
5. Muster Book of *Hind*, NA Kew, Adm 36/11152.

CHAPTER TWO **Learning the Ropes**
1. Muster Book of *Hind*, NA Kew, Adm 36/11153. Cochrane did not join as a midshipman as his biographers claim.
2. *ibid.*
3. Muster Book of *Thetis*, NA Kew, Adm 36/13179.
4. Cochrane's *Autobiography of a Seaman* gives much fascinating detail of these adventures, but alas his memory was faulty as he did not visit Norway in *Hind* but in *Thetis*. All his biographers have repeated this mistake even though the truth is easily established by consulting the logs of the two ships in NA Kew, Adm 51/452 and 51/1119.
5. *Autobiography of a Seaman*, 29.
6. Keith to Markham, 23 February 1803, printed in *The Markham Papers*, NRS, vol. 28.
7. Blackwood to Lady Hamilton, April 1800, printed in Leslie H. Bennett, *Nelson's Eyes: the Life and Correspondence of Vice Admiral Sir Henry Blackwood* (unpublished manuscript, May 2002).
8. Alexander Cochrane to Keith, 29 August 1801, *The Keith Papers*, NRS, vol. 90 (vol. 2).
9. *Autobiography of a Seaman*, 40.

Chapter Three **Master and Commander**

[1] *Autobiography of a Seaman*, 40.
[2] Printed in *Autobiography of a Seaman*, 73.
[3] Schedule of Head Money paid to *Speedy* by Thomas Ricketts, HCA 2/349; Navy Board to the Admiralty, 1 February 1802, NMM, Adm B 203.
[4] St Vincent to Admiral William Dickson, 1 March 1801, *St Vincent Papers*, NRS, vol. 55 (vol. I).
[5] St Vincent to Sir J. Carter, 17 Febuary 1801, *St Vincent Papers*.
[6] St Vincent to Keith, 4 September 1801, *St Vincent Papers*.
[7] *Speedy* Court Martial report, NA Kew, Adm 1/5357.
[8] Steel's *Navy Lists*, May to September 1801.
[9] *Autobiography of a Seaman*, 90-1.
[10] *ibid.*
[11] Correspondence between Rear Admiral Rowley and Secretary Marsden, January to March 1804, NA Kew, Adm 3/149.
[12] Monroe to Hawkesbury, 29 Febuary 1804, printed in *The Keith Papers*, NRS, vol. 2; Marsden to Hammond, 3 March 1804, NA Kew, Adm 2/639.
[13] *Autobiography of a Seaman*, 90.
[14] Log of the *Pallas*, NA Kew, Adm 51/1554.
[15] *Autobiography of a Seaman*, 92 and 97.
[16] Admiralty to Young, 14 January, 9 April 1801, NA Kew, Adm 2/1006; Admiralty to Cochrane, 12 January 1801, NA Kew, Adm 2/149.
[17] *Autobiography of a Seaman*, 115-7.
[18] John Sugden, 'The Honiton Election of 1806 and the Genesis of Parliamentary Reform', *The Devon Historian*, vol. 31 (1985), 3-10.

Chapter Four **Captain of the *Imperieuse***

[1] Quoted in Cobbett's *Weekly Political Register*, 12 (1807), col. 192.
[2] Richard Hill, *The Prizes of War, the Naval Prize System in the Napoleonic Wars 1793-1815* (Sutton, 1998), 111-3.
[3] *Autobiography of a Seaman*, 285, 292.
[4] 'Lord Cochrane and Abuses in the Adriatic', *Mariner's Mirror* (August 1954), 230.
[5] Logs of *Pallas* and *Imperieuse*, NA Kew, Adm 51/1554 and 51/2462.
[6] *Naval Chronicle*, XXXII, 201.
[7] *Naval Chronicle*, XXII, 15-18.
[8] *Times*, 6 May 1809.
[9] *Autobiography of a Seaman*, 285, 292.
[10] Report by Keats, April 1807; *Minutes of the Court Martial on the Rt Hon James Lord Gambier...from 26 July to 4 August 1809...taken by W B Gurney* (London, 1809).
[11] Gambier to Mulgrave, 11 March 1809, *ibid.*

CHAPTER FIVE **The Basque Roads Affair**
[1] Court Martial on Sir E. Harvey, 2 May 1809, printed in *Naval Chronicle*, XXI, 420-28.
[2] *Autobiography of a Seaman*, 221.
[3] The full story of the Basque Roads can be reconstructed from Gambier's complementary despatches of 14 April and 10 May 1809, and *Minutes of the Court Martial.*
[4] *Times*, 22 April 1809.
[5] *Times*, 6 May 1809.
[6] *Minutes of the Court Martial.*
[7] Cochrane to Surgeon Guthrie, 13 December 1809, NMM Greenwich, AGC/38/2.

CHAPTER SIX **Radical and Romantic**
[1] Tom Wareham, *The Star Captains* (London, 2001), 83-7.
[2] *Autobiography of a Seaman*, 279-281.
[3] The correspondence is printed in *Autobiography of a Seaman*, 283-294.
[4] Robinson Crabb, *On Books and Writers*, ed. Morley (London, 1938), 61.
[5] Maria Graham, *Journal of a Residence in Chile in the Year 1822* (New York, reprint 1969), 40, 188.
[6] Richard Hill, *The Prizes of War.*
[7] *ibid.*, 114.
[8] *Autobiography of a Seaman*, 127, 283.
[9] J. Carden, *A Curtailed Memoir of the Incidents and Occurrences in the Life of John Surman Carden, Vice Admiral* (Oxford, 1858), 314-5.
[10] *Times*, 9 June 1813.
[11] Charles Stevenson, 'To the Imperial Mind: The Secret War Plan of Lord Dundonald' in Tracy and Robson (eds), *The Age of Sail*, vol. I (London, 2002).
[12] Basil Cochrane, *A Statement of the Conduct of the Victualling Board and the Hon Basil Cochrane during his Transactions in India…* (London, 1820).
[13] *Autobiography of a Seaman*, 318.

CHAPTER SEVEN **The Stock Exchange Scandal**
[1] See evidence presented by brokers as reported in *Times* Law Report of 10 June 1814.
[2] For the unvarnished details of the conspiracy and trial as they were reported at the time see *Times* Law Report, 9 and 10 June 1814.
[3] *Law Magazine and Review* article (1861), reprinted in Lord Ellenborough, *The Guilt of Lord Cochrane in 1814* (1919).
[4] Statement by Farrer and Co., printed in *Law Magazine and Review* article (1861), *ibid.*

Chapter Eight Rebel at Large

[1] I am indebted to Dr John Sugden for this quotation.

[2] S. Bamford, *Passages in the Life of a Radical* (1844), vol 1.

[3] The minutes of the meeting are printed in full in the 11th Earl of Dundonald's *Life of Lord Cochrane* (London, 1869) vol. 1, 84-99.

[4] Richard Hill, *The Prizes of War*, 66-67.

[5] Dundonald, *Life*, 130-1.

[6] O'Higgins remained in power in Chile until 1823, long enough to see independence secured. But the financial sacrifices and turbulence of the wars, followed in 1822 by a terrible earthquake, led to political turmoil and his overthrow the following year. O'Higgins fled to Peru, helped Bolivar in the final campaigns against the Spanish and then retired quietly to a farm south of Lima. Chile meanwhile relapsed into 20 years of instability and war. It was not until 1842 that the country's new governors felt confident enough to invite O'Higgins to return from exile. Tragically, he suffered a heart attack on the day of embarkation and died in Peru at the age of 64.

[7] Bowles to Croker, no. 54, 28 November 1817, printed in Graham and Humphreys (eds), *The Navy and South America*, NRS, vol. 104. The idea that there was a vast Spanish fleet in the Pacific is erroneous.

[8] Alvarez to Zenteno, 12 January 1818, printed in Luiz Uribe Orrego, *Nuestra Marina Militar. Sua Organisacion y Campaña durante la Guerra de la Independencia* (Valparaiso, 1910), 174.

[9] *ibid.*

Chapter Nine Vice Admiral of Chile

[1] J. Miller (ed.), *Memoirs of General William Miller* (Spanish version), (Madrid, 1847), vol. 1, 217.

[2] Cochrane's annual pay and allowances as laid down in the *Reglamento* was $6000 − an amount confirmed by Cochrane's subsequent claims for half pay. See also footnote 12 below. There were approximately 5 Chilean dollars to £1 at this time.

[3] Quoted in Ian Grimble, *The Sea Wolf: The Life of Admiral Lord Cochrane* (London, 1979), 382.

[4] William Bennet Stevenson, *Historical and Descriptive Narrative of 20 Years Residence in South America* (London, 1825), vol. 3, 147.

[5] Lieutenants' Passing Certificates, NA Kew, Adm 107/25.

[6] Officers' Records, NA Kew, Adm 9/5 (no. 1533); William O'Byne, *Biographical Dictionary* (London, 1848), vol. 1.

[7] Zenteno to Cochrane, 7 January 1819, NAS, GD 233/39/261, printed in Orrego, *Nuestra Marina Militar*, 186-190.

[8] Bowles to Croker, no. 140, 21 December 1818, *The Navy In South America*.

[9] Bowles to Croker, no. 169, 15 March 1819, *The Navy In South America*.

[10] Cochrane–Pezuela correspondence, printed in full in *Gazeta Ministerial de*

Chile, 10, 17 and 22 July 1819, *Archivo de D Bernardo O'Higgins* (Santiago, 1953), vol. XIII.

[11] *Gazeta Ministerial de Chile*, 1 May, 10 May, 10 July, 17 July, 22 July, 26 July 1819.

[12] Cochrane to O'Higgins, 9 August 1819, NAS, GD 233/31/239. Zenteno to the Senate, 14 August 1820, printed in J. I. Zenteno, *Documentos relativos sobre la expedicion libertadora del Peru: Refutacion de las memorias de Lord Cochrane* (Santiago, 1861), 7, 12.

[13] *ibid.*

[14] Cochrane to Zenteno, 6 October 1819, *Gazeta Ministerial de Chile*, 12 November 1819, *Archivo de D Bernardo O'Higgins*, vol. XIII.

[15] Cochrane, *Narrative of Services in the Liberation of Chile, Peru and Brazil* (London, 1859), vol. I, 30.

[16] Zenteno to Cochrane, 14 May 1820, printed in Zenteno, *Documentos relativos*, 39–40.

CHAPTER TEN **Triumph and Tribulation**

[1] Zenteno to Cochrane (private), 26 November 1819, NAS, GD 233/31/238; O'Higgins to Cochrane, 29 November 1819, NAS, GD 233/34/252.

[2] Of the three versions available, the account of Cochrane's reconnaissance quoted here – Stevenson, *Narrative of Residence*, 212 – has the ring of truth. Cochrane's own version of entering the bay in the *O'Higgins* – thus losing the element of surprise – is typically dramatised but clearly incorrect.

[3] Zenteno to Cochrane, 27 Febuary 1820, printed in Grimble, *The Sea Wolf*, 209.

[4] *Narrative of Services I*, 71.

[5] Zenteno's letters, NAS, 233/37/256, 257, 258.

[6] *Narrative of Services I*, 74.

[7] John Miers, *Travels in Chile and La Plata* (1826), 493.

[8] O'Higgins to the Senate, 22 March 1820, printed in Zenteno, *Documentos relativos*, 23.

[9] *Narrative of Services I*, 129; General José de San Martin, *Manifiesto de las acusaciones que a nombre del General San Martin hicieron sus legados ante el Govierno de Chile contra el Vice-Admiral Lord Cochrane y vindicaciones de este dirigida al mismo San Martin* (Lima, 1823).

[10] Hoseason's Accounts, NAS, GD 233/260.

[11] *ibid.*

[12] There is confusion over the dates. The *Narrative of Services I*, copying Stevenson, *Narrative of Residence*, 243, says Cochrane's letter and resignation offer was dated 14 May 1820. But Zenteno, *Documentos relativos*, 39–40 (see footnote 13 below), which is carefully referenced, says the reply was dated 4 May 1820.

[13] Zenteno to Cochrane, 4 May 1820, printed in Zenteno, *Documentos relativos*, 39–40.

[14] Graham, *Journal of Residence*, 39–40.

[15] Cochrane to Guise, 19 Dec 1819, NAS, GD 233/36/255.

[16] Graham, *Journal of Residence*.

[17] Graham, *Journal of Residence*, 80.

[18] Stevenson, *Narrative of Residence*, 207-8

[19] Grimble, *The Sea Wolf*, 209.

[20] *Gazeta Ministerial de Chile*, 26 Febuary 1820, *Archivo de D Bernardo O'Higgins*, vol. XII.

[21] Charges against Guise, NAS, GD 233/36/255.

[22] Minutes of Spry Court Martial, NAS, 233/35/253.

CHAPTER ELEVEN **The Liberation of Peru**

[1] Zenteno to Cochrane, no. 293, 19 August 1820, NAS, GD 233/38/258.

[2] Hardy to Croker, 30 September 1820, *The Navy and South America*.

[3] Stevenson, *Narrative of Residence*, 291-5. See also J. P. Grenfell's contemporary account of the cutting-out of *Esmeralda* in University of Liverpool Special Collections (ULSC), Grenfell Papers 1-2.

[4] Searle to Hardy, 8 November 1820, *The Navy and South America*.

[5] San Martin to Cochrane, 26 January 1821, NAS, GD 233/35/252.

[6] San Martin to Zenteno and O'Higgins, 9 November 1820, printed in *Gazeta Ministerial de Chile*,15 January 1821, *Archivo de D Bernardo O'Higgins*, vol. XIV.

[7] Court Martial proceedings, 2 March 1821, NAS, GD 233/38/258.

[8] Grimble, 225; *Narrative of Services I*, 101-2.

[9] Court Martial proceedings, 2 March 1821, NAS, GD 233/38/258.

[10] Cochrane–Spry correspondence, 22/23 February 1821, *ibid.*

[11] *Narrative of Services I*, 103.

[12] Spry Court Martial proceedings, 3 and 5 March 1821, NAS, GD 233/38/258.

[13] Cochrane to Guise, 1 April 1821, NAS, GD 233/38/258.

[14] Report by Miller, 26 March 1821, NAS, GD 233/37/256.

[15] Cochrane to San Martin, 30 March and 14 April 1821; San Martin to Cochrane, 6 April 1821, NAS, GD 233/31/239. Cochrane's Letter Book, NAS, GD 233/32/240.

[16] Cochrane to San Martin, 7 August 1821, *Narrative of Services I*, 129-132.

[17] Hall to Hardy, 14 June 1821, *The Navy and South America*.

[18] Timothy Anna, *The Fall of Royal Government in Peru* (Lincoln and London, 1979), 184.

[19] Cochrane to La Mar, 9 August 1820, printed in San Martin, *Manifiesto de las acusaciones.*

[20] Cochrane to San Martin, 30 June,1822, quoted in San Martin, *Manifiesto de las acusaciones.*

[21] Cochrane to San Martin, 9 August,1822, quoted in San Martin, *Manifiesto de las acusaciones*. Printed in *Narrative of Services I*, 132-4.

[22] Stevenson, 352-5.

[23] Cochrane to O'Higgins, 24 October 1821, printed in Orrego, *Nuestra Marina Militar*, 370-1.

[24] Cochrane to Grenfell, 21 December 1854, ULSC, Grenfell Papers 15-155.

[25] Timothy Anna, *Fall of Royal Government in Peru*, 199.

[26] Zenteno to San Martin, 8 May, 1821, NAS, GD 233/31/240.

[27] Cochrane to San Martin, 4 August,1822, quoted in San Martin, *Manifiesto de las acusaciones*.

[28] Cochrane to O'Higgins, 24 September 1822, printed in Orrego, *Nuestra Marina Militar*, 366-7.

CHAPTER TWELVE **Farewell to the Pacific**

[1] Graham, *Journal of Residence*, 146.

[2] Echevarria to Cochrane, 4 June 1822, printed in Graham, *Journal of Residence*, 110.

[3] Basil Hall, *Extracts from a Journal written on the Coasts of Chile, Peru and Mexico in the Years 1820, 1821 and 1822* (Edinburgh, 1824), vol. 2, 60 and 64.

[4] Cochrane to Hoseason, n.d., NAS, GD 233/39/260.

[5] Receipts for money carried out in *Alacrity* and *Doris*, NAS, GD 233/39/261. Finance Papers, NAS, GD/233/20/450.

[6] Graham, *Journal of Residence*, 331-2.

[7] Both documents were subsequently printed in Peru as San Martin's *Manifiesto de las acusaciones*; *ibid.*

[8] Graham, *Journal of Residence*; John Miers, *Travels in Chile and La Plata*; Stevenson, *Narrative of Residence*.

[9] NAS, GD 233/20/450.

[10] Correa de Sa–Cochrane correspondence, 2 September 1822, NAS, GD 233/34/247, 233/31/239.

[11] Cochrane to O'Higgins, n.d., printed in *Narrative of Services I*, 229.

[12] Correa da Camera to Cochrane, 4 November 1822, printed in *Narrative of Services II*, 7.

[13] Cochrane to Chamberlain, 31 March 1825, NAS, GD 233/20/450.

CHAPTER THIRTEEN **First Admiral of Brazil**

[1] *Narrative of Services II*, 12-13.

[2] *Narrative of Services II*, 13-20.

[3] *Narrative of Services II*, 14-15.

[4] Portaria of 21 March 1823, printed in *Narrative of Services II*, 22. Note: the Portuguese phrase '...os mismos vencimentos que tinha no Chile' is mistranslated as '...the same pay and table money as he received in Chile'. Also NAS, GD 233/34/245, no. 31. In 1823, 5 Brazilian milreis were worth £1, and a thousand milreis (a conto) worth £200.

[5] See *Memorandum to the People and Congress of Chile*, 7 Febuary 1845, NAS, GD 233/21/238; and 'Account of Brazilian Pay and Half Pay...' submitted by John Moore and Co., 18 November 1856, NAS, GD 233/19/443.

[6] *Narrative of Services II*, 13.

7 see 4.

8 Maria Graham, *Journal of a Voyage to Brazil and Residence there during part of the years 1821, 1822 and 1823* (1824), (New York reprint 1969), 221.

9 Junta da Fazenda to Ministry of Marine, 10 and 26 April 1823, AN, Rio de Janeiro, XM 80.

10 Graham, *Journal of a Voyage to Brazil*, 222.

11 The *Narrative of Services II*, 27-8, says (and indeed complains) that *Pedro I* was abandoned and attacked the Portuguese line alone. This is untrue. That *Piranga* and *Niterói* were engaged is confirmed in many sources including the 'Diary of Fr Manoel Moreira de Paixão e Dores' (Chaplain of the *Pedro I*), printed in *Anais da Bibliotéca Nacional do Rio de Janeiro*, 1938, vol. LX, 204; and the report of Captain Pereira de Sá (of the *Princeza Real*) to Portuguese Commodore Félix de Campos, 5 May 1823, printed in *A Marinha da Guerra do Brasil na Lucta da Independência*, Anonymous (Rio de Janeiro, 1880), 72.

12 Cochrane to José Bonifácio (secret), 5 May 1823, NAS, GD 233/25/466, no. 1, and Cochrane's *Narrative of Services II*, 29-32.

13 Hardy to Croker, no. 77, 31 July 1823, NA Kew, Adm 1/28.

14 The *Narrative of Services II*, 42-4, says the *Pedro I* entered the Bay of Bahia alone. This is untrue. She was accompanied by the *Real Carolina* and *Maria da Gloria*.

CHAPTER FOURTEEN The Liberation of the North

1 Cochrane to Cunha Moreira, 2 July 1823, *Narrative of Services II*, 51.

2 Cochrane to the captains of the squadron, 1 July 1823, printed in Braz do Amaral, *História da Independência na Bahia* (Salvador de Bahia, 1957), 442-3.

3 *Narrative of Services II*, 55.

4 Sir T. Hardy's Journal: letters dated 22 August 1823, NA, Adm 50/151. Chamberlain to Canning, no. 112.

5 'Diary of Fr Manoel Moreira de Paixão e Dores', in *Anais da Bibliotéca Nacional*, 240.

6 Lord Cochrane says in his *Narrative of Services II*, 60, that the *Pedro I* arrived off São Luis flying Portuguese colours, and his various biographers have repeated the story. All contemporary observers (including the chaplain of the flagship and Maria Graham, repeating the information given her by officers who were present) say that the ship approached flying the British flag.

7 Cochrane to General de Faria, 26 July 1823, *Narrative of Services II*, 61-2, NAS, GD 233/24/463, no. 201.

8 Cochrane to Junta, 28 July 1823, NAS, GD 233/24/463, no. 11.

9 *Narrative of Services II*, 82.

10 *Narrative of Services II*, 79-81.

11 Cochrane to Grenfell, 5 August 1823, printed in *Narrative of Services II*, 76.

12 Grenfell to Cochrane, 11 September 1823, NAS, GD 233/25/465.

CHAPTER FIFTEEN **Politics, Prize Money and Rebellion**
1 Maria Graham, *Journal of a Voyage to Brazil*.
2 Of the 159 officers in the Brazilian navy in July 1824, 45 were British – Lord Cochrane himself, 3 of 9 captains, 2 of 24 captains-of-frigate, 5 of 19 commanders, 11 of 36 lieutenants and 23 out of 56 substantive or acting sub-lieutenants.
3 Cochrane to Echevarria, 21 June 1823, NAS, GD 233/32/240.
4 Villela Barbosa to Auditoria da Marinha, 17 Dec 1823, AN Rio, XM 678.
5 By the time Cochrane wrote his *Narrative of Services II* in 1859, these figures had risen to 120 ships worth 2000 contos of reis (105). The actual claims submitted by Cochrane in 1824 were for 1259 contos = £252,000 (Cochrane to Villela Barbosa, 31 January 1824, AN Rio, XM 254).
6 *Narrative of Services II*, 109.
7 Cochrane to Villela Barbosa, 31 December 1823, and replies of 3 and 12 January 1824, AN Rio, 1232.
8 Minutes of the Council of State, 12 February 1824, printed in *Documentos da Independência* (Bibliotéca Nacional, Rio, 1923), 45.
9 Intendencia to Cunha Moreira, 22 July 1823, AN, XM 101; Villela Barbosa to Auditoria da Marinha, 12 December 1823, AN Rio, XM 678.
10 Villela Barbosa to Cochrane, 28 February 1824, NAS, GD 233/34/245, no. 51.
11 'Kotzebue e o Rio de Janeiro em 1824', *Revista do Instituto Histórico Brasileiro*, 80 (1918), 517.
12 Cochrane's letter books, NAS, GD 233/33/243.
13 Cochrane to da Costa, 30 March 1824, *Narrative of Services II*, 126-132.
14 Da Costa to Cochrane, 20 April 1824, Arquivo SDM Rio (microfilm) 1/5/445.
15 Cochrane to Major William Cochrane, April 1824, NAS, GD 233/26/186.
16 Cochrane–London correspondence, 30 May 1824, NAS, GD 233/20/449.
17 Cochrane to Lima e Silva, 4 September 1824 and reply dated 5 September 1824, NAS, GD 233/20/448, no. 71.
18 Norton to Jewitt, 18 September 1824, NAS, GD 233/31/237.
19 Chamberlain to Canning, no, 108, 4 Oct 1824, NA Kew, FO 63/279.
20 *Narrative of Services II*, 169.

CHAPTER SIXTEEN **Goodbye to All That**
1 Cochrane to da Costa, 30 January 1825, NAS, GD 233/20/451.
2 Maria Graham, 'Escorço Biográfico de Dom Pedro I', printed in *Anais da Bibliotéca Nacional* (Rio, 1938), vol. LX, 143-8.
3 Cochrane to Teles Lobo, 11 and 20 January 1825, *Narrative of Services II*, 219-223.
4 Cochrane to Villela Barbosa, no. 291, 17 March 1825, printed in *Os Nossos Almirantes*, vol. I, 92-3.
5 Jackson's Diary, NAS, GD 233/31/237.
6 *ibid*.
7 Cochrane to Villela Barbosa, no. 290, 16 March 1825, *Narrative of Services II*,

241.

[8] Cochrane to Carvalho e Melo, 22 March 1825, *Narrative of Services II*, 244-5.

[9] T. Monteiro, *História do Império* (Rio, 1939), vol. I, 285-6.

[10] Cochrane to Chamberlain, 31 March 1825, NAS, GD 233/20/450.

[11] Cochrane to Villela Barbosa, no. 292, 14 May 1825, NAS, GD 233/34/245.

CHAPTER SEVENTEEN Home and Away

[1] Gameiro Pessoa to Carvalho e Melo, no. 3 (secret), 13 July 1825, *Archivo Diplomático da Independência*, vol. 2.

[2] Chamberlain to Canning, no. 18, 31 January 1825, NA Kew, FO 63/276.

[3] Gameiro Pessoa to Carvalho e Melo, no. 3 (secret), 13 July 1825, *Archivo Diplomático*, vol. 2.

[4] Gameiro Pessoa to Carvalho e Melo, no. 49, 20 August 1825, *ibid.*

[5] Cochrane to Gameiro Pessoa, 6 September 1825, *Narrative of Services II*, 254-5.

[6] Chamberlain to Canning, no. 73, 20 July 1825, NA Kew, FO 13/9.

[7] *Narrative of Services II*, 260-1.

[8] Cochrane to Villela Barbosa (Paranaguá), 5 November 1825, NAS, GD 233/32/241.

[9] Cochrane to Villela Barbosa (Paranaguá), 10 February and 16 March 1826, NAS, GD 233/32/241.

[10] Cochrane to Villela Barbosa (Paranaguá), 9 June 1826, NAS, GD 233/32/241.

CHAPTER EIGHTEEN In the Cause of Greece

[1] Ricardo to Cochrane, 9 September 1826, quoted in Dundonald, *Life*, vol. I, 358. Note: all the correspondence quoted in Dundonald's work can be found in NAS, GD 233/43-8.

[2] Harold I. Chapelle, *The American Sailing Navy* (New York, 1949), 351, 353, 362: includes dimensions and draught.

[3] Dundonald, *Life*, vol. 2, 29-30.

[4] Dundonald, *Life*, vol. 2, 99.

[5] George Finlay, *History of the Greek Revolution* (1861), vol. 2, 426.

[6] Thomas Gordon, *History of the Greek Revolution* (1832), vol. 2, 392.

[7] C. M. Woodhouse, *The Philhellenes* (London, 1969), 138.

[8] Finlay, *Greek Revolution*, vol. 2, 440.

[9] Cochrane to Eynard, 12 February 1828, quoted in Dundonald, *Life*, vol. 2, 159-9.

[10] Dundonald, *Life*, vol. 2, 117.

[11] See C. M Woodhouse, *The Battle of Navarino* (London, 1965).

[12] Kitty to Cochrane, 4 September 1827, quoted in Grimble, *The Sea Wolf*, 314-5.

[13] Cochrane to Capodistrias, 26 November 1828, quoted in Dundonald, *Life*, vol. 2, 177-8

[14] Cochrane to Dr Gosse, 17 May 1829, quoted in Grimble, *The Sea Wolf*, 315.

CHAPTER NINETEEN **Return and Rehabilitation**
[1] Strachey and Fulford (eds), *The Greville Memoirs* (1938), vol. I, 398-9.
[2] *Petition to the President and Congress of Chile* (1837), *Memorial to the President and Government of the Republic of Chile* (1845), *Petition to the Emperor of Brazil* (1847), *Memorial to the Emperor of Brazil* (1854), *Description of Services in Brazil* (1854), *Exposition to the Legislature of Brazil* (1856), *Petition to the Emperor of Brazil* (1856), *Address to the People of Chile* (1857).
[3] Quoted in Dundonald, *Life*, vol. 2, 284.
[4] Brian Southam, *Jane Austen and the Navy* (London, 2001), 326.
[5] A. C. Benson and Viscount Esher (eds), *The Letters of Queen Victoria*, vol. 2, 9.
[6] Cochrane to Grenfell, 1 March 1854, ULSC, G1-155.
[7] Stevenson, 'To the Imperial Mind' in *Age of Sail I*, 69-84.
[8] *ibid.*
[9] *Punch*, no. 724, 26 May 1855.
[10] *Law Magazine and Review*, 1861, printed in Ellenborough, *The Guilt of Lord Cochrane*, 311.
[11] Lord John Campbell, *Lives of the Chief Justices* (1849-57), James B. Atlay, *The Trial of Lord Cochrane before Lord Ellenborough* (1897), Ellenborough, *The Guilt of Lord Cochrane*, and Henry Cecil, *A Matter of Speculation* (1965).

CHAPTER TWENTY **Family and Inventions**
[1] NAS, GD 233/1/29.
[2] NAS, GD 233/2/32.
[3] Quoted in Dundonald, *Life*, vol. 2, 270.
[4] Roger Morriss, *Cockburn and the British Navy in Transition* (University of Exeter Press, 1997), 242-245.
[5] NAS, GD 233/4: correspondence quoted in *Observations on Naval Affairs...Including Instances of Injustice Experienced by the Author* (London, 1847). For plans of *Janus*, see NMM, NPB 4880-4.
[6] Cochrane to Grenfell, 9 December 1853, ULSC, Grenfell Papers 15-155.
[7] Kitty to Arthur, 11 September 1854, quoted in Grimble, *The Sea Wolf*, 364-5.
[8] *Illustrated Times*, 9 June 1855.

CHAPTER TWENTY-ONE **Settling Accounts**
[1] NAS, GD 233/51-4/109, 233/57-8/111, 233/59-60/113.
[2] *Narrative of Services I*, 271-285, NAS, GD 233/49/197, 233/60/122, 233/61/123.
[3] See *Observations on Naval Affairs* (1847).
[4] *ibid.*
[5] Caldclough to Hullet Bros, 29 July 1840, Correa de Sa correspondence, 28 June 1838, NAS, GD 233/31/239.
[6] *Memorial to the President and Government of the Republic of Chile*, 3 February 1845, NAS, GD 233/26/453.

[7] Cochrane to Dr Jenner of New York, 1855, NAS, GD 233/26/450.

[8] Cochrane to Grenfell, 19 May 1847–6 May 1858, ULSC, Grenfell Papers 15-155.

[9] *Narrative of Services II*, 263-273.

[10] John Moore and Co. to Cochrane, 14 and 23 February 1857, NAS, GD 233/19/445.

[11] *Petition to the Emperor Pedro II*, 12 October 1865, NAS, GD 233/19/445.

[12] Arbitration Papers and Award, NAS, GD 233/19/444. For details of Dundonald's negotiations see Brian Vale, *Independence or Death! British Sailors and Brazilian Independence 1822-25* (London, 1996), 183-5.

[13] Buckley Mathew to Dundonald, 22 December 1874, NAS, GD 233/19/444.

[14] *Times*, 2 November 1869.

Bibliography

The Cochrane version

Lord Cochrane, *Autobiography of a Seaman*, London, 2000 (reprint)

Lord Cochrane, *Narrative of Services in the Liberation of Chile, Peru and Brazil*, 2 vols, London, 1859

Lord Cochrane, *Observations on Naval Affairs...Including Instances of Injustice Experienced by the Author*, London, 1847

11th Earl of Dundonald, *Life of Lord Cochrane*, 2 vols, London, 1869

Printed sources

Anais da Bibliotéca Nacional do Rio de Janeiro, vol. LX, Rio de Janeiro, 1938: 'Diary of Fr Manoel Moreira de Paixão e Dores' (Chaplain of the *Pedro I*); Graham, Maria, 'Escorço Biográfico de Dom Pedro I'

Anna, Timothy E., *The Fall of the Royal Government of Peru*, Lincoln and London, 1979

Archivo Diplomático da Independência, vols 2 and 5 (correspondence with missions in Britain and the United States), Rio de Janeiro, 1922

Archivo Histórico Naval, *Vicealmirante Lord Thomas Alexander Cochrane*, papers in six volumes, Armada de Chile, 1993–9

Atlay, James B., *The Trial of Lord Cochrane before Lord Ellenborough*, 1897

Bamford, S., *Passages in the Life of a Radical*, 2 vols, 1844

Boiteux, Lucas, 'A Armada Brasileira Contraposta a Confederação do Equator', *Subsídios para a História Maritima do Brasil*, Rio de Janeiro, vol. 13 (1957),

Bonnar-Smith, D., *The Letters of Lord St Vincent*, Navy Records Society volume 55

Braz do Amaral, *História da Independência na Bahia*, Salvador de Bahia, 1957

Brown, D. K., *Before the Ironclad; Propulsion and Armament in the Royal Navy 1815-90*, London, 1990

Carden, J., *A Curtailed Memoir of the Incidents and Occurrences in the Life of John Surman Carden, Vice Admiral*, Oxford, 1858

Cavaliero, Roderick, *The Independence of Brazil*, London, 1993

Cecil, Henry, *A Matter of Speculation: The Case of Lord Cochrane*, 1965

Chisholm, M., *The Independence of Chile*, London, 1912

Clissold, S., *Bernardo O'Higgins and the Independence of Chile*, 1968

Cochrane, Basil, *A Statement of the Conduct of the Victualling Board and the Hon. Basil Cochrane during his Transactions in India*, London, 1820

Cochrane, Donald, *The Fighting Cochranes*, Edinburgh, 1983

Cubitt, Donald J., *Lord Cochrane and the Chilean Navy*, University of Edinburgh Ph.D Thesis, 1974.

Cubitt, Donald J., 'The Manning of the Chilean Navy in the War of Independence, 1818-1823', *Mariner's Mirror* (May 1977)

Dakin, Douglas, *British and American Philhellenes During the War of Greek Independence 1821-33*, Thessaloniki, 1955

Dakin, Douglas, 'Lord Cochrane's Greek Steam Fleet', *Mariner's Mirror* (August 1953)

Delano, Jorge Andres, 'The American Influence in the Independence of Latin America: Captain Paul Delano', *Derroteros de la Mar del Sur*, Lima, 1999.

Documentos da Independencia, Bibilioteca Nacional, Rio de Janeiro, 1923

Ellenborough, Lord, *The Guilt of Lord Cochrane in 1814*, 1919

Fincham, J., *A History of Naval Architecture*, London, 1851

Finlay, George, *History of the Greek Revolution*, 2 vols, 1861

Gazeta Ministerial de Chile, 1819–20, printed in *Archivo de D Bernardo O'Higgins*, vols 12, 13, 14, Santiago, 1946–53

Gordon, T., *History of the Greek Revolution*, 2 vols, 1832

Graham G. S., and Humphries R. A. (eds), *The Navy and South America*, Navy Records Society, vol. 104

Graham, Maria, *Journal of a Residence in Chile during the Year 1822*, London, 1824 (reprinted New York 1969)

Graham, Maria, *Journal of a Voyage to Brazil and Residence there during part of the years 1821, 1822 and 1823*, London, 1824 (reprinted New York 1969)

Grimble, Ian, *The Sea Wolf: The Life of Admiral Lord Cochrane*, London, 1979

Gurney, W. B., *Minutes of the Court Martial on the Rt Hon James Lord Gambier...from 26 July to 4 August 1809...taken by W B Gurney*, London, 1809

Hall, Basil, *Extracts from a Journal written on the Coasts of Chile, Peru and Mexico in the Years 1820, 1821 and 1822*, 2 vols, Edinburgh, 1824

Hill, Richard, *The Prizes of War: the Naval Prize System in the Napoleonic*

Wars 1793-1815, Sutton, 1998

História Naval Brasileira, vol. 3, tomo 1, Rio de Janeiro, 2002

Humphries, R. A., *Liberation in South America,* London, 1952

Jenks, Timothy, *Naval Engagements: Patriotism, Cultural Politics and the Royal Navy 1793-1825,* (University of Toronto Ph.D Thesis, 2001)

Lambert, Andrew, *The Last Sailing Battlefleet,* London, 1991

Lambert, Andrew, *Trincomalee: The Last of Nelson's Frigates,* London, 2002

Le Fevre, Peter and Harding, Richard (eds), *Precursors of Nelson: British Admirals of the Eighteenth Century,* London, 2002

Lloyd, Christopher, *The Keith Papers,* Navy Records Society, vol. 90.

Markham, C. R. (ed.), *The Correspondence of Admiral John Markham,* Navy Records Society, vol. 28.

Miers, John, *Travels in Chile and La Plata,* 1826

Miller, John (ed.), *Memoirs of General William Miller* (Spanish version) 2 vols, Madrid, 1847

Monteiro, Tobias, *História do Império: A Elaboração da Independência,* Rio de Janeiro, 1927

Monteiro, Tobias, *História do Imperio: O Primeiro Reinado,* Rio de Janeiro, 1939

Morriss, Roger, *Cockburn and the British Navy in Transition: Admiral Sir George Cockburn 1772-1853,* University of Exeter Press, 1997

Naval Chronicle, vols 21, 22, 32

Navigator, 'Cartas do Comodoro Sir Thomas Masterman Hardy', no. 5, Hardy's correspondence with the Admiralty, 1822 and 1823 in English with Portuguese summaries, Rio de Janeiro, 1972

Orrego, Luis Uribe, *Nuestra Marina Militar. Sua Organisacion y Campaña durante la Guerra de la Independencia,* Valparaiso, 1910

Pocock, Tom, *Captain Marryat,* London, 2000

Raikes, H. (ed.), *Memoir of the Life and Services of Vice-Admiral Sir Jahleel Brenton,* 1846

San Martin, General José de, *Manifesto de las acusaciones que a nombre del General San Martin hicieron sus Legados ante el Govierno de Chile contra el Vice Admiral Lord Cochrane y vindicaciones de este dirigida al mismo San Martin,* Lima, 1823

Southam, Brian, *Jane Austin and the Navy,* London, 2001

Stevenson, Charles, 'To the Imperial Mind: The Secret War Plan of Lord

Dundonald', in N Tracy and M Robson (eds), *The Age of Sail*, vol. I, London, 2002

Stevenson, William Bennet, *Historical and Descriptive Narrative of 20 Years Residence in South America*, 3 vols, London, 1825

Strachey L., and Fulford, R. (eds), *The Greville Memoirs 1814-60*, 8 vols, 1938

Sugden, John, 'Archibald, 9th Earl of Dundonald: an Eighteenth Century Entrepreneur', *Scottish Economic and Social History* (Spring 1988)

Sugden, John, 'The Honiton Election of 1806 and the Genesis of Parliamentary Reform', *The Devon Historian*, 31 (1985)

Turrado, G. P., *Las Marinhas Realista y Patriota en la Independencia de Chile y Peru*, Madrid, 1996

Urrutia, Carlos Lopez, 'Lord Cochrane y la Expedicion a Mexico 1822', *Derroteros de la Mar del Sur*, Lima (1999)

Vale, Brian, 'Lord Cochrane in Chile: Heroism, Plots and Paranoia', *The Age of Sail*, vol. I, London, 2002

Vale, Brian, *A Frigate of King George 1808-29*, London, 2001

Vale, Brian, *Independence or Death! British Sailors and Brazilian Independence 1822-25*, London, 1996

Varnhagen, Francisco Adolfo de, *História da Independência do Brasil*, Rio de Janeiro, 1917

Wareham, Tom, *The Star Captains*, London, 2001

Webster, C. K., *Britain and the Independence of Latin America 1812-30*, OUP/British Council, 1944

Woodhouse, C. M., *The Battle of Navarino*, London, 1965

Woodhouse, C. M., *The Philhellenes*, London, 1969

Worster, Donald E., *Sea Power and Chilean Independence*, Gainsville, University of Florida Monographs, 1962

Zenteno, José Ignacio (Jr), *Documentos relativos sobre la expedicion libertadora del Peru: Refutacion de las memorias de Lord Cochrane*, Santiago, 1861

Index